Advance Praise for
Of Roughnecks and Riches

"*Of Roughnecks and Riches* is a dramatic dive into an energy revolution that has upended the nation and the world…it's a rollicking ride that makes for a compelling read."

—Gregory Zuckerman, Special Writer, the *Wall Street Journal* and bestselling author of *The Frackers*, among others.

OF ROUGHNECKS & RICHES

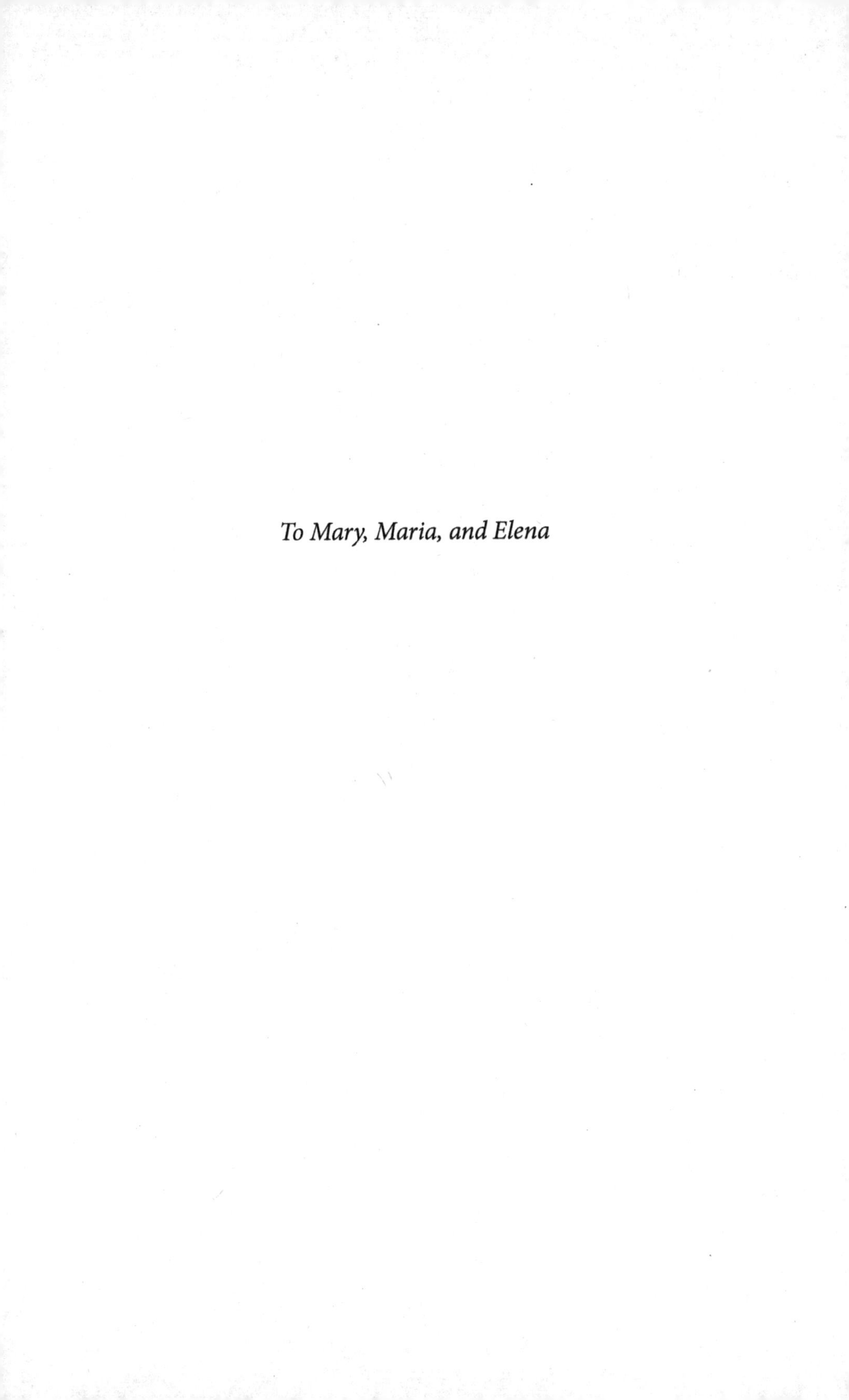

To Mary, Maria, and Elena

Contents

PART I

PART II

PART III

PART I

Everyone has a plan, till they get punched in the face.

—Mike Tyson

Chapter 1

NIGHT—NOVEMBER 2008

Pittsburgh, Pennsylvania

I didn't want to wake my wife.

I lay dead still beside her, fighting the urge to move, to sigh, to breathe. Our little terrier, Elroy, was lying stretched out on her pillow, over the top of her head like a Russian ushanka hat.

His wet, unblinking eyes were fixed on me, sensing something out of place. *Why wasn't I sleeping? What was wrong? A threat?* As much as I wanted to pet him to ease his worry, I didn't dare. He'd wag his tail, which in the still of the night would sound like a propeller blade beating the pillow. Mary would wake up. She, too, would wonder why I wasn't sleeping. I'd have to tell her. If I did, she wouldn't be able to sleep, either.

It felt like I was lying in a frying pan. My back was so damned hot; I was sweating through my T-shirt into the bedsheets. I could barely restrain myself from rolling to my left side, or my right side—toward the dog, or toward my wife—for fear of a waking reprimand. Then, in a fit, when I finally rolled right, the big wooden bed squeaked, and I froze and waited for the coming rebuke. When there was no break in the cadence of Mary's breathing, I finished my roll and reset my pillow. Ten seconds later, I was just as uncomfortable. Worse, because now my right shoulder ached.

The day before—I think it was the day before—my doctor told me I had bursitis in my shoulders. I asked him what we're going to do about it.

"Nothing," he said. "You're getting older. You're just going to have to deal with it."

Then he slid a finger in my ass, long enough to make a lousy joke, and told me my prostate was enlarged.

"You might want to lose some weight, too."

Fat? That, too?

All night long I was awake. Maybe I slept for a half an hour or so, maybe around midnight, but I'm not sure. Three hours later, I was still fully awake in our $800,000 Pittsburgh home that, a year from then, would go without a single offer when we listed it. The pool liner leaked, but the $11,000 estimate had me refilling it with a hose every few days instead, until I covered it over and ignored it. How long is the swimming season in Pennsylvania, anyway?

I tried breathing deeply, in long slow draws. That would be good for sleeping. I think I read that once. Or maybe that's wrong—who's sure of anything at 3:00 a.m.? So, I just lay still, trying to empty my head, trying to think of anything other than the trouble I had gotten myself into. But there was no getting away from it; my thoughts kept circling around and around the two sons of a bitches down in Creek County, Oklahoma—the two brothers—one a congenial incompetent, the other a conniving thug.

Inflaming my fears was the static hum of the baby monitor. Listening to my twin daughters sleeping, their tiny, rhythmic wisps of breath became like a chant, foretelling the calamity that lay ahead.

I was in trouble, real trouble, and had no way out, nothing to hang onto, no net. I was an entrepreneur, a moniker for people like me who work without nets. Entrepreneurs fall into holes of their own making. Some manage to climb out and start all over again. Others don't. For me, it was clear that I was falling into something without a bottom, an immeasurable dark and lonely abyss; and unconscionably, I was dragging my family down with me.

I pushed back, forcing myself to think of something different, anything that might bring on sleep as the nighttime minutes dragged by. Instead, my mind took a well-worn path to self-doubt, recrimination, and regret. All my stupidity...so crystal clear now, in an endless loop of *Why did I do this?* and *What was I thinking?*, my clairvoyance suddenly so damning.

All the lost money. My God, all that money—the money that I gave to the two brothers down in Oklahoma.

Two days before, I had called my loan officer, Emaline, but she didn't call me back. Instead, she emailed me a joke. I wanted to call a meeting, go to the bank, explain it all. But they must have known I was failing. All the signs were there—the NSFs, the drawdowns, the obliterated line of credit. Telling, their response was a cold silence. Altogether gone were the easy compliments bankers throw around in good times, all that fraternal camaraderie.

Emaline didn't bother responding to my request, the one where I asked that she release $100,000 in cash collateral. Of course she didn't respond to that. She must have been laughing. Or she was pissed, really pissed. She had stood by me because she believed in me. She had pushed her bank hard on my loan request. She'd prevailed, but likely spent a good deal of personal capital. Now her credibility was an issue. How would she handle that? How would I? She had to have been wondering if I would lawyer up, the same way I was wondering if she would walk me into her end-of-the-line workout department.

I tormented myself for blundering through unforced tactical errors as the bank waited for me to admit that my deal was falling apart. But if I did admit it—*it would fall apart.* If I blinked, if I showed any sort of weakness, the whole charade would fall apart. So I didn't. I hid it and hoped for pity. Maybe they'd feel bad for me and would act on my behalf. Maybe they'd save me—somehow.

It was a thread I hung onto for a few delirious seconds before I lost my grip and was dragged back down into the teetering, precipitous truth.

I may not make it.

Experience told me that my amplified self-flagellation would disappear in the morning. Daylight drives away all the nighttime vermin and despair. But on that morning, the sleepless, tortured night would just fade into a murky, sunless dawn.

Mary's eyes fluttered open, and she propped herself up onto an elbow for a better look—right through me. She wondered aloud the same thing Elroy had been wondering—why wasn't I sleeping?

I kept it simple and told her I had to go.

"Where, to work?" she asked.

"No, Tulsa."

"Huh? Tulsa? You're going to Tulsa?"

"I gotta go to Tulsa. I gotta go right now."

"Right now? Are you serious?"

That was it. She was up, too—every bit as shit out of luck as me.

Chapter 2

DELTA AIRLINES

Tulsa, Oklahoma

You can still show up at an airport with a credit card and a driver's license and get somewhere—as long as you're willing to pay for it. So, when I walked up to the Delta counter in Pittsburgh and asked for Tulsa and the soonest flight out, it was a simple transaction. Delta gave me a ticket and I overpaid for it. That was fine because at least it was familiar.

There were no lines at 5:30 a.m. No one had shown up yet, other than a few other overworked souls, pausing in front of the drawn and locked storefront gates, waiting for something with a newspaper or muffin in it to open. The presidential election between McCain and Obama had come and gone, but my insatiable appetite for the next news cycle continued. A rack of newspapers was just inside the security gate, and as I scanned the headlines, I took a grim comfort in not being alone in my current state of affairs. If I was going down, it seemed the whole world was coming with me. Every headline screamed of the tanking economy, plunging through recessionary levels right toward a technical depression. Jobless claims were soaring. Washington was bailing out the big Wall Street banks with taxpayer money and would soon be saving GM and Chrysler. The home mortgage meltdown that sparked earlier in the year was now kindling for a global macroeconomic firestorm. Bear Sterns had been the first domino to fall, and now Lehman Brothers was a pile of bones that even Treasury Secretary Hank Paulson and Fed Chair Ben Bernanke couldn't spread around.

And because fear never sleeps alone, there was the sudden worry of a similar and catastrophic shot to the commercial real estate market, a come-to-Jesus moment in the consumer unsecured debt market (credit cards), and a historic low in personal savings that would do nothing to offset the hinging crisis. And then, the most reactionary of all commodities, oil, was suddenly gravity-stricken, crashing 60 percent over the previous five months, on its way to an 80 percent wipeout.

The Baker Hughes rig count, the front-door barometer of drilling activity, was falling—like get-the-hell-out-of-the-way falling. Permits ceased to be filed, and drillers were stacking rigs in a swan dive of equity-for-debt deals. Patterson-UTI, one of the biggest on-land drillers in the United States, saw its drilling days fall by two-thirds in a few short months, and frack companies were discounting deep into the bone just to keep customers and crews.

Newly minted frack companies were lining up for failure. A statistic not lost on me as my start-up, Reliance Well Services, was a frack company. Already my projections were rubble, and I hadn't even made it out of the gate. Even some of the companies that had been around for years were doomed, so what chance did I have?

It was an astounding tide of failure, a catastrophically foolish time to start a hydraulic frack company from my little shop in Pittsburgh. But I was stuck. I was too far along.

I turned away from the newsstand and got to my gate as the plane was boarding. Wanting to spend as little time on it as possible, I waited until I was last in line, obediently bumping along the Jetway and through the first-class aisle where those of us on our feet stole glances at the big earners and beneficiaries already seated and served. It was only fitting that my last-minute ticket in a middle seat by the toilet cost more than the pampered seats up front. But hell, last time I flew first class, I didn't even know how to work the tray table.

We hit Tulsa International, and after a thirty-minute wait in a Thrifty line, I was given the keys to a neon-blue Dodge Nitro, as bright as the Blue Light Special on a Kmart endcap. This was to be my ride for my unannounced stealth mission into Bristow, Oklahoma, where I hoped to sneak in and uncover just what the hell the two brothers were doing with my money.

Three months had hardly passed on what was supposed to be a simple five-month build-out. I had hired the brothers and their start-up, STIM SOLUTIONS, to build a companion set of frack trucks, a pump and a blender, and paid them a $250,000 deposit. I was their first customer, and it was their company's first check for a straightforward matter that shouldn't have been falling apart but was. Four months later, I needed an explanation. I needed to see what was going on with the build and with them. There was no good reason for there to be problems, but problems had nevertheless found their way inside STIM SOLUTIONS.

The younger brother, Andy, was my main contact. He had some nebulous IT credentials, but it was his older brother, Bill, who had done it all before, out of his long-established oil-field equipment repair shop. Local behemoth Schlumberger was Bill's big customer. A mutual love affair, I was told. That was the thing that had sold me, that and Bill's ability to fix anything anywhere. The story was that Schlumberger had even flown him deep into Siberia, where he kept a fleet of pumps running in weather cold enough to freeze diesel fuel. He also built a few new trucks here and there but was mainly a guy cobbling together tired old equipment to make it through a few more jobs.

Closing in on Bristow, an hour or so west of Tulsa, I dialed the congenial little brother, Andy. I didn't call Bill because I knew he wouldn't answer. In fact, Bill had stopped taking my calls a few months before, about a month into the fabrication process. When I asked Andy why, I was told he was busy, that it wasn't me or him or anyone, just a good old-fashioned busy. Besides, everything was to go through Andy, anyway. That was the explanation. Now I saw it as a cover-up for a disaster in the making.

Andy had been emailing me in a desperate fit over the Thanksgiving holiday. It was now the Monday after Thanksgiving, a day that couldn't come fast enough after his emails over the long weekend. One of the emails was the crazy one that had kept me up the previous night—the one that took me from my warm wintertime bed, from my wife and infant daughters, to my iced-over truck on a desperate run to the Pittsburgh airport. This was the email in which he claimed to fear for his life.

> Dan:
>
> I tried to call you today with some important information. STIM SOLUTIONS is not doing too well in our management negotiations. Bill wants to be bought out of STIM but at a price far beyond its worth (please do not share this with Bill). Bill has told me that if he is to buy me out of STIM, then he would run STIM into the ground. STIM has paid Bill for the blender, transmission, hydraulic motor, none have been delivered yet, Bill has nothing to lose.
>
> Bill has placed higher priorities on his own clients rather than STIM. He has a job for STIM, in line now that was promised delivery to STIM for August 31, 2008. You can do the math (four months late). You can call Bill and just ask him outright when he thinks he will finish your units, please don't mention this correspondence, it would hurt things a whole lot and I could be a dead man (for real).

On my first reading, I was skeptical. Was this a joke? It had to be. Of course, it was. But it was from a guy who didn't joke around much. His email continued:

> Dan, the men I have made alliances or partnered with (in my new company) are all Christian men from my church with oil field, production, and welding expertise. They are all ready to get started immediately.... Now comes my big question for you, if things go sour for my pursuit of separation from Bill (he wants to be paid for a buyout from the next payment from Reliance), I have set up another company to work forward in, it is called STIM SOLUTIONS Mfg. Corporation. You have the power to move the operations from STIM SOLUTIONS, inc. and then hire STIM SOLUTIONS Mfg. Corporation. It would just take a letter from you.... I have the power to accept this and I can then guarantee you the delivery of the units at the remaining price that you were originally quoted....
>
> Dan, you can call me and I will tell you all of the reasons for the disputes between management. Anyway, don't send the money

until you decide how you want to move forward. PLEASE GIVE ME A CALL!

Sincerely,
Andy Brennan

I was slack-jawed incredulous. Dumbstruck. Speechless.

"Management negotiations?"

"Run STIM SOLUTIONS into the ground—"

"I could be a dead man (for real)."

"Christian men from my church—"

"PLEASE GIVE ME A CALL!"

I read it a second, then a third time, but nothing changed. There was no disappearing ink or holograms or misunderstandings here. I wasn't being pranked or ribbed. It wasn't even a bad joke. This guy was as serious as $250,000 gone missing could be.

I called Andy from my parents' home in Erie, Pennsylvania, just about to sit down for a second Thanksgiving meal. He immediately answered with a buoyant undertone, wondering aloud how I was on such a fine day.

I was taken aback by his levity. His spirits were flying high after nine rounds of golf with his family down in Tulsa. It was a great day, he told me—golf, laughs, soup and appetizers, save a little room for dessert—that kind of day. Then he blithely asked me how he could help. Astonished, I reminded him about his email, the one that was only a dozen hours old, the one in which he feared for his life.

"Oh, yes, that."

We talked through it but only briefly. Andy downplayed it all, which made it worse. Do we have a problem or don't we? Is your brother going to kill you? Is STIM really going down in flames with my deposit? My assumption was that these two were ordering parts and putting them together, not drawing lines and preparing for a standoff. What I got back from Andy were reassuring comments, in soothing tones, as though I was the hysterical one. I was talking to a guy that wasn't engaged in reality; that, or he was a drunk or a drug addict or at a level of dishonesty I couldn't comprehend. Or maybe it was something simpler. Maybe he was miffed that I was calling at the end of a long holiday break, messing with his time-off mojo. That, or his wife was listening in, the one who may have warned him against going into business with his Neanderthal brother.

Either way, I was so dumbstruck I apologized for calling.

"It's okay. Call anytime," he assured me.

Now I was hauling ass through Oklahoma toward his shop and fearing the worst. As I closed in on Bristow, I had to call. When Andy answered, he was upbeat and happy to hear from me. That was the new normal for him, extreme highs and lows. Having the better half of him on the line, we started in on the perfunctory exchange of Oklahoma genialities, an exchange in which I didn't mention I was ten minutes away. Then, as we drifted into matters at STIM, Andy's bearing darkened as he morphed into his paranoid side, into the chrysalis of Hyde. Drifting behind the scenes into the melodrama at STIM, he rambled of right and wrong and redemption in the face of adversity, following the theme of his crazy email from two days back, the biblical part about atonement and a few good Christian men, proclaiming he didn't need Bill, how Bill had no intention of building my trucks, how Bill never intended to build my trucks, that I would be in better hands, his hands, should I choose properly and make a stand. All the while, I was quietly making my way toward his shop, wondering when I should spring the news of my whereabouts, wondering if he would stay, run, or go dark, as his brother had.

Trying to wrap my head around the whole STIM SOLUTIONS gambit, around its incubation, my growing sense was that Andy had come along and explained to Bill how he was missing out on the real money in the "build it new" market. Bill likely heard him out and agreed because he thought he'd make a fortune jumping into the bum's rush of shale. He'd let his little brother walk in with piles of executed sales agreements. What was the risk? Bill only had to make a little room at his shop for the new company, and Andy only had to come up with a name and a splashy logo.

They were going to make a killing, until they didn't, right about when I was hauling ass through Oklahoma, looking for my money and answers.

The questions I wanted to ask kept rolling through my head.

"Why didn't you tell me there were problems with your partner?"

"What have you done with my deposit money?"

"How much has gone to procurement?"

"How much has gone to shareholder distributions?"

Or, "How much have you and your shit-heel brother sucked out of my account for pizza and wings and Jet Skis?"

But Andy kept on, laying out a plan of how he would fulfill our contract, how the good men from his church would succeed even if oil went to zero, how like an old-fashioned barn raising they would turn my money into frack trucks. He explained that it was all doable, that a change in management was all that was needed. He was starting his own company, one without the nuisance of a knowledgeable partner, the one whose back he had built the first company on.

"Andy," I interrupted him, having heard enough.

"Huh?"

"I'm here. I'm in Oklahoma. I'm on my way to your shop."

"You're here? My shop? You're at my shop?"

"I'm on my way. Like ten minutes away." After a long and pregnant pause, I spoke up. "Andy, you there?"

"I hope you didn't come down because you don't trust me, Dan."

The truth had no place there, so I bit my tongue. "No, not at all, Andy," I lied. "I just wanted to make sure you're okay."

With that assurance, he was overjoyed. In his devotedly Christian way, his manifest destiny was coming to be. His prayers were answered, and his path to salvation was about to be paved by my dollars. To him, I would be on hand, in person, to sign this new deal with him and his new company.

A hastily arranged plan came together: I was to meet him in forty-five minutes at a gas station in downtown Bristow, next to the Indian casino—easily the smallest casino ever built, smaller even than the gas station.

"It's called the Kum & Go. You can't miss it."

"The what? The Kum & Go?" I asked.

"Right. The Kum & Go. It's like a fixture in Bristow, but they have this really good breakfast sandwich there. Hurry up and we'll break a little bread with a few."

"Great, Andy. Looking forward to it."

It wasn't lost on me that he was still at home and not at work as it crept toward noon. But as I had no Plan B, I had no choice. I had the single option of playing along and seeing where it went. Good due diligence—had I done it—would have ferreted this out. I would have had other options, other places I could go. Instead, I skipped it all. I was in a hurry, for no good reason other than having something bottlenecked inside me, something that made me need to get a deal done.

With Oklahoma blowing past me at seventy-five miles per hour, I was rushing all over again, this time rushing to find a way out of the mess my hurry-up had put me in. I didn't have the resources to weather a fight, either. I had self-funded my deal, because I didn't want to go begging for money or dilute myself any more than I already had. Everything I owned I had leveraged, right down to the second mortgage on my oversized, underfilled house.

I coasted off the Bristow exit and onto Main Street, through its five or six stoplights, and passed the police station that would soon enough become familiar to me. Things couldn't be as bad as they seemed, I was thinking. These were reasonable people. They had all presented themselves as reasonable. Surely they had to be.

Maybe I was just overreacting.

Chapter 3

KUM & GO

Bristow, Oklahoma

I had met the older brother, Bill, four months back, when he made a last-minute trip up to Pennsylvania. Right off the bat, my partners decided they wanted him to build our trucks. A month after that, I flew down to Tulsa to see him and his little brother, Andy, and to look over their operation at Sooner Fleet Service, Bill's long-established oil-field build-and-repair shop and the new home of STIM SOLUTIONS.

Had I not been so out of my league, I would have immediately seen Sooner and its little tagalong, STIM, for the abhorrent shithole they were: sharing an open-air, three-sided shop packed full of junk motors and pumps and a scattering of parts that were no better than scrap. The surrounding yard was filled with stripped-down trucks, engines on pallets, power tongs, pumps, transmissions, trailers, tanks, and other pieces of iron oxidizing into red piles of rust. Being such a cipher, I didn't know that fab companies shouldn't look like this. Reputable places are generally clean and well-kept, with an apparent sense of order. They have a "picked-up" look, with shelves and sheds and employees who meet your glance with a nod or a smile. Not so at Bill's. There, you were ignored by averting eyes and stoop-shouldered gloom.

With thirty minutes to kill before meeting Andy, I decided to take a drive past STIM and have a look, the entire point of jumping on a plane in the first place. As I came upon it, I saw the familiar, rusted-out perimeter fence, hoping to God my trucks were inside it. If they weren't, I was going to have real problems, lawyer problems. But then I saw them for the first time. My two brand-new International Paystar chassis parked right there, right behind the fence, giving me the feeling for the first time that I had done something right. They were enormous, hulking pieces of equipment, every bit the same as a semi-tractor but bigger. What started three months back as a deep blue, almost purple paint chip, was suddenly real.

But my feel-good moment faded as quickly as it came on. The trucks may have been delivered, but on second glance nothing had been done. To Andy's point, the trucks were sitting in the same place they had been dropped off. The long, black frame rails were absolutely bare on both trucks. These were the rails to which $1.5 million of frack equipment was to be bolted—the ones with a due date five weeks away.

Andy had told the truth. The two trucks were months and months away from being finished.

Not wanting to be seen—not with what I suspected Andy was about to drop on his brother—I rolled past Bill's ratty office trailer and what I suspected was his pickup truck, then spun around and headed back to town. A few minutes later I found the Kum & Go and saw Andy's shiny black truck parked in the side lot, hard to miss with the STIM SOLUTIONS logo emblazoned on the doors—way cooler than my white Chevy back home with crank-up windows and manual door locks.

I parked and consciously patted the keys in my pocket, remembering where they were in the event of a quick exit. Then I sucked in a breath of cold Oklahoma air and walked into the Kum & Go.

The place had the look of any other gas station in America. Hotdogs spinning out grease on a revolving carriage. Lottery tickets and cigarette lighters with etched-in pot leaves and Confederate flags packing the countertop.

And then there he was: Andy, hunched over and eating something in an orange, plastic-laminated booth that bore a strange resemblance to an orange Creamsicle. You could see he was a tall man, but he looked smallish in a coat that was two sizes too large for him, the collar creeping up over his neck, looking as if it might swallow him whole. Catching me between bites, he was immediately on his feet and coming at me with an outstretched hand.

"How are you, Dan? So glad to see you," he said, grinning through a mostly full mouth.

"You, too, Andy. You, too," I said as we shook hands like two men who wanted to be with each other.

Impossibly polite, Andy wanted to know how my flight was, if I wanted a cup of coffee, maybe one of the Kum & Go's famous sausage-and-egg biscuits?

"I love this place," he said, choking down the last of his, likely bought on my dime. "You sure you don't want one?" When I said no again, Andy went on, "I'm so glad you came down. You kinda surprised me, but you couldn't-a come at a better time. Everything's just crazy, you know," he offered as we sat. "I just want to work, and my brother started playing these games and…" Andy trailed off as his attention wandered past me to the counter. "I might get another sausage-and-egg, you sure you don't want one?"

"Pretty sure, but thanks. Don't let me ruin it for you, though."

"I better not," he said patting his stomach. "You wouldn't think a gas station could make such a good croissant," Andy said, making it sound French, until he gave up on the sandwich. "I can't work with Bill anymore. I've really tried. It's impossible. He just doesn't care. He sort of cared in the beginning, and then he just stopped caring. He doesn't care about anybody but himself. Now he's saying he's got to do all the 'real work,'" Andy said, making air quotes, "so why's he only getting half? That's just him. He's always been just like that."

"But you're trying to work it out with him? Right?"

"I tried. God knows I tried. It's just, how do you fix someone that threatens to shut you down?" Andy asked, anxiously watching a customer open the counter-mounted heating cabinet and pull out a handful of breakfast sandwiches.

"It seems that shutting the one company down to start another—it seems like a lot of unnecessary effort," I offered. "Can't you just work out some other arrangement with Bill? Like a consultant or something. We still kind of need him, right?"

"That would never work. He's not like that. He always has to have all the control." Andy stood abruptly. "You mind if I go and get that sausage-and-egg?" he asked, not really looking for an answer. "They only got like one left." Andy pushed ahead like a runner in a set of starting blocks and grabbed the last sandwich. He paid for it and was inhaling it by the time he sat back down. "I already told you," he said through a full mouth, "Bill said he'd run STIM right into the ground. He says he's got his reasons, which means he thinks he can do it all on his own. So, now I'm thinking that's what he's going to do."

"But what do you mean? You still have my trucks to build. Right?"

"Bill says he's done, so he's done. He's not going to build your trucks. Did I tell you about his customer in Denver? Bill still hasn't finished his cementer, and it's been like a year. He's not going to build your trucks, Dan. I'm telling you. Because the way it is with him, I can't build them, either. They're at his shop. There's no way he's gonna let me build them there, and he's not gonna build them there, either!"

Andy mistook my idle panic as me being a sympathetic listener. He lowered his voice to a conspiratorial whisper. "Besides, he can't," he said. "He's been writing himself checks from the STIM account. There's nothing left," he added, forgetting it was my money.

"What do you mean, 'nothing left'? What do you mean, he's 'writing himself checks'?"

"I'm only saying—"

"You're out of money? You can't be out of money! *I just gave you—*"

"Dan, Dan, please," Andy cautioned, alarmed by the embarrassment of an outburst but not so much by the money gone missing.

"Fine. Fine," I said trying to calm myself. "What'd he take the money for, Andy? Please tell me it was for my trucks."

"He took it to buy parts off himself. He's supplying most, most of the parts from his other company. It's just he's buying things off himself we don't need yet."

"Like what?"

"Well, like everything."

"Jesus, Andy. You have everything, then? At least you have all the parts, right?"

"Yes. Well…no. Yes, and kind of no. Some things are still coming. Mainly like the pod."

"How much was that?"

"That was sixty thousand dollars."

"Sixty thousand dollars? Is that what you agreed to?"

"Well, Bill agreed to that part. It was his pod. But, yeah, pretty much, yeah."

"You're getting it, though, right? I mean, Bill's going to make good on all this? You don't think he's ripping me—I mean us—off?"

"No, no. Absolutely not. Maybe. I don't know. Some things have gone up in price that he's selling to us."

"What!? How's that? What? What's gone up in price?"

"The transmission."

"How much?"

"For the transmission?"

"Yeah, the transmission."

"That was like thirty thousand more than what he and I discussed, you know, back when things were better."

"Thirty thousand more? Thirty thousand dollars more!? You shitting me, Andy?"

"I know—"

"You gotta be kidding me!"

"It's doesn't help, you getting mad, Dan."

"This is crazy, Andy. I mean…I don't…we got to talk to him, Andy." I made a move to stand up. "Let's go talk to him. Now. Right?"

"I don't know if you've been hearing me, Dan," Andy cried, panicked. "You don't understand my brother."

"Understand what?"

"That you don't want to get him mad."

"You mean like he might kill you, like that part?"

Andy said nothing, resigning himself to how absurd his email sounded in the light of day.

A wave of nauseating hopelessness caved in on me. Our government doesn't have social programs to help entrepreneurs pick up the pieces of their lives. Congress isn't out lobbying for life support on behalf of us. They know you can't help yourself, so why intervene with legislation? So I did what I always do. I punished myself. I'd failed myself, my wife, my infant twin daughters. The rest of the world would soon know what I already knew about myself. That I was bullshit, a ne'er-do-well, a failure. That's the bottom for me. It's not living in a car or on floors. I've done that. It's failing and giving away my freedom to two other entrepreneurs hell-bent on stealing my money, my future, my family, my second mortgage.

"Dan, this is a blessing in disguise."

"Really?" Still in my stupor. "How could that be?"

"You're gonna be the first customer of my new company. That's what I'm hoping for, anyways. If you'll, you know... Bill was never really as essential as you thought. He had me kind of overselling his abilities before. It was the engineering I brought in that made the difference. Not Bill. And the trucks, Dan, they can be—no, *they will be*—they'll be in my new shop within a few hours, with your blessing. Together we can do this. It's a blessing, I'm telling you. You gotta see that!"

Dumbfounded, just too dumbfounded to respond, I simply nodded as Andy rattled off reasons why my luck had just changed. Logic would dictate that I concentrate, that I listen closely, that I hear him out. But I'd hit some sort of muddled saturation point. Everything Andy said sounded like the cacophonous adult chatter in a *Peanuts* cartoon. Nothing made any sense.

Sure, Schlumberger was flying Bill to Eastern Russia's oil fields to pull rabbits out of his ass, but now, skeptically, he was no longer needed at STIM SOLUTIONS. His once vaunted mechanical skills were suddenly replaceable. Instead, Andy had a very talented hydraulics engineer onboard. He had sourced every item going on the trucks. He had arranged to rent a building down the road. He had what it took. He had the team—*four good Christian men.*

Looking at my lousy options, I was steeling myself for the fact that Andy and his merry band of Christians would have to get some of the work. It was that or place all my faith in Bill, the guy who was ignoring me. But still, I needed to get with Bill. I had to get his side of it. Broken contract or not, he could block this, too. For all I knew, the two of them could have taken my money and bought a weekend cabin down on the lake together.

I couldn't see it. I couldn't see a way to make a clean—and *cheap*—break from STIM. What was another builder going to do with all the parts I bought, with their inflated prices and peculiarity—parts that made a vortex blender that no one else built? But sticking with Andy: *My God! What a choice!* He wasn't even the key man. I had aligned myself with the weaker partner, the runt of the Brennan litter who had never in his life even worked on a frack truck, let alone built one.

"Work will begin immediately, tonight even—as soon my team gets out of their day jobs," Andy continued.

"Their day jobs?" I heard myself saying as I woke from my fog. "Your employees have other jobs?"

"Well, yes. I told you. This is a start-up! I can't just go in whole hog. There's no money. We're going to have to talk about a deposit, too, so I can get going."

"What do you mean, a 'deposit'? I already paid you a deposit."

"What deposit?"

"What do you mean, 'what deposit'? You're joking, right? The two hundred fifty thousand dollars, Andy. The *deposit* deposit. Remember? I get credit for all my deposit, right?"

"That's been spent. I told you."

"Right, but do I get credit for it? All the parts come over with you? This isn't going to cost me a dime more, right? Like you said—no matter what Bill charged. Like you want to start over, but all in, everything, this is going to cost the same one-point-five million? Right?"

"You mean total?"

"Yeah, I mean total! Everything. Between both your STIMs. You're going to live by our deal? The one we have right now?"

"I told you. Everything will be the same if you stick with me."

"So, that's a yes?"

Andy paused, like he was thinking it over. "I told you I'd cover everything. Even what Bill took, if you think that's what's fair."

"Yeah, I think that sounds pretty fair, Andy."

"So, you'll do it, then?"

"Come on, Andy," I responded. "I don't know… What if you just let me walk away? What about that? I have every right, Andy."

"That's exactly my plan!" Andy lit up. "You tell Bill he hasn't lived up to the contract, so you're pulling out, then I come in and agree to shut down STIM."

"Yeah, right, Andy. Bill's going to go for that."

"Bill's not going to build your trucks, Dan."

"You already said that. And it still doesn't make any sense."

"And there's another thing. He doesn't like you."

"What do you mean, 'doesn't like me'? What's that? Why would he not like me?"

"You promised him a bigger deposit. He says you changed the deal on him."

"That's right. I did. Thank God I did. Otherwise, he'd have stolen it all. Thank God, in hindsight, right?"

"Well, that's how he feels."

"What a bunch shit, Andy—"

"I'm just telling you, Dan—"

"That was my bank's call, to change up the deposit. Thank God for my bank, right? With all this bullshit, at least I got title to the engine and pump. That's like another four hundred thousand dollars. With all this going on with you guys—thank God the bank didn't just hand it all over to you and Bill, and made me go direct, instead."

"I know, but he still says you made a deal."

"So, the guy who's ripping me off is offended? That's really something! This is crazy. It's just crazy. It's like…like…" Stammering, I floundered for words. "You're putting me right in the middle of this. Second, don't you think your brother is going to see right through it?"

"How would he know? I'm not going to say anything. And you have every right. It's right in the contract—I wrote it! You have every right. Nothing has been done on your trucks. You have the right to pull them, or you have the right to exercise the penalty option. And Bill hates the penalty option. This is the only way, Dan. It's this, or let your trucks sit and rot. And believe me, he's gonna keep telling you you owe him more money! You gotta go see him and tell him you're taking your trucks back. He's not gonna make his deadline. Tell him nothing's been done on the trucks. And he's only got five weeks to go before the penalties start. I'll come in after and let you out of the contract. I'm the president of the company! I can do that."

Andy took a long expectant breath. "Dan, listen to me. Bill'll be happy to be rid of STIM. Trust me. He's already sold me all the parts. There's nothing left for him to make any money on. I mean, not without having to work for it."

"And now I'm right in the middle of it. You're putting me right in the middle of it, Andy."

Andy shrugged. "It's the only way."

"And you're not going to come along with me, are you?"

"That would ruin everything. I mean, that would only make Bill suspicious."

"Yeah, okay, Andy. We sure wouldn't want to make it look like you're up to anything."

"It's the only way, Dan. You'll see. Bill's bark is worse than his bite. When you go in there, just don't get alarmed by anything. Okay? He's got a big bark, is all. All intimidating and all-a that. I'll come along right away, but just don't get alarmed if he does anything—"

"Alarmed at what?"

"Just Bill being Bill, is all."

"What does that even mean, Andy? What do you mean, 'Bill being Bill'?"

"Like just stupid stuff, like, say, he pulls a gun on you."

I stared at Andy. For a long while. I didn't think I'd heard him right. "You say a gun?"

"Yeah, but he won't actually use it," Andy added as a quick consolation.

"But a gun? You mean like a *gun*, gun?"

"Yeah, but he's not gonna shoot you with it or anything."

"He's going to pull a gun on me? Your brother's going to pull a gun on me?"

"Yeah, just like a little gun. Like, it might not even be loaded."

"You gotta be kidding me!"

"Well, no—"

"For what?"

"It's just his way, Dan. It's just how he kids around."

Chapter 4

THE SETUP

Reno, Pennsylvania

A little less than a year before, my twin daughters had been born, and instantly, right at the hospital, my reaction was magnitudes beyond any expectation I had. A spirit awakened within me, a sense of gratification—love, I would guess—that I never could have otherwise comprehended. But there was more to it. Equally alarming was being struck with the feeling that I needed to do better, that I needed to make a better life for my wife and daughters.

The company I had started ten years before had topped out and was no longer growing or capable of growth. We were at the top of our class, but our industry had run straight into a Warren Buffett maxim: "Better to be a mediocre business in a strong industry than a strong business in a mediocre industry." Being the latter and running a sideways business, with two infant daughters, took on a profound sense of unacceptability. Sitting still felt like I was shirking my duties as a newly minted father. But there I was—stuck and static—and crawling out of my own skin.

Lightspeed Grip & Lighting was the company I was bemoaning, a Pittsburgh-based grip and lighting rental company that I had started ten years before, with an unsecured $5,000 loan from a big-hearted banker. Lightspeed rented lights, cameras, rigging, portable power, and trucking to the film and television industry. All our revenues came from the film industry and from long-established print and broadcast ad agencies. After years of old-line stability, upstart digital agencies were suddenly running circles around their precursors by producing cheap and precisely targeted internet ads. Money was fleeing expensive broadcast television and its blitzkrieg approach, which was in turn starving out suppliers like my grip and lighting company.

I began casting about for opportunities. When nothing came my way, I created one by convincing myself I could start a frack company. Forget that I had never worked for a frack company. I also hadn't fracked a well in almost twenty years, back when I was raising money and drilling wells in Colorado, Pennsylvania, and West Texas, in what seemed like another life. I had studied geology in school and had drilled wells way back when. I had even been around plenty of frack jobs, but that hardly made me knowledgeable, let alone an expert that financing would require. Add twenty years, and I had forgotten everything; yet I had talked myself into it, and that was that. It became something I had to do, at first for me, then, I convinced myself, for my family, too. Such a leap of faith was a worrisome habit of mine. Like any other naïve and ill-advised entrepreneur, I felt as though I could always land on my feet. Incredibly, the enormous, outsized risk of it all didn't even give me pause. My abject stupidity wouldn't allow it.

So I made the most impractical, capital-intensive decision I could. I'd move ahead and start a frack company. Shortly thereafter, I signed off on a highly leveraged $1.7 million loan, which in time would prove to be far short of the final cost. But I was nostalgic for the oil and gas business, and that won out over a fear of debt. The only thoughtful decision I made at the time was deciding I couldn't do it all on my own. Even in my wet-behind-the-ears blitz to get something done, I needed operational help and started to think about some brothers I knew in Oil City, Pennsylvania. I wondered if I approached them, if they might just listen.

These were the Kane brothers, drillers and frackers who also had their own oil production. They were hard-as-nails fixtures in the Northwest Pennsylvania oil fields. Back when I was raising money, drilling my own wells, and contracting out the frack jobs to Halliburton and Dowell (later to become part of the Schlumberger empire), my driller suggested I try a couple of upstarts in the frack business, brothers Eli, Wallace, and Daniel

Kane. They had a set of trucks and were catching more and more jobs. So I gave them a try, and they got it done in a no-frills kind of way.

Years later, finding the Kanes wasn't easy. Independent oil men don't advertise. Most don't even put a company name on their pickup trucks, let alone have websites, media presences, and all the other marvels of look-at-me branding. Eventually, though, I did find them, and when I got through to Eli on a twenty-year-old phone number I found in a notebook, we picked up right where we left off, reminiscing about his old Camaro and the girls who used to drive by my well sites looking for him—back when he had a full head of hair. He filled me in on who had come and gone and who was still around. It was old times all over again, Eli treating me like an old friend, and me feeling the pull of something I needed. Talking to him reminded me that I didn't leave the oil business because I didn't like it. The oil business left me and hundreds of thousands of others when it went into a decades-long decline through almost all of the '90s.

We finally got to it, and I asked Eli if he was still in the frack business. He told me he was but wasn't. He and his brother Wallace still had the service rigs that stand over a hole, but they were out of the frack-truck business. Their trucks had gone through a flood, a rollover, a punishing decade of low oil prices, and a severely deficient maintenance program. But what they wanted, what they talked about all the time, was getting back in.

Kismet, karma, or coincidence, it was music to my ears. I enthusiastically explained my thoughts to Eli. I told him I was thinking about fracking, too, and that we should meet. I'd fill him in on my thoughts when we saw each other, and that was probably intriguing enough for him to say yes. A few days later, I jumped into my dented white Chevy shop truck and raced north to the tiny town of Reno, Pennsylvania, just south of Oil City where the Kanes had settled. This was the area I used to run around in when I was just out of college, in an old family station wagon, chasing rumors and oil and gas leases.

All along the way I had expectations of making a deal. I suspected Eli did, too. In the rush of excitement to get something done, I never once questioned why I was in such a hurry, why I was hauling ass up to the same woods I had walked out of nearly two decades before, when the market turned against me.

But twenty years later, oil was hitting all-time highs, with Wall Street calling for more, and I wanted to be a part of it, just like I did back when I was a kid wanting to get in. Like everyone else with oil on the brain, I was looking forward and not back. I was pushing down on the pedal, thinking the only risk was to risk missing out. FOMO had corrupted my thinking, filling all my thoughts, pushing out any sense of prudence or circumspection. *Never get in on the highs* is what should have been going through my mind. Let things settle down—wait, just wait—don't be the guy that jumps in on market tops. Let the private equity guys do that.

Patience. Patience. Sure, but there was just no time for patience. Not with babies at home and a frivolous need for more.

Chapter 5

SOONER FLEET SERVICE

Bristow, Oklahoma

I felt sick at the sight ahead. I'd driven through Bristow and its vaguely familiar pockmarks of industry and was coming up on its eastern horizon and the unavoidable presence of Bill's fenced-in yard of oil-field junk. I fought the impulse to box it out, mash down on the accelerator, and escape into the false hope of hiding. Yet I had to keep moving, but moving against my will. Because this is how I would be judged. If my clock were to stop right then, it was going to stop on an incomprehensible level of idiocy, and that is how I would forever be remembered.

Being at Bill's place for the first time was being at the headwaters of my stream of unforced errors, of trusting because I didn't verify, of being so pathetically green and taking on the single-celled form of a pleaser, because my operating partners—the ones safely ensconced in Pennsylvania—had to have a vortex blender, and I had to dutifully oblige them. Be careful of being a pleaser. You'll end up a doormat on a dirty trailer floor in Oklahoma—or dead cold with a bullet in your head, forgotten and buried out on the dusty plains.

Like the team player I had become, I turned left through a break in the cyclone fencing, fearing that my fool's errand would end with a terminal jump into the obituaries—me, another martyr in the history of humans knowingly walking into their own destruction.

I rolled straight up to Bill's ratty office trailer and spun around and parked so that my grille was pointing straight out. If I were in a hurry to get out, I'd want to be ready, but, lamentably, my Nitro had no ass. I could get away faster on a bicycle.

Stepping onto the stoop of Bill's office trailer, moving to the beat of my own thumping heart, I saw my hand rise in slow motion in front of me, as involuntarily as a breath of air. Then, without prompting, my clenched fist knocked on the grease-stained trailer door and pushed it open. Right in front of me was Bill's secretary, sitting at her desk wedged in behind the door.

"He's on the phone," she said without greeting or surprise, speaking up to be heard over Bill roaring into his phone in the back of the trailer.

That was it. There was nothing cordial like "have a seat" or "there's the coffee." Nothing.

Trying not to look bothered or confused or terror-stricken, I made my way along the narrow corridor between her up front and Bill in back. A few chairs were arranged in front of his desk, but that seemed like too much, impolite even, so I stood back by what looked like a schoolhouse desk lodged between a few file cabinets. That was Andy's desk, I would come to learn, ground zero of STIM, when STIM wasn't operating out of his kitchen. I pretended to busy myself with my phone as Bill jabbered on in the submarine of a trailer. He was in no hurry, which meant he'd already begun negotiating with me, letting me know he was a busy man, that the pecking order had me on the bottom.

I spun around when the trailer door swung open behind me. Filling the doorway was a guy in blue Schlumberger coveralls, instantly chatting up Bill's secretary, who was now a perfectly amenable, gregarious, fun gal. Once their flirty banter ran its course, the Schlumberger man brushed past me without so much as a nod or even an eyeball. He took one of the two seats at Bill's desk without any of my hesitation, seemingly without any concern for propriety or good breeding. Given my heightened state of paranoia, I wondered if Bill had filled him in on me, the wet-behind-the-ears prick from up in Pennsylvania who had shorted him half a million dollars on a deposit.

Bill hung up and gladly engaged with his paymaster, Schlumberger. There was a relationship there he obviously intended to keep, given that he was screwing them, too. They just didn't know it yet. Neither did I, though soon enough I would. So I continued to wait, a discarded idiot standing in the middle of a fifty-foot tube—yet somehow ignored—as I surreptitiously listened in on shit-heel Bill entertaining oil-field powerhouse Schlumberger from his throne.

Nothing I ever saw in the *Harvard Business Review*, back when I had the money to buy it, covered what to do if a maniac pulls a gun at a business meeting. Not that it's a very erudite thing to do, to pull a gun; but likely it's just too far out of the purview of the elites up in Cambridge, people unlikely to even conceive of anything so out of balance as this.

But on my side would be reason and righteousness, as Andy explained it. STIM's self-imposed penalty, a rolling 2 percent per week against the $1.5 million contract cost—$30,000 per week—was too much for Bill. He'd bend, Andy was sure of it, so long as I played the pawn. That left me squeezed into a trailer in the middle of a budding war between a needling con artist and a hairy, fat, feral man with a gun and my money, waiting my turn and thinking about how exactly was I going to get my trucks, my 15,000-pound deck motor, my 12,000-pound triplex pump, and all the rest of my parts out of Bill's shop.

The trailer door opened and, true to his word, in walked Andy. *Too soon* was my first thought as I watched his short exchange with the secretary, looking for some sort of tell, something conspiratorial between them, maybe a shared glance my way, a raised eyebrow, anything indicative of a setup. I didn't see it. But that didn't convince me it wasn't there. Then Andy pretended to see me for the first time, grinning and buoyant and feigning a first meeting as he raced in with an outstretched hand and a big, winning smile.

"What are you doing here, Dan? You didn't tell me you were coming! Holy cow!"

"I was in the neighborhood," I answered stiffly.

After a few "what a surprise" comments and perfunctory questions about my flight down, the same questions I just endured at the Kum & Go, Andy rambled on about missed timelines and vendor difficulties, just loud enough for his brother to hear in our little dog and pony show.

He was playing it as he said he would. Nothing about it suggested collusion, just the flimflammer levering his brother out of the deal.

Fortunately, even Andy exhausted himself and gradually trailed off into silence. When I turned down his offer to take a seat, he instantly folded himself into the little desk between the file cabinets—STIM SOLUTIONS's global headquarters—where he quietly remained while his older brother made money twelve feet away.

Eventually the dick from Schlumberger left, and Bill's concentration on everything other than his brother and me came to an end. Acting as though he was surprised, Bill magnanimously waved us two losers over like a throned king greeting two court jesters. Obediently, we approached in small steps, and I shook hands with Bill, eyeing him and his brother for some kind of tell. As with Bill's secretary up front, I didn't pick up on anything other than the sense that Andy might have been honest after all. He truly was scared stiff of his brother. And, right then, so was I.

"How're you?" Bill asked. "Didn't know you were coming. Good to see you."

He was buoyant and convivial, and I was stumped. This was not the Bill I expected. After a back-and-forth about my partners in Pennsylvania and their well-being, Bill wound down on his charm offensive, and Andy and I were invited to sit.

"So, what is it brings you down, Dan? Andy didn't mention you coming."

"I didn't know, either," Andy interjected and turned to me, "did I?"

"No. Just an unannounced visit."

"Well, good," Bill said, leaving it at that.

"Yeah." I turned to Andy, who was staring into his lap. I didn't sense any backup there, so I stepped out over the ledge on my own. "I just wanted to see how it's going down here."

"Good, good. Plugging along, you know."

"I was just out looking at my trucks.... It doesn't look like a whole lot's been done."

"It doesn't?"

"Not really. I haven't seen any of the progress pictures I was supposed to get, but I've been getting progress-payment requests, so I thought I'd come down and have a look at what, you know, could have been in the pictures."

"Okay. Well, what do you think?" Bill said, boring a hole in me in an unspoken challenge.

"It looks like nothing's been done."

Bill laughed uproariously, "That's because nothing can be done, Dan."

"Oh. Okay. But why's that?"

"Because I'm still waiting on parts," Bill smiled. "I can't get started until I've got everything I need on hand. You understand that much, right?"

"Yeah. I get that, Bill," I said, ignoring his shot at me. "But you can't set the engine? Or the pump? They're out there sitting on the ground."

"Not without the driveline." Bill turned to Andy. "You got that ordered, right?"

"I did," Andy said defensively. "Back in October."

"Everyone's busy. I can't do anything about back orders. It takes a lotta time, Dan. This's nothing out of the ordinary, just typical oil-field bullcrap."

"You can't set them off a measurement?"

"I wouldn't. You might, but I wouldn't." Bill laughed.

"How about the subframes? You at least get them made?"

"Not until everything's here. It wouldn't make any sense. Besides, my best welder's off on a job. You wouldn't want anyone but him, so why push ahead with anyone else?"

"So only one guy in your shop can weld up the subframes?"

"He's the best and I figured you'd want him."

"How about at least the bumpers or the manifolds? You build those? You don't need your best welder for those."

"When everything's here."

"So you can't even build the bumpers? Nothing special there, right?"

Bill just shrugged. He truly didn't care.

"You have any plans we can look at? You know, any drawings or modeling, workups for the pump or blender? You got anything I can look at?"

"I don't need drawings, so I don't do 'em."

"Then how long to build them, Bill? How long d'you think?"

"Long as it takes."

Bill's magnanimity was wavering. His thin smile wearing away, replaced by a creeping tension, a nuanced bit of annoyance washing over him. He was becoming more of the Bill I expected.

With just a hard stare, our meeting seemed to have come to an end, or to a confrontation. I thought of mentioning Andy's septic email of murder and intrigue, of using it as an icebreaker. But people don't usually warm up to being called murderers, so I dropped it. I thought, too, of appealing to Bill's sense of fair play, but because I didn't think he had a sense of fair play, I dropped that, too.

"You guys…I don't think this is working out," I started in, having decided to just wing it and stick with the insinuating truth.

"Really? You don't?" Bill asked.

"Sorry, but not really. You guys are like five weeks away from running out of time, and it doesn't look like you've even started yet. We've got work lined up for the trucks back home, starting in January, right when we're supposed to get them. The way things are, I gotta have that money and everything else back."

"You got work in January? Congratulations. You'll be the only guy working in the oil business," Bill said, deadpan.

He knew I had nothing. Nobody was working at fifty-dollar oil. With Wall Street saying it was going lower, Bill stopped just short of laughing at me. Looking for a little support, I looked to Andy but got nothing.

"Listen, I didn't come down here to make a big deal out of this, but you got this two-percent penalty coming. You do the math—"

"That's his deal. Not mine," Bill stated flatly, nodding toward Andy.

"Well, it's a STIM SOLUTIONS deal, right? That's both of you, isn't it? That's like thirty thousand dollars a week penalty you're gonna give up? Right off your bottom line? I don't see it. There's no way."

"That's a problem on his side. Talk to him about it."

"So, the two percent a week you signed off on was just Andy's deal? The big reason we went with you guys? So, you don't think there's any penalty anymore, you guys miss your date?"

"Not on my end," Bill said, staring a hole straight into me. "Tell me, Andy. Dan here caught up on everything he owes? He paid up to date on everything?"

"Um, yes," Andy said, feigning innocence.

That was the trigger, this sham openly ruminating about payment schedules, failing to mention the quarter million dollars I'd already surrendered.

"This is kinda bullshit, isn't it?" I stated.

Andy remained consistent. He didn't say a word.

"Let's just call this thing off now," I said.

"Okay. I'll build 'em then," Bill said, folding his arms across his chest.

"Okay... That's all I'm asking for, then," I said. And then I waited, just long enough to understand. Bill wasn't saying STIM would build them. Bill was saying *he* would build them, without his brother. I glanced at Andy but got nothing back, not even as his big brother cut him out of the deal, right in front of him. It was unimaginable. These two brothers couldn't be more alike. A perfect retelling of Cain and Abel. Each was trying to screw the other, one quietly, the other right out in the daylight.

"This isn't working. This just isn't working out. There's no way this is going to fly. I need those trucks, and there's no way—I got to pull my trucks out. That's it. The contract you guys gave me said I could get a full refund of my money. I think that's what we're going to have to do. We got to cancel this deal. If you got the keys, I'll drive those trucks away myself."

That one hung in the air. It could have been a couple of seconds or a couple of minutes, but we all sat there in dead silence.

"I'll have a truck here in a few hours to get the engine and pump," I continued. "Sorry, guys, but that's how it's going to go."

Andy buried his head back inside his enormous coat, like a roadside turtle retracting at the sight of an oncoming truck.

His face glowing red, his palms turned down on his desk, Bill did exactly what his brother said he would. He stood over me and glowered dramatically. Then purposefully, slowly, he opened his desk drawer and began fishing around in it…and fishing and fishing. His hard stare began fading into confusion as he was forced to turn his full attention to the drawer, his anger becoming more pronounced as he rifled through it, scattering its contents, unable to find it!

It was astonishing to me, utterly unbelievable. He had lost his gun. *How much bourbon, rum, tequila, whisky, and fucking painkillers do you need to choke down before you lose a gun?*

I shot a glance Andy's way. He was pushing back in his chair, skittishly unnerved, probably wetting his pants and praying this whole put-on wouldn't derail into federal time.

When I turned back to Bill, he was grinning demonically. He was waving a knife around. He had found a knife instead of the gun. *Jesus, a knife instead of a gun! What a break!*

Bill parried and thrust it, making motions like he was gutting something. It was all bravado, but it worked. He had me terrorized, especially when he stepped closer.

"This is what I do to guys like you."

The knife was of the woodsman's style—a long, upturned, stainless-steel blade with a serrated edge running along the top, good for sawing through bone and sinew. I stared at it, then at Bill making his thrashing motions, hoping he didn't trip over his big gut and drive it through my heart. *What a son of a bitch*, I thought, *him and his bullshit Wild West show.*

This guy flew up to Pennsylvania and sold my partners simply by virtue of having shown up. He sold us on his hyped-up vortex-blender technology that I'd soon enough learn was stolen right out from the obvious. He took my money, but wanted more, and now he was trying to back me down and teach me a lesson.

Screw him. Screw his knife. He wasn't going to stick it in me. Shoving a knife into me would put an end to his line of credit, the one he had no intention of repaying. It was all a jacked-up bluff and I was pissed. I wasn't buying into it any longer. I was getting the hell out of there, and this asshole wasn't going to stop me.

Summoning something from somewhere—the unchecked stupidity of anyone who gets pushed around once too many times—I stood and jabbed my finger into Bill's fat belly, right into his hardened liver.

"Take it easy, chief," I told him.

That astonished even me. *Where'd that come from? Why'd I do that?*

I waited for Bill to act on a lifetime of threats, bullying, and malfeasance. It seemed to me that I stood there forever, paralyzed as much by fear as I was by fear of failure, standing there in the dark basement of entrepreneurism, willing to risk everything to go on, to monetize all my poorly drawn ideas.

Bill stopped waving the knife. His bluff had been called. Deflated, absolutely emasculated, he let go of his demonic expression for something less baleful. It was almost sad to watch, all the bombast hissing out of him like a leaky tire as he haltingly placed the knife back in the drawer and dropped down into his chair.

And that was that. It was over. Bill had surrendered. The tension in the back of the trailer was gone. The three of us were just sitting there quietly, almost contemplatively, as the trailer shrank in around its master.

Though I was contained, I was also crazy with relief. And there was Andy, hiding a grin, certain that he, too, had just scored a victory, pulling his own metaphorical knife from his big brother's back.

"Where you takin' the trucks?" Bill asked softly.

I caught Andy's sharp glance, betraying a terror that I might tell the truth.

"I'll know in a couple of hours," I said. "I gotta see."

Watching Bill accept my answer with a simple nod had me oddly concerned for him. Most bullies have a damaged, soft core. I never would have bet that on this one, though. I saw him as the real thing, a bully's bully, which had me wondering if this was just a pause in the action, a brief respite in a gathering storm.

"Dan, do you plan on staying here or you heading right back to Pittsburgh?" Andy asked.

Oh, brother, I thought. The truth was I'd be meeting with Andy as soon as he could dispose of his brother's body.

"I was thinking of sticking around," I said, playing along.

"Well, do you mind if I meet with Bill, just the two of us? Maybe I could call you later?"

"Sure, Andy. I'll stay close by."

"I'll call you then. We understand your concerns. I'll call you."

"Okay," I said and extended my hand to Bill as an offer of no hard feelings. He took it, probably wondering what the hell had just happened.

I turned and walked down the long trailer corridor, staring intently at the secretary ahead, waiting for her to duck from something developing behind me, notably Bill finding his gun and opening fire on the guy with the open checkbook ecstatically walking out of his life. But I saw nothing telling, just more typing, her head forever down and permanently taking cover.

Barely able to contain myself, I picked up the pace and walked right out the door and down the steps into my perfectly positioned Nitro. I punched the gas and took off down the blacktop until I had some real distance between me and him, so damned happy to be alive in beautiful Creek County, Oklahoma. It could have been raining hot lava and I still would have been giddy with joy for that small moment, my first victory in three months of knockdowns.

But because the truth is so damned relentless, so omnipresent, it didn't take long before its buzzkill effects grabbed hold. My fight-or-flight compulsion moderated and my high dissipated as I squared up with the fact that I had made it out but my trucks hadn't. A glance back confirmed that my money was still on Bill's property and was quickly fading in the rearview mirror. What were the chances that on my return I'd run headfirst into a locked gate, or into some shit-bird lawyer palming my truck keys? All he'd have to do was stall to make me collapse. He and Bill would both know that elapsed time was my death knell.

So I headed for the Kum & Go only because it was familiar. There, in the parking lot, I spent the next two hours on a flurry of phone calls, each one a piece in a larger puzzle, all of them directed toward unraveling the tangled mess my start-up, Reliance Well Services, LLC, had become.

Chapter 6
THREE MONTHS BEFORE, AUGUST 2008

Oil City, Pennsylvania

Any start-up has multiple fronts. Oil price collapse or not, I had to execute on all of them. I needed partners and key personnel, customers, suppliers, crew, and capital. The capital part was coming from debt, and that was all mine. Wallace and Eli Kane, my Pennsylvania partners, were to bring in the customers and crew and mostly run our jobs. I'd figure out suppliers over time. But it was equipment that had the longest lead times. Building frack trucks in 2008, back in the middle of the boom, was taking a year or better, if you could even get on a fabricator's schedule. With nearly all the core pieces of a frack fleet being custom-built, I needed to get in line quick.

Unfortunately, one packager—STIM—was running ads in a trade newspaper, like an *Auto Trader*, but for ragged-out oil-field equipment. Equally unfortunate, one of my partners in Pennsylvania saw it.

My first call to STIM SOLUTIONS went well. I met Andy over the phone and told him my project was small, just one pump truck and one blender, but I needed a builder and was funded and ready to go with a set of partners that had a long history in Pennsylvania's shallow oil fields. That was an attention-grabber—the part about money in hand. Enthusiastically, Andy launched into a spirited explanation of his company. He was the guy at the helm, while his brother, a mechanical wunderkind, covered their operations. Like mine, theirs was a start-up, and they were actively looking for work, too. More conversations followed, and soon enough we foundered our way into a deal, me and two brothers in Pennsylvania joining with two more brothers from Oklahoma as our fabricators. Between both sets, one a perfect retelling of Cain and Abel, and the other just plain old dysfunctional, I would soon be the odd man out. Like many things, I just didn't know it at the time.

"Dan, there isn't a piece of equipment in the oil field that my brother Bill hasn't built or repaired. Schlumberger even flew him to Siberia to keep a fleet of Detroits running. To Siberia, Dan. Think about it! *Siberia!*"

After Andy rattled off a few more selling points, the clichéd pitch of smaller companies bettering bigger competitors, he hit me with his knockout punch, the thing no lucid business owner would ever guarantee. He promised a four-month build-out with a guaranteed delivery date. Backing it up was a self-imposed penalty if they missed it, STIM's standard 2 percent per week gun to the head.

"That's compounded, Dan!"

This is what is known as too good to be true. I realized it at the time but was almost salivating at the thought of them running late. Thirty thousand dollars a week! But they were cheap, fast, and knowledgeable, and that was exactly what I wanted to hear. The bum's rush was sealed when, several calls in, the phone was passed to Bill and I was suddenly talking to the man himself—Siberia! Flying first class! Schlumberger! He was attentive, heard me out, and let me know that he had already thought his way through our build. It was like Elvis was suddenly in the room, asking me if it were okay if he caught a flight that night to see me first thing in the morning. In Pennsylvania.

I called my partners, and we quickly agreed that this would be a great way to talk things over. Wallace Kane and his younger brother Eli had a business running frack rigs (derricks that run pipe in and out of a well during a frack job), and they would have one on a well that was being fracked the next day. A set of frack trucks would also be there, owned by our soon-to-be competition, Universal Well Services. Given that we wanted to build a pump truck very similar to Universal's trucks, a hands-on visit by the builder would be incredibly constructive.

At first light the following morning, I picked Bill up at an airport motel in Pittsburgh. He stepped out of his room into the parking lot where I was waiting—me, a short and eager guy, friendly and wanting things to work out. And there was Bill—tired, dark, and pissed off for a hundred different reasons, not the same guy that was on the phone the day before. He'd had something like two hours of sleep, but no one sleeps much in the oil business. That's part of the deal, making Bill a natural, with his look of someone who didn't sleep much, anyway.

He may have been looking forward to a snooze on the three-hour drive to the frack job, but reality won out when he had to sandwich himself into my cramped 4x2 Chevy Silverado truck, a step down from the full-sized Ford 150s and 250s typical in the oil field. Ticked off, he brooded the entire way. For three hours I played nice and tried to engage him in dead-end, one-way conversations. To his credit, though, he came alive when he talked about his son and their cross-country runs, chasing a motocross series around North America. Bill would drive all day and night so his boy could sleep beside his motorcycle in the back of their van. He'd wrench so his kid could race. You couldn't help but appreciate a guy like that. But the silent treatment, the disregard...it all left me wondering.

The late-summer sun was out when we got to the frack job in northern Pennsylvania. Right away, Bill was answering Wallace and Eli's concerns about the trucks. He was coming up with solutions and offering up insight on things they hadn't even thought about. It was ingratiating and became a tractor beam for Wallace—to be in the presence of the only guy in America still actively building the fabled vortex blender. He had seen them on the Dowell trucks that had long ago left the area, but for some inexplicable reason they had become an obsession of his. To him, they were the cat's ass of blenders. It was technology that had come and gone for good reason, one in which sand is dumped directly into an open-sided centrifugal pump, where it mixes with water and chemicals before being pushed off to the frack pumps. Conventional screw-type blenders auger sand up from ground-level hoppers into mixing tubs. More parts are required, but they work and remain the industry workhorses. Vortex blenders, on the other hand, are fickle and tricky to run and have been more or less bypassed. But to Wallace, they were revolutionary. He had to have one, so certain he was that they would pave our way to frack glory.

We all stood in the field and from a distance watched as the single Universal frack pump and blender revved up and drowned out our voices. Under the roar of their big Cummins engines and clutch fans, we watched as the trucks fracked a small stage.

If you knew what was going on, you'd know that sand was being dumped out of a covered dump-style truck into a hopper hanging off the rear end of the blender. Augurs screwed the sand upward into a tub where it mixed with water and chemicals and was stirred into a slurry, then injected through hoses into the back end of the frack pump. There, up on the truck's frame rails, a quarter-million-dollar triplex pump run by a 1,500-horsepower diesel engine supercharged the slurry to a pressure in the thousands of pounds per square inch. After that, it was pushed out through high-pressure iron pipe to the wellhead, and then downhole where it met the resistance of the rock below.

Watching it unfold, you didn't want to get too close, not with the throttled-out roar of the engines and the big chromed plungers on the back of the pump punching away at the rock formation a thousand feet below.

When the stage abruptly ended, the trucks idled down and a small rig crew moved in. They gathered on the rig and lowered the frack pipe down to the next targeted depth, setting up the next "stage" to be fracked.

Able to hear again, I sensed a presence next to me and turned for a look. Reflexively, I jumped back at the sight of an enormous bearded man, covering me in his shadow and staring down at me. The guy looked like Gandalf the wizard, except he was built like he'd played in the NFL, six-five or six-six with long red and gray hair and a grease-stained fluorescent-orange hunter's cap. I was told it was the Kanes' mechanic, Ken Carson. Neither one of us said a word for a moment, until I said hi and he grunted something back. A few months later, Ken would stick by me after most everyone else had left. But right then, looking up at him, my only thought was, What the hell is *this*?

At the end of the day, when Wallace and Eli said goodbye to Bill, there was little doubt STIM would be building our trucks. Wallace was absolutely convinced that a vortex blender would make us stand out, and Bill knew that as long as Wallace wanted a vortex blender, STIM was getting the work. No one else in North America was building them any longer, at least according to Bill, which right then and there eliminated every other builder from consideration.

On the ride back to the airport, Bill didn't bother talking much. There was no goodwill effort, like a "let's get to know each other" ride to the airport. To him, I was just the money guy, a good observation because it was mostly true. But it was my money.

No, that's incorrect. It was my debt.

Chapter 7

KUM & GO

Bristow, Oklahoma

Mary and I were the only signatories on Reliance's loans, meaning we leveraged everything we owned, including Lightspeed, my film equipment rental company that I owned with a few partners. The bank wanted its assets as collateral, which meant I had to cross-collateralize all of it, my interest and my partners'. To compensate for the drag on its balance sheet, I passed around small interests in Reliance. No cash came in from my Lightspeed partners, but their permission to leverage Lightspeed did.

And right at that moment, I needed to keep my Lightspeed partners onboard.

As I worked my phone from the Kum & Go parking lot, my first call was to one of my Lightspeed partners, my old friend Dave Good, a CPA and valuation expert, and once the owner of the largest independent accounting firm in Pittsburgh. He knew I'd be calling, so I didn't need to preface the conversation with being in Oklahoma on a life-support mission. When he answered, I got right into the Andy-and-Bill brotherly intrigue and misplaced gun, doubling back a few times on the knife, only because it was so bugged-out.

"No, I'm not joking," I kept repeating. "The guy pulled a knife on me. I don't think he was going to use, but he pulled it."

I told Dave that it seemed like Bill was going to let us out of the deal. But we needed to move quickly, before he rethought it and concluded that he should have stabbed me when he had the chance.

Dave and I quickly agreed that we were bound to Andy to some degree. If we walked, we'd never see a dime of the money paid in. On the other hand, if we stayed in, Andy had never built a frack truck. It was a huge risk—a damned-if-I-do, damned-if-I-don't one. But the money was paid in and gone hard, and I couldn't walk away from it.

It didn't take long to determine that Andy would have to get the vortex blender. That was only because we had already paid STIM, and STIM had already paid Bill for the heart of it, the pod portion, with its big and unwieldy centrifugal pump. Besides, the new generation of builders didn't even know what the hell a vortex blender was. When I explained the technology to one of them, the builder was perplexed.

"Why would anyone want to build that?"

Since I needed to move on to other calls to shippers, truck drivers, and my lending bank, I was hurrying along my conversation with Dave, until something in his tone stopped me. He was hesitant and had something to say. I began sensing that my day hadn't seen bottom yet as I heard Dave telling me that he'd been thinking about something recently—that he was a father and a grandfather, and a lot of people counted on his support. Then it came, when he told me it was best for him to withdraw from the company. It was already top-heavy with partners, and maybe I could sell off his interest to raise money. But to continue like this, taking one gut punch after another, and feeling victory only in the fact that we were still standing, wobbling really, was too wearying. And to hear it from my old mentor and partner felt something like blunt-force trauma.

I promised Dave that I'd sleep on it and did my best to hide the glum onrush of something beneath depression.

Twenty-five years my senior, Dave had been a friend and a mentor and a foundation of support throughout my entire working life. Twenty years back, he had been an early investor in my first Pennsylvania wells, right after I busted out of college with an English degree, two classes short of a double. The other degree was geology, but waiting out another semester to finish up felt like damnation. After that, Dave came in on wells we drilled together down in Texas, outside of Abilene, in a company we called Migration Oil and Gas. Then it was Dave again, investing in my film rental company, Lightspeed. This, right after my decade-long, post-oil stint at New York University's graduate film school (yes, I know, film school), and the subsequent obliteration in the movie business in New York and Los Angeles, trying to talk producers into making a movie with me about the oil business. As that capitulated into failure, it was Dave again, in Reliance. All those years, we'd been working together.

Until this.

After we hung up, I fell into a dim, rayless hole. This marked our end, with coming capital calls and continued pain. After nearly forty years of overseeing endless businesses in crisis and helping clients climb out of holes, he had never seen one quite like this. I knew a part of my life had just come to an end, and that I was now truly alone.

There was nowhere else to turn. My operating partners up north, the Kanes, weren't the kind of guys you'd ask for advice. That wasn't them. They weren't business strategists. They just knew how to frack. Besides, they were looking at me to put the business together, not to cry on their shoulders.

Before my next call, to a freight dispatcher, Mary called. She had just gotten back from the grocery store. After loading the girls into the big metal cart and filling it with groceries, then unloading it onto the checkout conveyor belt, our personal credit card was declined. And that was her best shot, the only personal card we had with any room left on it. Carrying checks was pointless, as I had mostly raided that account, as well.

Thinking on her feet, Mary pushed two containers of milk toward the cashier and asked her to run the card again. To her joy, there was just enough left on our $32,000 limit for two gallons of it. The wife of an entrepreneur, Mary saw the milk as a blessing, that and the kindly cashier insisting she'd restock everything else. Then she told me to get back to work and to tell her later how I was doing "down there."

When I got a trucking company on the line, I told the dispatcher I had about a half million dollars of equipment that I needed to get out of Bristow immediately.

"Where's this equipment going, sir?"

"I'm not sure yet."

"You're not sure yet, but you need it moved immediately?"

"It's a little unusual, I know. But I need a tractor and a drop-deck trailer, like right now."

"Do you want us to store this then? Is that what you're—"

"That's a great idea. Yeah. Please. Store it, but don't unload it. The important thing, though, is we get this equipment picked up right away. How long, you think, before you can be there?"

"Bristow? Probably a couple hours. I need to assign a driver and a truck and trailer." Then the dispatcher went quiet, until finally asking, "Sir?"

"Yes?"

"Do you own this equipment? Would you have proof of ownership?"

After talking through weights, widths, and heights, and proof that I wasn't stealing the engine and pump, the dispatcher ran my company credit card. As I waited, all my worries shifted from getting my equipment out of Bill's to there being enough room left on the card. *Please work. Please, please work* was my refrain after Mary's card didn't. A few seconds later, she told me to watch out for the driver, which meant my card was still good.

The next decision was who would build the pump truck. Taking a shot, I called a guy down in Texas who I thought I had a fifty-fifty chance of getting on the phone. That was generous, given that the last time we spoke, he'd hung up on me.

Some people's expectations become their reality. That was Douglas Campbell, a swaggering Texan full of stories about bar fights and edge-of-your-life skirmishes. Wallace found him at a fab shop called Tribute Oilfield Solutions on the outskirts of Fort Worth. He had quoted the trucks three months back and assumed without pretense that the work was his. Because he'd built a frack truck for the Kanes back in the '80s and still remembered that "ol' son of a gun Wallace," he just figured he'd do it for him again. When I gave the job to STIM instead, because they built vortex blenders with guaranteed delivery times, and he didn't, he got pissed and hung up on me.

This time, Douglas graciously accepted my call. If he was harboring any resentment, he didn't show it. A downturn in the oil business will do that to you. It'll force you to drop all those pretenses and prejudices. He simply said hello and asked how I was doing, and how were his old friends the Kanes. I told him fine on all counts, then told him just what it was that he wanted to hear. I needed a frack-pump builder...again.

"Listen, I'm pulling the frack pump away from STIM SOLUTIONS, the builder I went with up in Oklahoma. And I was wondering if you could build it?"

"Well, sure, Dan—you need a builder, I've always been right here for y'all. You know I'd love to build that truck for you," Douglas said, kindly not asking what had gone so wrong and me not offering. That would all come later, when I got around to my admission of stupidity.

"So, I don't know if this will work, but I bought a fifteen-liter Cummins deck engine, and I know you're a Detroit shop, but you think we can work around that?"

"I don't see that's a problem, if you got it all paid for."

"It is. I bought it direct. Cummins Southern Plains."

"I know the fellas at Southern Plains. Be happy to work with 'em. I can call 'em and s'plain the minute we're done here, if y'all'd like me to."

"Yeah. Good. Good. There's also the controls, though. I need some consistency between the trucks, so everything is talking to each other, and I was hoping for the same manufacturer on both trucks, or some, you know, reliable work-around," I said.

"Well, they use Quantum up there, don't they?"

"Yeah. How'd you know?"

"Small world, Dan. An' I happen to know Quantum very well."

"You think they'd work with you?"

"I know they would. I put 'em on my trucks, too. Lemme ask. Andy up there tell you they wouldn't?"

"Nah, he...I just thought he had some kind of exclusive with them," I said, hiding my embarrassment that Andy had claimed an exclusive on the controls, another of his selling points that just bit the dust.

"Got a pencil? I'll give you Zahir Kahn's number up at Quantum in Enid," Douglas offered. "He's the number-one man at Quantum Controls. Fact, he owns the place. You might want to call 'im for yourself. An' make sure an' tell him you got that number from me."

From there, Douglas assured me he had room in his shop and could start right away on our truck, with me remaining noncommittal, thinking this time I might do my due diligence and stop myself from closing another deal on the quick.

"How about I come down and meet you, finally have a look at your place?" I offered.

"Well sure, Dan. Absolutely. Love to show the place off to you. When're you thinkin' you'll make it down?"

"Tomorrow. You'll be my first stop in Texas," I added, pretending I actually knew other builders in Texas. "I was thinking tomorrow morning, if that's all right?"

"Tomorrow mornin'? Damn, son. Well, okay, come on down then."

Chapter 8

CUP OF MEMORIES LUNCHEONETTE

Bristow, Oklahoma

I was working through my call list, my phone hot to the touch, when Andy finally beeped in and animatedly told me he was alone and could speak and was driving out of Bill's place. He wanted to meet right away, somewhere in Bristow, anywhere as long as it was out of Bill's orbit. He suggested Cup of Memories, a little café run by a few genial grandmothers, private and quiet and not at all a joint, making it the perfect place not to run into Bill.

I got there and found a few tables in a makeshift room that was dressed up in doilies, knickknacks, and antiques. Andy arrived a few minutes later with his silly grin and laptop, energized and exhilarated after having gone mano a mano with his brother.

"It's all good, Dan. It's all good. Honestly, it couldn't be better."

Surviving a kind of Shakespearean coup d'etat, the man was all jacked up on the bliss of undivided ownership. One more step, one more contract, and he'd be off to the races without the burden of his brother.

"This just feels…so good."

Itching to launch a new and revitalized rendition of STIM SOLUTIONS, he fired up his laptop and began throwing out ideas, improvements, terms.

"Andy, Andy, hold on! Just a second!"

"What? What's wrong?"

"Nothing's wrong. It's just…I don't know, Andy. I know he's your brother…but I don't know. He seemed a little shocked."

"You just surprised him, is all."

"You mean *we* surprised him."

"Yeah, but he was surprised. It's all good now. We got our way." Andy leaned back in his chair, basking in the glory of sweet deceit. "This is so great. Such great news, I should call my wife. She's never gonna believe this," Andy blathered with unchecked glee, until he remembered I was sitting with him. "You did really well in there, Dan. I can't believe you stood up like that. It was great. It was—what were you seriously thinking?"

"I don't know. I wasn't. But you believe Bill pulled a knife on me," I stated more than asked.

"I know, but I told you he wouldn't use it."

"That was the gun. You said that about the gun."

"Yeah, but I told you he wouldn't use that, either."

I dropped it.

"It's all good, Dan. You're gonna be fine. He doesn't care. He even gave me advice on building the trucks."

"You told him?" I asked, shocked.

"I did. And he doesn't even care. He said so. This is just what we needed, Dan. Both of us, I'm telling you."

"But you told him?

"Of course I did. He's gonna help me. He wants to see me get on my feet with this. This is like—this is way better than I could have expected." Andy smiled. "Starting STIM was my idea. He doesn't want anything to do with it. I'm telling you, all Bill wants is to get bought out."

"I thought you said it wasn't worth anything."

"It's not. That's just Bill. He said he lent his name to it. That's why it has value. That's just Bill. He put a little time in on thinking through the trucks, but that was it. I'll probably have to give him something for that."

"But you paid him for everything, right? You gave him the transmission money, the pod money, right? No bills from Bill, right? You paid him the money I gave you?"

"Dan, I paid him. I mean, he paid himself. I don't owe him anything. STIM doesn't owe him anything."

"Okay. As long as he's not going to come back on you. There's no way he can tie you up, right?"

"I don't understand. Why do you think he's gonna come back on me?"

"Because you said he wants you to buy him out. You know, buy-him-out. Pay him money."

"It's not worth anything, Dan. I already told you that."

"Andy, for Christ's sake, then why's he want you to buy him out?"

"I already told you, that's just Bill being Bill. The company isn't worth anything. Maybe like a parting gift for thinking about it, is all. For the trip up to Pennsylvania. But trust me, he's already done pretty good."

When the waitress came along and took our lunch order, I watched as Andy loaded up on more—the two sandwiches at Kum & Go gone, and already another big pile of food. Who would pay for it suddenly became my overarching concern.

"And you really think he's going to let me pull my trucks out? You really don't think he's going to block me?" I said, having determined there was no way in hell I'd let myself get stuck with the bill.

"He said so," Andy responded giddily.

"And my engine and pump? The transmission? He's going to load it all? He said that?"

"Absolutely, Dan. He's fine with it. I mean, you never know with Bill. He's just—I mean, you know Bill. I don't think he even cares."

"All right," I said. "Long as we can get the trucks out. I have a drop-deck coming for the engine and pump later today."

"Already?"

"Yeah. Don't you think so? I thought that's what you wanted."

"Absolutely I do."

"I don't want it to get stuck there. You know, get while the getting's good."

"I'm not ready, though. I mean, I can be. I don't have any way to unload that engine. Not even the pump. That engine weighs, like, sixteen thousand pounds. We'll need to get a skid steer...."

"Yeah. Andy—"

"You think your freight company has a skid steer we can rent?"

"Yeah. Listen, Andy. I gotta talk to you about that."

"I wish I knew someone. That'll be expensive.... That's going to have to go in the new contract."

"Andy, we have to talk about the trucks."

"Maybe Bryson. You'll love Bryson. He's going to be my foreman; maybe he'll know someone, like maybe a friend or someone, to keep the cost down."

"I'm really sorry about this, Andy. But all these problems," I said, trying to get his attention. "Listen. I gotta tell you...I've been talking to a builder in Texas and...well..."

Andy looked up from his computer screen.

"And I think I'm giving him the pump. I mean, I am giving him the pump to build."

"Huh?"

"Andy, I'm sorry, but I gotta split this up."

"No, no..."

"I can't risk—"

"No, no. You can't."

"I'm sorry. But you get the blender, Andy. It's a good deal. You've never built a truck before. This's a good start. I mean, Andy, you understand, all these problems—"

"But, Dan."

"You do a good job—"

"But, Dan, Dan! That's not a good idea. You know that. You're going to have two different sets of controls. There's not gonna be any redundancy. What about all this talk about redundancy? You don't want to do that. I build both trucks, you won't have that problem. It's my dream!" Andy cried. "I told you that. You know it's my dream. I don't need Bill—"

"Listen. I know, Andy. But listen, your business partner just pulled a knife on me. There's kind of a confidence issue here."

"*I* didn't pull a knife. *I* didn't do that. I was just as surprised as you. Come on, really. How can I be taken seriously as a fabricator if I don't have both builds in my portfolio? Wouldn't you be insisting, absolutely insisting, if you were sitting in my position? If this is about me not having Bill, I can assure you I have good people. Bryson—"

"You're getting the blender. That's gotta be good enough. It's way more complicated. You can cut your teeth on it. Word will get out. You do a good job, word will—"

"But what about the same controls? That was your big concern. You don't care about that anymore? Suddenly, you don't care?"

"Andy, the other group down in Texas uses Quantum controls, too."

Andy looked as though he'd just been sucker punched. "No they don't! They can't."

"They say they do. Quantum Controls. Out of Enid, Oklahoma. Guy named Zahir runs it. That Quantum, right? Apparently, I'm hearing he doesn't know about any exclusives with you."

Andy looked sick. Whether he had been lying to me or was simply kidding himself, I didn't know. But he sat there, caught, traumatized, and now his jaw was hanging open.

"Is it Tribute Oilfield Solutions? The other builder? In Texas? In Granbury?" Andy asked pensively.

"Yeah, it is. Douglas Campbell's company."

That was it. Andy's mind was turning, but he didn't offer anything else.

"You do a good job on the blender, Andy, and I'll be building more," I promised. "If you can build a blender, you can build anything."

Following was a long-winded pause. Nothing was said, just Andy slipping into a dumbstruck, cheerless admission of guilt.

"You okay?" I asked as I reached to grab his arm and shake him out of it.

"If this is what you want…." Andy stared right into me. "This is what you really want?"

"Come on, Andy. This is a good deal. You pull this off, you can pull off anything."

Andy turned back to his laptop, audibly sighing, looking as if he were going to deflate as he pulled up a template for our next contract.

"I'll keep the guaranteed delivery date, but not the two-percent-a-week penalty. You wouldn't want to enforce that anyways," Andy said, trying to regain some ground.

"Yeah, sure. But how about something monthly? Enough to cover my interest payments in case you go late, which I know you're not going to do, right?" I smiled and thought I saw Andy nod, but left it at that. The truth was his guarantee wouldn't be worth the paper it was printed on. He'd have to be watched, with a payment schedule matching performance markers. Photographs of work completed would trigger the next payment, not arbitrary dates on a calendar.

As we worked through it, the resuscitated STIM SOLUTIONS was going to build the same blender at the same price. Nothing would change there, as Andy didn't know enough to make any changes. What did change, though, was the finish date. My start-up would be starting all over again, with the build clock resetting to zero for both the blender and pump. As much harm as that would cause—thwarted income and principal payments coming due before the trucks were finished—it was a relief.

"It can be more or less the same as our first one," Andy said about the contract. "Except I guess we have just one truck now."

Grudgingly, Andy continued striking out everything to do with the pump truck, with me pushing him along, anxious to get back to Bill's yard before he sparked when the tractor-trailer arrived for the engine and pump.

As soon as Andy finished his edit, he wanted to run off and get it printed. I stopped him, though. It would have to wait until later, until I got the blender and pump out of Bill's shop. Once I was able to get the blender to Andy's new yard, and the pump on the road, I'd sign his contract.

But first I had to pay our lunch bill.

Chapter 9

ROADSIDE

Bristow, Oklahoma

I'd found a lookout spot, a half mile up from Bill's place on the rural highway running alongside the front of his shop. I had already been there a few hours in my Nitro, watching it and my trucks, waiting on the driver to show and free me forever from at least one of the Brennan brothers.

As I waited, I was also pinned down by my phone. Every call I placed generated several-fold more, in a back-and-forth crossfire. Everything that was set in motion had some ramification, some complication, some obstacle somewhere that required more follow-through.

My most recent string of calls revolved around a friend with a bird problem. I needed someone to drive the pump truck to Texas. That's how I landed on Woodstock, a truck-driving hippy stagehand from Pittsburgh. I knew that with an out-of-date license on the truck and absolutely no credentials, he was just the man, with his long hair, omnipresent shorts, a metal plate in his head, and a lifelong aversion to authority. When I told him I needed to steal a truck away from a son of a bitch in Oklahoma, he was all ears. When I framed my problem as an adventure—a quest, really—a possibly illegal foray down in Oklahoma in which the good guys (us) had to outrun the bad guys (them), he was all in.

"Yeah, man, why not? When you thinking?" Woodstock asked, casual as hell about it all.

"Like right now. Today. Like right away."

"Wow, right away. Okay, man. Ummm…I'm flying down, right? You don't need me to drive down?"

"No. You gotta fly. To Tulsa. Just show up at the airport and ask around for who's flying there next. Trust me, someone'll sell you a ticket. I'll pay you back when you get here."

"Yeah. All right. Tulsa, cool. I never been."

"Woodstock, I have to tell you," I nearly shouted, so overwhelmed with relief. "I'm gonna really owe you for this."

"No problem. I just gotta find someone to watch my bird, man."

"Your parrot?"

"Yeah, man, my macaw."

"You can find someone, you think?"

"I don't know. Prick bites everyone, even me! And I'm the asshole who feeds him! Hahaha!"

That began another unending string of calls, with me stuck on the Oklahoma roadside, and Woodstock in his Pittsburgh sound studio searching for someone to feed his gigantic blue-and-green macaw for the next handful of days. Trying to find someone who knew enough not to get bit.

Then there was another call, a returned call, this one from my banker, Emaline. I had inadvisably called her earlier and left a message, explaining that I was *unexpectedly* in Oklahoma and wanted to talk. "Unexpectedly" is a bad omen for a banker. I should have framed my trip another way—something that was scheduled, just a normal part of my rigorous due diligence.

But a storm had already been building. In fact, Emaline had been bracing herself against it—something I could feel right over the phone when she returned my call. We started off well enough, but as I steered our conversation toward why I was sitting in my Nitro in a barren field, littered with wind-blown garbage, I knew the days of our breezy and empathetic repertoire were over.

The easy banter I once had with her had mutated into something more exigent and less sportive since the downturn in oil. I needed more money, but I also needed to secure the access I already had to the funding I had in place with her. Emboldened reassurances weren't going to work anymore. Regardless of my rehearsed explanations, I still sounded like a guy clinging to the cliff's edge, trying to soften why I wanted to redirect the bank's progress payments from one company that I had spoken so highly of to two companies utterly unknown to her (and me).

STIM SOLUTIONS had been a selling point to my lending bank, with its depth of knowledge and history in the oil field. They all loved that guaranteed delivery date—an outsized factor in the loan approval. And having cinched myself to the Brennans and their guarantees in order to get the loan, I couldn't very well torpedo them without incurring some collateral damage. What would that say about me and my own due diligence? My reputation would sink right alongside theirs.

"Dan..." Emaline began haltingly. "How could things have changed so drastically in such a short period of time? I think, Dan, on my organizer—I think, like, six days since our last conversation?"

A loan going bad tends to sharpen bankers' tongues, so there was very little beating around the bush, even as I attempted to circle around it and tamp it down. Finally, and tacitly, Emaline stopped me. She wanted another set of ears, to get someone senior on the phone. In other words, she was looking for dilution. Continuing alone would put it all on her. If she were lucky, she might get someone else to jump on this fumble early enough to spread the blame. Emaline was as stand-up as they come, but in a scrum it's hard to tell who's punching and who's getting hit.

For a brief moment, the phone went silent, just long enough for me to realize that my time might be coming to an end. Over the past few months, I had been able to dance around tanking commodity prices, portraying them as something other than the wretchedly miserable cancer they were. I demonstrated that the committed loan with its progress payments was still good. I harped on about how falling material costs would lower our frack prices but not our profits (fib), and that savvy operators would still drill and frack (fibbish). I told of how the smart money on Wall Street was calling the bottom on oil prices (fact and fib). I explained our positioning relative to weaker pressure pumpers (lie—we were a start-up, for God's sake!). And I spoke of the work my operating partners (the Kanes, an outsized influence on our loan) and I could do on our own behalf, right down to forty dollars per barrel (fibbish nonsense). My partners and I didn't have two nickels to rub together, let alone to launch an in-house drilling program (fact). Hell, I was having trouble even putting groceries on the table (fact).

There was no more room for a sales job. That would make me an over-the-top bullshitter. Boxed in, I had to play this one straight. My guess was that my bank would, too. They'd want the truth, and they'd know if they didn't hear it. They had agreed to the loan but would likely be dusting it off the second we hung up, doubling-checking on how much wiggle room they'd written in.

The phone line abruptly came alive as Emaline and her co-lenders and bosses joined in on what was suddenly an exceptionally well-attended, last-second conference call. No one wanted to hear my take on commodity prices, operator behavior, or strategic positioning. They just wanted to hear about the once-vaunted STIM SOLUTIONS and what the hell was going on down in Bristow County, Oklahoma.

If you know bankers, you know that most do not yell. They're as well trained in polite business etiquette as they are in risk. Because they don't yell, there is too much room for contemplative thought and consideration. Sadly, in my case, they became quietly inquisitive, like people at the wake of someone who has died far too young. Preferably, they would have yelled at me. But instead, they took turns, one banker after another, dissecting my endeavor and the decisions I had made to date. Each was civil, a few of them even encouraging, but the appetite to continue making the advances I needed was gone. If a loan agreement weren't in place, the call would have been over, and the bank's workout department would have been gearing up to take over and wash away this stain. But because there was a loan agreement, which had tethered them to the legal obligation of funding the trucks (regardless of what company built them), we continued with the dolorous unmasking of my start-up and the faltering, expensive failure it might just become—for all of us.

I pushed on as requested and defended myself as best as I could, but I could just as well have been pitching a reality show to Universal or Paramount or any of the other patrons of the barmy fringes of society. My story was just so damned crazy—a guy with a knife, another guy with a parrot, and another guy, a lightweight, with his crew of good Christian soldiers at the ready. It was understandable why they wanted to hear every last bit of it, as unfathomable as it was to a group of risk-averse bankers.

When there is no money, hope becomes your currency, so I pushed that to the bankers, too. Unfortunately, hope also was in short supply. In fact, there was so little hope that it was beyond the balance of odds. I was occupying an anomaly that wouldn't right itself. That was becoming perplexingly obvious to everyone on the call, including the executive vice president who had just joined us.

"How much of it can you get back?" he chimed in, referring to money, his money, the unspent dollars that he'd like to see me return.

An uneasy silence settled over the call, until it was broken by a voice I recognized as my own. In an involuntary impulse, I found myself speaking, telling the executive VP where the money was and that it likely wasn't coming back, not even with an expensive, go-nowhere lawsuit. I ceded that some money had been lost, but not enough to capsize our effort.

Rushing not to be interrupted, I explained that I was splitting the work between the newly minted STIM SOLUTIONS and a known company down in Texas. Better deals were being negotiated due to the downturn in new builds, and we were minimizing any further risks on a single shaky fabricator by forming these new relationships. To inject a little enthusiasm, a bit of conviction and determination, I added that this was not the end, it was just a hard beginning.

Strangely, that was good enough for him. Maybe I had restored the VP's faith after my pandering and musings on hope and hard work. Maybe he was satisfied that my abundance of Lightspeed collateral would cover the coming rout.

He never said, and I never asked, though we both knew he was stuck with an agreement that his own lawyers had prepared.

Chapter 10

BILL'S PLACE

Bristow, Oklahoma

Three hours it had been and still no one, even though the dispatcher had already assured me on my last two calls that a driver was on the way. In a day that was running out, I became certain I was attracting trouble as I sat weakly along the roadside, in a foreign land, making me a foreigner unaware of small-town allegiances and a hundred other reasons why the trucker might not show up. Who's to say the dispatcher wasn't a drinking buddy of Bill's, or one of Andy's sore-kneed parishioners—that she wasn't part of this conspiracy of Okies making me wait and wait and possibly forfeit every bit of ground I had taken back?

"Hey, it's me again, Doyle—the guy in Bristow waiting here for that truck," I said into the phone on my third check-in.

"Yes, sir," the dispatcher impatiently responded.

"Still no driver, so I'm just calling to see if you had any more information?"

"I think I tol' you already, sir. You prepaid, so you'll see a truck. All right, sir?"

She hung up and I waited a fitful wait. Then, after another long wait, I heard something distant and growing. I stared up the road and saw it coming my way, abruptly shaking me from my self-pitying gloom. My small buzz of hope escalated into unchecked bliss as it came on like a mirage on the thin, rolling horizon: a big tractor and drop-deck trailer headed right my way, passing twenty feet in front of me, pulling along a vortex of dust and garbage. A turn signal came first, then the brake lights hit, and then the raucous sound of the truck's jake brakes shaking right through me as it slowed and turned into Bill's shop.

My God! I thought to myself. *My credit card worked!*

I dropped my Nitro into drive and shot ahead, my elation quickly morphing into anxious dread. Enough time may have gone by for Bill to rethink his situation and see gold by hiding behind a locked gate. Add charges of trespassing, along with newly printed unpaid bills, or whatever else he could cook up, and let a court prove him wrong. Just kill some time as he buried me with the absolute certainty of default. Such were my thoughts as I climbed Bill's office trailer steps for the second time that day, feeling my freight company's big Kenworth filling the view behind me.

When its clutch fan kicked on, it roared, just as I stuck my head inside the trailer, into what felt like a guillotine. There, in the dim light, was Bill's secretary, head down and hammering away at her keyboard. I stepped in without an invite and saw a diminished Bill unhappily pondering me from his throne in back. Stupidly, I said hello and announced the obvious—that I was back—having to shout over the Kenworth and the rattling windows inside.

"Hey, Bill. Truck's here for the engine and pump," I shouted, ridiculously. "All ready for you to load it." Then I added, as a matter of fact, "I'll drive the two chassis away after."

Bill did nothing but glare. He had regressed from the kindly, concerned Dr. Jekyll–Bill to the more familiar and socially challenged Mr. Hyde–Bill. All the goodwill that Andy gushed about back at the Cup of Memories was gone. It was just cheerless Bill now, not the guy Andy promised me would happily load my truck and see me off with best wishes and a slap on the back.

I dropped a "Thanks for everything," and stepped back outside to the hulking truck, glancing over my shoulder, fearful that I had just pushed a guy into taking a second shot at finding his gun.

I met the truck driver and told him what we were doing, but he already knew. He just wanted to see my credit card and ID. Two minutes into my first call earlier in the day, and they had already figured me out. A minute later, I caught sight of one of Bill's guys driving in on a loader.

Backing him up were the rest of Bill's crew, wandering out of the darkened hole where they worked. I was immediately struck with the thought that they might be hoping to catch a show—the one where their boss's reputation was finally put to test, where he'd meet, or even exceed all their wanton expectations and channel a lifetime of rage, chaos, slights, and derision into a single violent focus.

Me.

Like a close-by crack of thunder, Bill's office door banged open and out he came like a gorged bull, covering the considerable distance between us in a few strides. Those in his way jumped back as I braced myself against the approaching wrecking ball. But Bill blew right past me, like a subway train on the express tracks. He shoved the loader driver out of his seat and instantly found a higher gear as he loaded my engine and pump in a rushing onslaught. I could only hope nothing would get damaged, that Bill's skid steer wouldn't accidentally drop the engine from ten feet up, or that the spear-like forks—in a tragic mishap—didn't pierce the $200,000 pump. As much as I wanted to ask him to slow down, I didn't. I just jumped back like everyone else and watched.

As soon as Bill finished the load, the truck driver hurried to chain down the engine and pump, wanting to get the hell out of there as badly as I did. No such luck, though, not as Bill pushed himself off the loader, steaming to the point of bursting and looking directionless as he paced back and forth without reason, muttering over and over, "This is bad. This is bad. This is bad."

I plucked everything I had out of my wallet, nearly a hundred dollars in mixed and crumpled bills, and held it out to him as a magnanimous offering for loading the trailer. It only provoked him all the more.

"I'll be billing you," he promised as he stopped just short of dismembering me. Then he stomped past me and disappeared inside his trailer, where I prayed he would stay.

With dashed expectations and an ass-beating no longer on the agenda, Bill's crew grew disheartened and gradually faded back into the dimness. I didn't trust that Bill wouldn't burst back out the trailer door, so I jumped in with the trucker and hurriedly helped him ratchet down the engine skid and pump with his rusty chains that smeared our hands and clothes orange.

"I'll let you know where it's all going. I just need to get it all out of here for now."

"Don't blame you," the driver agreed as he vaulted up into his cab, dumped the air brakes, and spun around where the dirt road allowed.

Next was the blender. I started for it and tried to make my run look more like a walk.

I did stop, though, and took a picture of the truck with $600,000 of my equipment rolling past me on the free side of the chain-link fence. If anyone else were to look at it, they would have seen nothing more than a tractor-trailer and a load of big, odd-looking parts. But to me it was a different image. It was a life of working nights and Saturdays, Sundays, and holidays, of skipping all the good things people are supposed to do with their time off. It was passing on buying a boat and a brand-new car, on taking a weeklong vacation, on hanging out with friends, on double dates, on all the things normal people do. It was waiting interminably to get married and start a family so I could instead fold myself over a desk to work and think alone. All this passed through my head in a few seconds, yet hung on long enough to be irrepressibly liberating.

This was a victory for me. I knew that. But it would be a Pyrrhic one.

Chapter 11

NEWLY MINTED STIM SOLUTIONS MANUFACTURING

Bristow, Oklahoma

I remained giddy, absolutely giddy, as I walked up the dirt road toward my two big International Paystars. Irrationally, I was succumbing to an overwhelming sense of relief that this dogfight, this lawless bit of brotherly intrigue, was finally behind me.

My soaring emotional state was a strange counterpoint to the fact that my work wasn't done yet, that my two chassis were still inside unfriendly territory and still susceptible to being locked in for the night, the week, or for however long Bill needed to shove another stick into my spokes. There was still a chance the trucks had been sabotaged, or the keys "lost," the batteries borrowed, the oil drained, the tires flattened, or countless other bits of mischief that could have stopped me in my tracks.

I got to blender truck and climbed up its cab steps and tried the handle. To my enormous relief, the door was unlocked and the keys were hanging in the ignition. That was two blessings in a row. But trucks are not like cars. Truck batteries bleed off and die if they sit too long, and this truck had been sitting for nearly three months. Absent cold cranking amps, you might turn the key and hear a fuel pump ticking or the starter straining to turn the flywheel. Or you might hear nothing. And asking Bill for a set of jumper cables wasn't going to fly.

Haltingly, I turned the key just enough to engage the fuel pump, praying that no one had siphoned it off. Then, when I turned the key to start, there was a slow roll, slow enough for me to lose my breath. Then the flywheel caught and spun the crank as the big 15-liter, 600-horsepower Cummins engine rumbled, then burst to life.

"Thank God. Thank God," I repeated as I impatiently sat still, making sure the truck didn't stall.

With the air pressure up and holding, I hurried to the second truck, the pump, and repeated the same methodical procedure. It could have been booby-trapped or jinxed, too, but the motor strained to roll, then caught, and to my absolute jubilation, started.

I left the pump truck running so that there'd be no slow-ups on my return and ran back to the blender truck. The air pressure was in operating range, so I released the air brakes, found low on the shifter, and dropped it into second gear. Nearly stalling out several times, I kept going with a bit of luck and ground my way past Bill's pickup and office trailer, then right out of his woebegone wasteland.

Hallelujah! I silently proclaimed. *One down and one to go.*

Lurching and halting, grinding and cursing, I followed Andy's directions through Bristow. I had a Class B commercial driver's license (CDL), but that didn't make me much of a truck driver. In fact, I was a damn hazard, with no aptitude at all for shifting gears on big, double-clutch trucks. Downshifting gears is how you really slow down big trucks. But I couldn't downshift worth a damn. I was never able to match up rpms to gear ratios, meaning I couldn't stop a rolling truck, which was a real problem for a guy who was on a runaway mission in big trucks.

After miraculously making it through downtown Bristow, a white-knuckle ride all the way, I hit the outskirts on the western edge of town and saw Andy's shiny black pickup right where he promised it would be. I turned into a lot and shouldn't have been surprised. But I was.

It was a disaster. If Bill's yard was bad, this place truly was a shithole. In front of me was a metal-sided building that you could count the holes in, holes big enough for pigeons to fly through. Off to the left was a grown-over yard with junk scattered all around it, likely dropped and forgotten by whatever tenant had last been run off. Spent power tongs and engines, blocks, elevators, Chiksans, pipe, and wellheads were stained rust red, like thousand-pound compost piles leaching back into the earth. It was a preservationist's dream, with the exception that it was all worthless crap whose only purpose was to hold down the weeds.

As per form, Andy stepped out of the building in his big jacket, waving at me with that winning smile, and welcoming me to his rebirth on the opposite side of town. I opened my door and there he was, a bit too close and wanting to shake hands as I dropped down into his dusty lot. Normally, a man would apologize for the condition of his business, or at least make a joke. But Andy was proudly ecstatic and pleading that I follow him on a grand tour of the place.

I resisted, wondering if this inclination toward open-air buildings was a Brennan family tic or an Oklahoma thing that I just didn't understand.

"Thanks, Andy, but I gotta go get the other truck. We gotta keep moving, you know."

I started for Andy's pickup, but he didn't move.

"You're driving me over, right?" I asked.

"Me? No. Bryson's gonna give you a ride over. He's one of the men from my church I told you about, who's gonna run the shop for me. He should be along any minute now."

I stopped in my tracks, thinking how to respond, until I found the right mix of words. "Kinda in a hurry though, right, Andy?"

"I don't think it would be appropriate for me to drive you over. Just not proper with Bill there and all. It'd be more appropriate to have Bryson do it… You'll love Bryson, Dan. I told you. Great guy."

Then we waited. Like the crop-dusting scene out of Alfred Hitchcock's *North by Northwest*, we just stood there, two guys across from each other, waiting on a guy named Bryson in a barren junkyard, with nothing left to say. A long five minutes later, we both caught sight of a Chevy Silverado heading our way. Andy waved and announced it was Bryson and reminded me again how much I would love the guy, friendly and competent and just the man he needed to run his able crew.

"Truth be told, I never built a frack truck," Bryson offered as an ice-breaker, after I jumped in his Silverado with him. "Truth is, I never run one or worked around one, but God willing, we will get this done."

"What is it you do, Bryson?" I asked. He told me, and I can't quite remember, but he was right in that it didn't have anything to do with building frack trucks, particularly a blender with all its hydraulics, actuators, pumps, controls, and in-line sensors. If I weren't scared shitless of the return to Bill's, I would have been a bit more concerned.

"We want this to work for Andy," Bryson proclaimed. "It if works for him, it'll work for all-a us."

"Who's us?"

"Our congregation. Lotta them are hurtin' an' they're tremendous people an' Andy thinks we can help a whole lot of 'em with this."

He does, does he?

Bryson went on about his church and its "no man left behind" faith while I politely asked him to hurry. As we closed in on Bill's shop, though, my new friend's chatter tailed off. Whatever Andy had said about his mercurial brother—most if it probably downright worrying—it must have been playing out in his mind, because his sudden change of mood was startling as we closed in.

Stricken with the same fluttering unease that Andy had, Bryson whipped the truck off the highway onto the graveled apron outside Bill's gate. Just like me, he wanted to get the hell out of there.

"Best-a luck to you, Dan. Best you run along an' get that truck now," Bryson advised.

We shook hands and I think I heard "good luck" again as he sped off down the blacktop, cleaning out his carburetor and dumping a long trail of black soot behind him. A fainthearted mess, but pretending I wasn't, I walked back into Bill's place. If this were a cartoon, I would have seen eyeballs in the dark staring out at me from the dim fabrication "shed" that forever looked like a meteor shower, with sparks flying from grinding wheels and an arc welder bursting in flashes of light. But in the rayless gloom, I couldn't see a thing. In fact, it was quiet. Other than my still-idling truck in the distance, it was almost serene, like being out on the water after a brief and brutal summer storm.

I climbed into the idling truck, grabbed a gear, and jolted ahead. Nothing on it had been altered, drained, locked, or gone missing. Freedom, and maybe even solvency, was only fifty yards ahead, a distance I covered in fits and starts as I bounced my way past Bill's trailer and—in my prayer of prayers—his life. As a departing touch, my last goodbye, I reached to give a blast of my air horn, then thought better of it. That would seem like gloating, and I was in no position to gloat. I'd just stick with relief and redemption as I hit the blacktop.

My Nitro was still sitting in the litter-strewn lot up from Bill's yard. I'd left it there because it looked like neutral territory. Taking on the significance of a checkered flag, I pulled in alongside it and shut down the pump truck. I still didn't know for sure where the pump was going, but I couldn't take it to Andy's and tempt him. It would only sit down the road from Bill's shop for a few hours and should be safe, I hoped, as I slipped into my Nitro and took off for the Tulsa airport and Woodstock.

Chapter 12

THE KANES

Reno, Pennsylvania

On first glance, Eli Kane was still tall, but time seemed to have pressed down on him. He was stooped and bald under his ball cap, but was smiling and waving when I found him, and that made it feel like a reunion. Of the three Kane brothers, Eli was the one I always got along with, the introspective and smart brother whom I had last seen twenty years ago. I'd made the drive up from Pittsburgh to meet him at his hydraulic hose shop in Reno, Pennsylvania, and had just found it—a sagging, whitewashed, two-car garage in a sparse residential neighborhood.

We shook hands and caught up while we waited for his brother Wallace to arrive. Eli told me he was still drilling and completing wells, and along the way had got married and had dogs but no kids. I told him my story—a rental company down in Pittsburgh that was paying the bills, and a wife and newborn daughters and a growing feeling that I needed to do more.

Catching up fell short when we both caught sight of a big water tank truck—a vac truck, as they are known—heading our way.

"That's him," Eli offered. "'Member his son, Ford? Little Ford?" Eli asked, holding his hand a few feet off the ground, about where a little boy's head would be. "Wait'll you see him now. He grew up a little."

Twenty years back, little Ford was a four-year-old boy running around frack jobs—the first and last time I ever saw something so dangerously harebrained. But now, as I could see through a mud-caked windshield, he looked to be a big guy with a reddish beard who, I would come to learn, wasn't in the driver's seat because of a DUI or two. His father, Wallace, was behind the wheel. I remembered Wallace as quiet and sullen, with the look of a "heavy" from a Sergio Leone western—his walrus moustache and ever-present ball cap substituting for a Stetson. In a few minutes, I would see that nothing had changed, that Wallace was still a brooder with an expansive list of people he no longer talked to. But he was still hard-working and had never done anything but drill and frack wells, which made him my ideal.

The vac truck braked to a stop in front of us, and Wallace stood up so that he was half in and half out of his idling truck, almost like he was shielding himself. He was a big, solid man, grayer now, but still watchful and suspicious, and forever faithful to his demeanor of unapproachability. We said our greetings in that way, shouting a little over the low rumble of the truck's engine before he finally shut it down and joined me and Eli on the ground. He never smiled or waved or even offered a handshake. He just made room for his son, Ford, and his dog, Spike, not bothering to introduce them, either.

When I asked if the third brother, Daniel, was going to make it, I was met with silence. Eli curtly explained that their other brother wouldn't be joining us. In due time I learned of the missing brother's departure—something about cross words, brotherly challenges, and a black eye at the hands of Wallace.

It was hard not to draw a few quick conclusions about my soon-to-be partners and our surroundings. Time had not been particularly kind or rewarding to them. They were definitely not rich; I could see that by the vac truck Wallace was driving. Run-down and exhausted equipment isn't typical of a service company that is doing well. That, and the Kanes weren't even particularly busy at a time when oil was hitting historic highs. But they were upright and breathing, and at the time that was good enough for me.

We settled in over the back of my pickup, leaning on the bed as is the fashion when drillers and frackers, investors and roustabouts gather to shoot the shit in the oil field. I wanted to know what was going on in the hills around us, and I learned that there was a lot of work out there, but also a lot of service companies doing it. Still, there was work, and the Kanes would be my connection to it.

I let the Kanes know that I wanted to be on the service side. I didn't want to raise money and drill wells as a promoter, like I had before. I didn't want to meet with dentists and doctors, and I didn't want to have countless lunches and breakfasts with lawyers and business owners looking for deductions. I didn't have any appetite for promising anything I wasn't certain I could deliver. Instead, I'd risk my own money and signature. But what I needed were operational partners who would run the field while I took care of the administrative back office. The operational partners could be them, the Kanes. They'd drive the trucks to their existing customers' frack jobs, where they were already running their service rigs. Their crew could jump off a rig once they set the pipe and packer downhole and onto our frack trucks to pump the job. Back and forth they'd go through the job, letting us control the entire completion package, their service rigs and our frack trucks, seamlessly working together and making a lot of money.

My simple question for them was, "Are you in?"

They were. No question about it. They were in nearly as big a hurry to make something happen as I was.

Four more meetings with the Kane brothers followed, each one giddier than the last. We would go fifty-fifty on the frack trucks and name the service company Reliance Well Services. I'd pay for the trucks and infrastructure, and the Kanes would oversee building them. Once completed, they'd run them and all field operations. They'd train their existing crew, supervise jobs and maintenance, and would sell us through their long-established customer base.

As a stand-alone deal, this one was bad. Picking up the entire bill was stupid. But the Kanes didn't have the money. They were like old Virginia plantation owners, rich in land and poor in cash.

To balance it out, I proposed a second, concurrent deal. This one we called Arcade. It would be another fifty-fifty setup, with me chipping in a small amount of cash and the Kanes providing everything else—

drill sites and all their equipment and services to drill and complete our own in-house oil wells. With the exception of frack trucks, Wallace and Eli owned bulldozers and backhoes to build roads, a drilling rig, service rigs, vac trucks, roll-off trailers, flatbeds, tanks, and tractors. If we came to a deal on the frack company, we'd collectively own about everything you needed to drill and complete a well—including the land. And as I remembered, the Kanes had ground, good ground. That is, they had oil leases in areas with good production. They also had an inventory of pipe, pumpjacks, tanks, and tubulars needed to complete a well.

When not fracking for third-party operators, we could utilize our spare capacity for our own wells through Arcade. Our cost for putting in a well would be a fraction of what other operators—good, in-the-black operators—typically paid. This would take the sting out of the Reliance deal, a negotiation that on its own gave me the halo of an idiot for giving away 50 percent of a highly capitalized company.

At the time, though, I was proud of the fact that I was able to reconnect with the two brothers after twenty years and put the whole deal together in five meetings. As the months rolled on, though, as events pushed me to deconstruct it, I wondered if a sixth meeting would have helped me avoid the coming maelstrom. Providence would have made me see that mixing with two sets of brothers, one in Pennsylvania and the other in Oklahoma, was two too many. Surely I'd have seen that mixing with blood that wasn't my own was a fool's errand. And then, soon enough, I'd be leaning on two of my own brothers and one of my sisters to get me out of the coming tide of familial calamities, all of it occupying a level of dysfunction previously unknown to me. But I needed to make a deal. Because, after all, that's what entrepreneurs do.

We make deals.

Chapter 13

TULSA INTERNATIONAL

Tulsa, Oklahoma

Slow-rolling through arrivals, I caught a glimpse of Woodstock in camo shorts and combat boots and a cloud of steam billowing out of his mouth. Cold as it was, he was chatting up a few open-minded travelers, until he saw me and sprinted my way, howling, with his long, graying, braided hair whipping along behind him.

"That was close, man," Woodstock said as he jumped in.

"What, getting a flight?"

"No, I got held up by TSA. The damn plate in my head kept setting off the alarm."

Woodstock roared with laughter as he gave me a hug. "How you doin'? Not so fucking good, I guess."

"Hahahahaha!" I roared back, so happy to see a familiar face, a friend.

I pointed my Nitro toward the airport exit and we took off, cutting through the cold Oklahoma night, a good part of our hour-long ride consumed by who was doing what back in Pittsburgh, and by Woodstock's bird.

"My chow got loose from the basement and scared the shit outta my bird. That cost me like at least an hour, man. I couldn't get it to eat!"

"Who, the dog?"

"No, man, the bird. The dog'll eat anything. He'd eat your arm, you let it. I mean the bird; the bird eats like a bird, man."

That and the craziness of it all had us belly-laughing all the way through Bristow and into the lot alongside my pump truck.

I jumped out to do a quick lap around it, looking for anything missing, leaking, broken, or deflated. Finding nothing out of sorts, nothing curiously broken or punctured, I returned to Woodstock, who was still sitting in his seat, gawking up at the truck.

"Whatdya think? You like it?"

"No, man. I don't."

"What do you mean?"

"This truck is huge. It's like twice the size I was thinking. I didn't know it was gonna be this big!"

"Yeah, I know. Little bigger than the grip trucks in Pittsburgh," I said, trying to make a joke.

"I don't know, man. I don't know...."

"What're you thinking?" I asked when Woodstock remained in his seat.

"I'm thinking it's pretty big, is what I'm thinking."

We had already talked over the lack of rear lights and license plate, even the outdated dealer papers. All that was funny on the phone, but confronted by it, Woodstock's enthusiasm for our adventure was seeping out of him.

"You want to see if you can drive it?" I asked. "You want to start there?"

"How 'bout you drive it?"

"Me? I can't drive that eighteen-speed, not all the way to Texas. I'd kill myself. Probably someone else, too."

Woodstock still wasn't moving. Just staring.

"Listen, Woodstock, if you're not comfortable—"

"Nah, I'm all right," he stopped me. "I can drive it. But, man, you really need such a big truck?" he asked, forcing a chuckle.

"Go big or go home, right?" I said, referring to a popular saying among grips and gaffers like Woodstock, and the size of the movie lights they'd set.

"Yeah, funny, man."

"Don't worry. It's not like you'll be legal or anything."

"Yeah, why would I want to start worrying about that?" he said as he got up out of the Nitro for a closer look. "I just don't need some cracker cop locking me up."

"Hell, Woodstock. You're used to that!"

"Yeah," he grinned. "Just not in Oklahoma."

He pulled himself up into the truck's cab and flicked on the dome light, illuminating what looked like an airplane console as he worried over all the knobs and dials and gauges, levers, lights, and pedals.

"Hey, man, this thing is like a jet, with all these damn gauges and controls."

"Yeah. We better take some time and figure it out."

"Screw it, man, I'll figure it out. Let's roll." He pulled the door shut and started the truck. The low baritone roar of the four-hundred-pound crankshaft turning in a cradle of cold bearings caught and rumbled to life. "That's some power!" Woodstock shouted from his open window as he pushed the truck into gear and grinned. "You better follow me out of town. I don't need some Okie cop rear-ending me without any lights back there."

"I will," I shouted as I jumped into my Nitro. "Good luck, my friend."

Woodstock strapped in, dimmed the cab lights, and found a gear the same way I did, by grinding and lurching his way toward town, with me sticking like glue to his rear-end frame rails.

Ten minutes later we were on the interstate, and a few minutes after that we hit an exit with a motel and pulled off, just as we had discussed. I got Woodstock a room, and when I returned, he was chocking the tires with stones to keep the truck from rolling off.

"I'll call when I know where you're going. Hopefully soon," I promised as Woodstock pulled me in for a bear hug.

"That's fine, brother. I got plenty to do."

"Gonna figure out the truck?" I asked.

"No, man," said Woodstock, looking like some strange apparition in shorts and combat boots, with all that hair and his breath like cigar smoke. "No, man, I'm gonna sleep, and try not to think about your truck and your fucked-up deal."

Chapter 14

I-35 SOUTH

Oklahoma

All night I drove, heading west until I hit Oklahoma City, then south on I-35 toward Dallas–Fort Worth. For the last hour or so, I'd been looking for a place to take a leak, but had long ago left behind gas stations and convenience stores with bathrooms. Into the stillness of rural Oklahoma, and bursting at the seams, I gave up and braked hard for a barren exit. Once stopped in the weeds, I jumped out and went.

Standing there and draining out, I could see a tower of dull yellow halogen lights off in the endless, nighttime distance. It was a drilling rig rising off the Oklahoma floor. The top lights were flickering, experience telling me it was from an American flag up in the crow's nest, casting about in the breeze and big enough to block and unblock the light behind it.

I zipped back up and a few minutes later was hurtling through space and time and feeling the relief of an empty bladder and maybe some better prospects ahead. The volume on my Nitro's radio didn't have much to go, but when the Marshall Tucker Band came on, I pegged it to the point of a crackling howl, listening to lyrics about a man climbing a mountain…then jumping off…and nobody would know…

How fitting, I thought, as I came upon the glowing and otherworldly Chickasaw Nation Riverwind Casino. All those kilowatt-hours gave the impression of a nuclear blast mushrooming over the earth's surface—or maybe that a white-hot spaceship had landed just off the otherwise desolate highway. In the wee hours, I wondered why the need for so much amperage, given that there wasn't another car on the road. Then I saw the parking lot, packed full of cars, RVs, and tractor-trailers, and realized that a light show made sense—something for all the other gamblers like me, most of them with better odds.

Watching it fade away in my rearview mirror, I caught sight of a bank of flashing lights coming up on me. Closing in was a brilliant, hard-to-look-at, red-and-blue LED display, accompanied by the high-pitched whine of a siren growing louder. In my diminished and dreamy state, I wondered what it was all about before realizing it was all about me. Glancing down at my speedometer, in the hope that I was traveling somewhere around the speed limit, I saw that I was doing 92 mph in a speed zone I never noticed. What was it anyway, 55, 65, 70?

Dammit! I'd take the ticket and points, but I was running so fast, I worried they'd take my Nitro, too. *Damn!*

The bullshit vortex blender! One guy in the world wanted it: my partner Wallace. One guy in the world made it: my now-ex-builder Bill. All the ungodly losses, and my go-along-to-get-along bearing put me on this highway. Had I not been such a pleaser, I would have pushed back. Now this cop was right on my ass—me, the fun, well-liked guy with deep pockets stuffed full of borrowed money! Being the owner's not what it's cracked up to be, not with the grille of the trooper up my ass and his flashing luminous-flux light bar blinding me.

At 92, I had to let wind resistance slow me enough before I began tapping the brakes. The Oklahoma State Police car was right there, keeping it tight with its high beams and strobing lights as I rolled into a run of grass and gradually stopped. Regrettably, I was no novice to any of this. I knew exactly what to do. I rolled down my window, turned on the cabin lights, and rested my hands on the steering wheel. I didn't move as I waited and wondered just what in the hell was coming next.

I jumped. A rap on the passenger-side window scared the bejesus out of me. Of course it was the trooper, but I was expecting him on my side, not the other. And then there was his face, planted against the glass, right there across from me. Cautiously, I pointed to the window controls and very slowly and deliberately rolled down the passenger's side window. What I saw was a young guy dressed up in a trooper's uniform, every bit as weary and worn down as me.

"How're you, officer?" I offered over his long silence. "I guess I was going a little fast.... Sorry about that."

I waited for the invective to begin, the part where you take the lecture and the ticket, never just one or the other. But it never came. The trooper just kept staring. Maybe he was waiting for me to reach for my wallet and my driver's license, or for the glove compartment and a car registration? Hopefully, Thrifty had left it there. I didn't know; I hadn't checked because I was in a hurry.

"Would you like to see my license, sir?" When he didn't answer, I went on. "It's a rental car, but I bet there's a registration in here somewhere. I can check. Officer? Officer?" I asked in an unsettled way.

"Sir," the trooper finally said.

"Yes, sir?"

"I want to thank you for turning on your cabin lights...I want to thank you for putting your hands on the steering wheel where I could see them."

"Well, I wouldn't want to walk up on a dark car, either."

"No, I don't like it. Not one bit. I can never get used to it... Be careful," he added, pulling away from the window. "It's dark out here."

With that, the trooper turned and disappeared back into his car, leaving me dumbfounded and wondering what had just happened and what to do next. Should I stick around for a ticket? Assist him through his breakdown? I didn't know, so I sat there for a minute, watching my rearview mirror and growing more convinced that he wasn't coming back, that he was letting me go. I turned on my left-side turn signal and waited for some form of protest. When none materialized, I accelerated slowly ahead and left behind a kindred soul every bit as confused as me.

God help the pressed-upon and weary, I thought, as his flashing lights became a faint pinprick in my black and featureless rearview mirror. In another five minutes I was up over 80 mph, hoping that was fast enough to get me to Granbury, Texas, by the start of the business day.

Chapter 15

TRIBUTE OILFIELD SOLUTIONS

Granbury, Texas

Dawn broke as I came upon the Texas Motor Speedway, a NASCAR mecca where crowds the size of my Pennsylvania hometown make a yearly pilgrimage. As I passed by, it was quiet and still, with none of the wound-out rpms of race day audible all the way out to the highway.

Another twenty minutes of driving, and traffic became as thick as ants on a dropped popsicle. With my destination only a few miles ahead, I was hit with a wave of exhaustion that had me looking for an exit. Salvation would come by way of a Cracker Barrel and their Uncle Herschel breakfast special, my go-to staple when I was on the road.

When I got there, I crawled out of my Nitro and limped across the lot. Fifty hours had passed since I'd last slept for more than an hour straight, and I couldn't remember where or when I had last eaten. Oddly, I wasn't even that hungry, but I knew I should eat as a rote response to sunrise. And while I sat and ate, I would think about how to deal with Douglas and his company outside of Fort Worth.

In my favor was the undeniable truth: It was an apocalyptically bad time to even think of starting a frack company. The river of money flowing from private equity, stock offerings, and debt placements had hit a dam. If oil producers were in trouble due to lower prices, the first thing they would cut was me, and the first thing I would cut was Douglas. He knew it and I knew it, and the fact that he didn't hang up on me again was as big a tell as I needed.

To my way of thinking, that had him dropping his price. Or so was my thought and hope, especially since I had only so much money left. Substituting lower fab costs for missing money—stolen money—was the only way to claw back what I had lost. So I'd bank on that, I half convinced myself, aware it was a stretch, aware of my own foolishness, and aware, too, of exactly what my father would say: *"If 'if' was syph, we'd all have it."*

Finding Tribute Oilfield Solutions came quickly enough. When I did, I was immediately impressed—and equally crestfallen. In front of me was a newly built steel building with four sides and no rusted-through holes—a real departure from the two bootstrapped shitholes I had just left behind in Bristow. The dichotomy between this and the others was galling and, of course, made me feel stupid for having handed hundreds of thousands of dollars to two guys working out of a lean-to.

Stepping out of my Nitro had me feeling a little dread, carrying with me my side of a rocky relationship with the guy within. Driving down, I had been sure Douglas would be in as much trouble as I was, but looking around at all the fresh concrete and brand-new fencing, I wasn't so sure any longer. He wouldn't be the one walking in with no sleep and wearing the same clothes from two nights before, hoping for redemption through a reset and a reprice so he could claw back his money and his reputation.

Douglas's AA, Lisa, met me at the door and walked me into the clean, well-kept office. She was exceedingly pleasant and accommodating, undoing all my unease as she worried over me and my ride down and promised that Douglas was looking forward to meeting me, just as soon as he was off the phone. When she put a cup of coffee into my hands and offered me a seat in a small waiting area, I felt as though I were home.

As soon as I was alone, though, I stood up. I'd been sitting for the last twelve hours, but more so, I didn't want to be diminished by getting caught sitting. I'd stay on my feet and busy myself looking over all the framed pictures on the walls of Tribute equipment and the builds completed, a few of them including the smiling owners.

A few minutes later, the front door swung open and a stout, middle-aged, Middle Eastern man walked in. Without a word or glance, he walked right past me to Lisa's desk, where the two of them spoke in a familiar chitchat way. When they finished, the Middle Eastern man returned to the hall across from me. There we waited, each of us pretending the other wasn't there until I couldn't help myself any longer. I glanced up and was instantly caught. The Middle Eastern man was staring back at me. Given that he was six feet away, I gave up and awkwardly asked how he was doing.

"Fine," he said and slowly revealed that his name was Zahir, and that he, too, was waiting for Douglas.

This was Zahir Kahn, I realized, the man prefaced by both Douglas and Andy as the genius founder of Quantum Controls. We shook hands and I introduced myself, though I didn't need to. Zahir already knew who I was. That's why he was there. Probably called in by Douglas to let me know Andy was lying when he said he had an exclusive on Quantum's products. My thoughts were validated when Zahir asked me how Andy was doing and if he and his brother had worked out their differences, letting me know with a smirk that he knew all about it.

I was saved from getting into it when Douglas entered the hallway. Tall to begin with, he was another three inches taller in his cowboy boots. Sixty or so, he was loud and all Texan, with the big silver rodeo belt buckle to prove it. Apologizing for keeping me waiting, he shook my hand with tight-gripped gusto. As far as I could tell, he wasn't harboring any ill feelings, not with him backslapping me and eagerly pushing me down the hall, with Zahir tagging along behind.

"Why don't I show you aroun' first?" he suggested as we strode, double time, toward a steel door. "Show you what we're up to."

Douglas wasn't wasting any time as he passed around hard hats and safety glasses and pushed through the door to a grated platform. Below was his shop, a panorama of a well-put-together place, full of perfectly aligned frack trucks and trailers.

Surely Zahir had told him about the third-world appearance of the STIM SOLUTIONS operation up in Bristow, maybe even of Andy's scrap yard with its ventilated, shot-up, warming-hut appearance. By comparison, he knew I'd be drop-dead impressed, making STIM SOLUTIONS look Stone Age by comparison.

A dozen or so men were at work welding, grinding, and assembling pieces onto the five or six trucks in various stages of production. All of them were wearing safety glasses and fire-retardant clothing. No sleeves had been ripped off shirts. No one was wearing wifebeaters, or smoking over the acetylene tanks. Not a soul was sporting bloody, bandaged-up tattoos. This group didn't give me the impression of Gulag laborers on a bread-and-cigarettes diet. None of them was peering out from dim shadows, leering with the look of wanting to beat me into the dirt.

I thought I even heard polite laughter.

We descended the steps onto the shop floor and out an open bay door into a lot where an operator had a remote-control box on a stand. He was running a cherry-red, trailer-mounted frack pump a hundred feet away, testing the transmission solenoids, and grabbing one gear after another.

When Douglas stepped out and leaned into him for a word, the operator instantly stuck a higher gear on the 2,500-horespower colossus with a 20,000-pound pump on its back. Its sixteen-inch chromed plungers started beating out shockwaves—*thump-thump-thump-thump*—that I could feel right in my chest, as a digitized rpm needle pegged deep into a flashing red dial.

Out in the distance came a percussive *bang* when the lid of a 20,000-gallon steel tank slammed open and a geyser of water shot up out of it, like water from an enormous straw. Immediately, the operator dialed it down and turned back and grinned an "oops" kind of grin.

"Don't make me clean up that mess," he shouted at Douglas over the engine's heavy throttle. "All yer fault!"

Douglas laughed, and I thought: *Mission accomplished.* His show was working and was further fortified when he leaned into me and ingratiatingly confessed, "Another damn red trailer. Everyone wants red these days. Let Halliburton keep their damned red."

I was all smiles, but relieved when we ended up back in Douglas's office. Any more gushing on my part wasn't going to help the coming negotiation—not in what was going to be a lopsided effort, with me feigning strength where I had none.

We took up positions around a conference room table with Douglas's go-to guy, Clayton, joining us with a file. He dropped it on the tabletop, but everyone ignored it, settling instead into two oil-field favorites: talking over the state of the industry and politics. A new president was about to be sworn in. This one, Obama, wasn't a Texan and didn't have roots in the oil field like the last president. No one knew what to expect, which resulted in ten minutes of back-and-forth filled with uncertainty and doubtless doubt-filled speculation.

Finally, when a discussion about my pump truck became unavoidable, Douglas offered something positive. He had a talk with Cummins the day before, and they would support him if I'd be willing to offer up some testimony that I was pulling my deal from STIM. A grievance letter would do it. Easy enough, and with that, the largest barrier to my working with Douglas had fallen.

My second concern, electronic controls, was settled seconds later when Zahir, unprompted, let everyone know that Andy had no exclusive on his controls.

"Had he, Dan, I would be out in the streets begging for food!" Zahir bawled.

Douglas, not Andy, was buttering Zahir's bread, so Andy was out and Douglas was in, and my seat was barely warm. With two of my concerns allayed, the third—price—would have to be brought up by me, principally, because why would they?

"Listen, things have changed," I started. "I mean, I'm not even sure we'll have work for these trucks, the way things are. But I want to keep things moving ahead. That's why I'm here. But I gotta make some changes."

"You talkin' changes to your design?" Douglas asked. "Other than a Cummins package?"

"I'm talking about some changes to the truck design," I said. "Find some ways to help you save some money. But I gotta build this cheaper. I have all the major stuff, the engine and radiator and transmission. And the pump and the fluid end, both Gardner Denver. It's all ready to go. There wouldn't be any waiting for things."

"Well, what you got in mind, Dan?"

"I only have so much money. And truthfully…I need to cut a hundred and twenty-five thousand off your quote," I said, letting it all out.

"That's it?" Douglas blurted out, incredulous.

"Well, one more thing. I need the truck in three months. All the time I lost up in Bristow—"

"Really? A hundred and twenty-five off an' three months to get it done?" Douglas laughed. "Anything else?"

"No. Nothing else. That's it. Sorry. It's a lot, I know. But it's what I need."

"You need one of those famous guaranteed delivery dates, too?" Douglas exclaimed. "What is it, half off every week? Fifty percent a week?"

"No. No," I laughed along sheepishly, taking my medicine, because Andy and Bill's discount was every bit as ridiculous as it sounded. It didn't surprise me, either, that Douglas knew about it.

"That's good, because that is just damned silly. 'Round here we jus' work on keepin' our word, 's all."

"Let's see what we can cut out of the truck," I offered, trying to pull the conversation back in between the rails. "Maybe there's a way to save you some money."

Even with the cat out of the bag, I couldn't help but notice that no one was pushing away from the table. One hundred twenty-five thousand dollars was not so arbitrary, either. It was exactly half of what I figured had been lost or stolen up in Bristow.

"Hundred an' twenty-five, seriously?"

"Yes, sir…I only have what I have. But I have it in cash."

That got Douglas, Clayton, and Zahir to begin privately deliberating on how to build my truck cheaper. Oil prices may have been falling, but their costs weren't. Douglas's mortgage wasn't dropping, nor were his steel or labor costs. Like me, Douglas probably had partners to keep happy, too. So why should I get a discount when his shop was still full?

But…but…but… How many more customers would be walking in the door if oil prices didn't get up off the floor? How many of his ongoing jobs out back would be cancelled midstream? How many unpaid balances would be answered by bankruptcy notices? And as I would soon learn, too, sometimes in the oil field you have to take work at cost just to keep your crews, just to buy time.

The three of them began talking over a few ideas to save money, and I did my best to convince them that this build would be different. Everything—the big items—were all on hand. The long lead times plaguing the industry wouldn't apply here. They could get right into it, then right out of it.

"You'll push the truck right through your shop," I argued. "It won't even have time to get dusty."

Through the back-and-forth, my intractability came through because it had to. "Just make it good enough."

We were all chipping in something, me with concessions on the build, Douglas and Clayton with a different approach, and Zahir—because Douglas said so—would be dropping his price on controls.

Zahir looked ready to shrug it off until he jolted upright. In a kind of pre-planned "aha!" moment, he blurted, "Dan, if you are so concerned about integrating controls, why don't you just give Douglas the blender, too? You could get to your better price if he had both trucks."

So much for Andy. The guy not in the room was just dragged out and shot by his vendor.

"Have you been to Andy's new shop, Dan? Kinda windy inside, isn't it?" Zahir giggled, slapping his own knee. "The birds can fly right through the entire building! Hahaha! Big birds. Big, big birds!" he kept laughing.

Me, the butt of the joke, I tried laughing along. "I already thought of that," I said. "But you guys don't build vortex blenders. My partners, the Kanes, they want a vortex blender. I gotta build a vortex blender."

"And you think Andy can build that for you, huh?" Zahir smiled, a wink-wink smile, meant for Douglas and Clayton. "You're not so worried, huh, Dan?"

Based on Andy's claims that he had already paid Bill for the parts, I was shit out of luck. Getting a refund from Bill had the distinct ring of "go screw yourself" to it.

"I'm sorry. I can't."

The same contemplative silence returned to the room, until Douglas pushed back in his chair and stood up. The meeting was over, and my first thought was that I had failed.

"Dan, you mind if me an' Clayton an' Zahir here try an' figure this out in my office?"

"No, no, not at all. I have plenty I can do here." I held up my phone as though I had calls to make, hiding my relief that Douglas wasn't walking out of the meeting the same way he'd ended our phone call three months before.

With that, they left, leaving me alone with myself—a bad place to be at that moment.

Chapter 16

DEAL

Granbury, Texas

With a self-incriminating dread, I remained in my seat in the Tribute conference room, hoping to God Douglas wouldn't call me out on my legless bluff. Surely he saw through it—all those other fabricators I had to call. He had to have known I was faking it, juicing up my side of the negotiation, pretending that all the other truck builders in Texas were just salivating for my call.

When my phone did ring, I was surprised, more so when I saw it was NOV Rolligon, a large and premier builder of frack equipment. Months back, I called them after I saw their placard on a Universal pump truck back home, but they were expensive and a year out, so idiotically I moved on.

It was their salesman Ryan, a young Texas A&M engineer, returning my call and telling me he could build my trucks but still had a year-long backlog in his three-hundred-person shop. When I pushed back, begging for relief for the little guy, Ryan apologized, wishing that he could, but then wisecracked, "Yeah, but ours will work."

Even his bad news was better company than my own thoughts as I sat alone with little else to think of besides my loan and the bankruptcy lawyer I'd be hiring if this didn't play out. I could see it, the final resolution, the lawyer telling me, "Never mind the stigma," pushing me ahead into it: "Just look at all the twenty-something kids in Silicon Valley. A few failures, so what? It's *tout la rage*, a rite of passage, is all."

But mine wouldn't be. I was neither a whiz nor a kid. Failing with Douglas would be a financial bullet to the head. Besides, lawyers say all sorts of things. Then they move on, leaving you stuck to your mess.

I called Mary to tell her I was alive and well, and apologized for leaving her alone in Pittsburgh with our two infants and no help.

"I've been cleaning for a solid hour," she told me. "Maria took off her diaper and was whipping it over her head. It was full, and Elena was rolling it all through the house in her jumper—all over the place. I hid in the bathroom. My hands are raw. When you coming home?"

My next call was to Woodstock to tell him to grab some breakfast. I didn't have any news yet, but I thought I would soon enough.

Later, Lisa the AA drifted in with two cups of coffee. Kids and family came up, and I told her of the warm place I had back home, where my wife and I were raising little daughters who had stolen our hearts. Lisa had a similar story. Two teenage daughters that she was raising on her own. Doing it on her own didn't matter to her. Life to her was a blessing, and right then it was filled with an upcoming prom and prom dresses and shopping trips into Fort Worth. I got the feeling that relishing the challenge of finding just the right dress for her oldest daughter, nothing could bring this kind, ebullient woman down. Though something seemed amiss in the way she told it, something more she was about to say, until Douglas, Clayton, and Zahir entered the conference room.

Without fanfare or explanation, Douglas handed me two identical signed documents that I didn't bother to read at first. I was only interested in his number, and right away I found it.

I didn't jump and cheer or pump my fist. I didn't celebrate survival. I skipped all the fanfare and kept my head down, quietly thanking God.

Every dollar I had asked for, I got. Douglas had hit my number, and the longer I stared at it, the more I had to suppress an overwhelming urge of revelry.

The details, though. That's where the harm would come. Hiding in them would be the add-ons, outs, and omissions that would put me right back at Douglas's first number from the halcyon days of three months ago.

I had to read it. Everyone's eyes were on me, but nothing so intrusive that I didn't read it all the way through, then a second time, dragging through every sentence, studying the truck design, the components, the schedule, and payment due dates. Nothing was hiding in the cracks, other than the hard realization that Douglas was no different than me. He was just as bad off, taking work for cash flow alone.

"That's a good deal, Dan. You can't go wrong with that deal," Douglas said, breaking the long silence.

"You got a pen?" I asked as I looked up at him. "We got a deal."

"Very smart, Dan. You will be happy," Zahir chopped in.

Matter-of-factly, I signed both agreements—one for Douglas and one for me—and smiled, unable any longer to hide the astonishing relief I felt. Because I had asked for it, half my lost money was just returned. And for Douglas, he had just covered his payroll, all of which pushed us into handshakes and the goodwill of a shared effort.

"How long you think until I can get that truck-a yours, an' all those parts?" Douglas asked as our celebration wound down.

"Tomorrow, I was thinking. Maybe this evening."

"How's that?"

"I got a driver in the pump truck, and I've loaded everything else on a flatbed. Both the drivers are just waiting on the go-ahead."

"You already got everything away from Bill?" Clayton joined in.

"Yeah," I grinned.

Douglas laughed. "I guess you're not in much of a hurry, huh?"

"I didn't have a choice," I said. "I got everything out but my money."

Chapter 17

HOME

Pittsburgh, Pennsylvania

With the promise of sleep only a few hours away, I turned my Nitro north for the DFW airport and called the Oklahoma freight company holding my engine, transmission, and pump. They took down Tribute's address and promised a departure within a few hours. My second call was to Woodstock to let him know he was good to go.

"Great news, man. Now I can go and kill myself on the highway," Woodstock said with cold-footed reticence.

When I laughed, he didn't join in. I asked, "You gonna be okay?"

"No. But the hell with it. I'll just keep it at five miles an hour."

He made it all the way down, though, and later that night, after Woodstock rolled unscathed into Tribute, Douglas drove out to meet him and put the truck away. The two of them hit it off, an unlikely alliance between a proud, blustering Texan and a self-effacing hippy from up North. Douglas even drove Woodstock to the airport and waited around to make sure he was able to book a flight out. His kindness likely due to seeing something in Woodstock, a man jumping into a fight that wasn't his own. Go through life and count how many times someone has done that for you. Get past two and you're rich.

Half a day ahead of Woodstock, I had also shown up at DFW and bought another ruinously expensive one-way ticket. A few hours later, and light years away, I got some sleep in my own bed. When our girls woke early the next morning, I left Mary sleeping and snuck downstairs and fed them. We took a short stroll around the neighborhood and got back just as Mary was waking up.

"When you coming home?"

"Right after work."

"So, is that, like, tonight?" Mary joked, getting used to it.

"Let's hope so," I said in a way that asked for forgiveness.

I needed to get to my Lightspeed office, to start back in on scratching around for money. I may have just saved $125,000, but that didn't put it in my pocket. I also needed to tell my Lightspeed employees that we were okay. Like Mary, I had surprised them with my unannounced trip to Oklahoma. Undoubtedly, they had been wondering if they still had jobs, if I had to sell the old company to fund the new one.

Driving to work, I felt the heft of my surroundings. December was coming, and a featureless, overcast sky had settled over Pittsburgh. As I turned into the browns and grays of (ironically) Uptown, the dim and hopeless streets were mostly empty. This late in the morning, far past the wee hours, the prostitutes had all receded from sight, disappearing as though they didn't exist. But my neighbor Bernie kept at it, a lone and plastered sentinel blocking traffic in the middle of the street, doing the Sangria slur. After an exchange of hellos and a few indecipherable words, I turned into my lot and stepped over the used tampons and spent needles that would randomly appear as I walked past the house where Emilio lived. He was a neighborhood kid, an abandoned boy in a home full of foster kids. Later, he would get a full ride to Carnegie Mellon, and after that, a master's in finance from Pitt. But before all of that, Emilio was just a kid who would stick his head out his third-story window and wave and shout, "Hey, Mr. Dan. Mr. Dan! How you doin', Mr. Dan?"

It was late now, though. He was already off to school. I'd see him later, I knew. He'd want to know what was going on, too.

I dragged myself into Lightspeed and up to my employees to tell them I hadn't sold out Lightspeed or their jobs, nor had I liquidated parts of it to pay for my newest, craziest entrepreneurial endeavor. I filled them in on the spectacularly bizarre facts of the last few days—the Christian redeemer, the knife-wielding maniac, the milksop state trooper, the new deals, the savings, the lower build costs, Woodstock—all of it.

As everyone drifted back to work, I settled behind my "desk"—a door propped up on two file cabinets—and dug into the work piled up in front of me, one pile but two companies. I'd start with Lightspeed, the faction that had the money to pay its bills. If a free dollar showed itself, I'd swoop in on behalf of Reliance and grab it. That's how I spent my first day back—generously reappropriating capital from Lightspeed to Reliance, trying not to think of the day when I had to pay it all back.

The whole time, Adam, my rental manager, watched. He did it with some skepticism, but without judgment, trusting me as I trusted him—an arrangement that pundits in our astringently polarized world would see as eccentrically impossible. Naturally, they'd be wrong. Adam was politically on the far side of left, while I was trying to be a fracker. Adam was also gay—neither here nor there—but a perfect fit in our catch basin of a neighborhood. Between the two of us, the whip-smart gay socialist and the newly minted fracker, we had grown Lightspeed into the largest grip and lighting rental house in Pennsylvania, even with all those dollars flowing out to another, brand-new enterprise.

Chapter 18

PENNSYLVANIA OILFIELDS

Reno, Pennsylvania

On my second day back home, I made the two-hour, north-by-northeast drive to meet with my partners, Wallace and Eli Kane. They wanted to hear more about my doings in Oklahoma and Texas, and I wanted to see how they were coming along with the five oil wells we planned for our other company, Arcade.

If we could get all the roads cut and graded; level and build the stone locations; drill, case, cement, log, and notch all five wells; dig in and bury the flow lines; set electric poles and run the line; and plumb-in the separator and tanks, we could roll in with our brand-new frack trucks and complete the wells for our own account. No one on the outside would see our learning curve play out. We'd keep it quiet and pray the work we did would be good enough to bring oil to the surface. Me—the cipher—would run the blender, without the normal two or three years of training first. The Kanes would shake off their rust, familiarize themselves with the new equipment, and—my hope of hopes—we'd have five wells flushing oil. And with little frack work likely at low oil prices, Arcade's oil income was looking more and more like my last refuge.

Once I got into Reno, I turned off the highway and drove back to our shop, a metal building whose useful life had mostly come to an end. It was cold and dark, cheap and forgotten, a perfect fit for us. Plus, we had the additional benefit of being at the base of a steep hillside, on top of which we'd put our wells.

Ahead were Wallace and Eli. I parked alongside them and stepped out.

"You're alive," Eli grinned as I joined him and Wallace idly leaning over the back of Wallace's pickup.

"Yeah. Barely."

"So what the hell happened down there?" Wallace asked in his gruff way.

I repeated what I had been telling them over the phone, but juiced it up by adding a few crowd-pleasers and details, answering the "what did he do then?" questions and the "tell us that part again" requests.

"Why didn't you tell us what was goin' on? We'd-a come down," Wallace offered.

"You're lucky you didn't get stabbed," Eli added.

We all laughed, because we all knew my deal in Oklahoma was more of a rough-up than a murder-in-waiting. But framing it otherwise made for better theater, so I ran with it until it gradually lost steam and we lapsed into an awkward silence. My hope of Wallace and Eli taking over with stories of all their progress on our wells up on the hilltop didn't materialize. Instead, the two brothers stayed mum, until Wallace groused instead about crummy oil prices and a newly elected president who, it was beginning to appear, didn't like us oil and gas people all that much. Naturally, we spent some time on that. And then a little more time on our do-nothing Congress and entitled senators, with a few choice words for movie stars and Silicon Valley start-up heroes. When that died off—to my relief—Wallace gave in to the obvious, conceding to what he knew I was after.

"You wanna see what's goin' on so bad, we could take a ride up the hill, we don't get fuckin' stuck in all-a the mud up there."

I perked up. "Yeah, let's have a look," I responded, anxious to check the progress.

What I thought I'd be seeing was a crew cutting locations and roads ahead of the drilling rig, maybe a few guys trenching in pipelines or building a tank battery. My hope, too, was to see the Kanes' drilling rig, if not drilling, then at the very least, mast-up and ready to spud. Instead, as we crested the steep hill in Eli's Ford, I was met with the stillness of an undisturbed winter scene, a quiet and eerie emptiness where the only signs of progress were tire and 'dozer tracks and bygone ruts in the mud. But otherwise, nothing.

"Where's the rig?"

"Yeah, we were gonna talk to you about that," Eli quietly offered.

"We got a job," Wallace said.

"You had to pull off?"

"Yeah, guy we know needed a well done."

"There's not much work right now," Eli added, trying to add reason to my onset of disappointment.

I didn't own the equipment, and I wasn't making the decisions, but I was paying for the labor as part of my participation in Arcade. And, so far, the Kanes had just used a bulldozer to collectively drag a few hundred thousand pounds of rig parts and equipment up the hillside and over a rocky ledge, only to get a call for a job, then skid and drag it all the way back down again, without ever touching a bit to the ground.

It was deflating, two rig mobilizations and nothing to show for it.

That lump that grows in your chest, that pushes into your ribs and lungs—anxiety or an early-onset heart attack—was flashing its sweaty early warning signs. It was the same lump that triggered my impromptu flight to Tulsa. It's the sort of lump that makes it hard to breathe, like you're running flat out and sucking air through a straw.

Frustrating as it was, I did my best to shut the hell up. The Kanes had to make a living, and we had never agreed to exclusivity. No one agreed to shutting down their own income in favor of our venture. I had to acknowledge, too, that there wasn't that big of a hurry. The frack trucks were being built—finally—but they were three more months out, assuming no one ran off the rails again.

Still, they had me wondering—their lack of progress, the lack of concern. If they weren't fully committed, if they didn't have the cold sweats right alongside me, it was because of me. I had let them off the hook with a dumb deal. If it worked, we profited equally. If it fell apart, only I would be left broken. That left me with the singular hope that good character would cause them to act as I thought they should. But that's a risk, isn't it—asking people to behave as you think they should?

As good a time as any, given that there were really no good times, Wallace brought up something that had been on his mind.

"I been thinkin'," he said.

"Yeah? What about?"

"I don't know...just...I don't know."

Feeling the lump again, I waited for the guy who had no filter.

"Some-a these guys are gonna wanna run more sand. Just the one dump, I don't know. We'll be too limited on sand."

"What do you mean?"

"One truck's not gonna do it."

"You think we need another sand dump?"

"Yeah... Don't you?"

"Hold it. You mean you really want another sand dump?" I asked confoundedly, then turned to Eli. He said nothing in return, his way of agreeing with Wallace.

"Why you guys think we need it now? We didn't need it before. We didn't need two sand dumps before."

"We get a call to go up in the big woods, we gotta go. We're gonna need two dumps. An' those bigger guys, like EnerVest, they ain't gonna stand there with their dicks in their hands wonderin' what we're up to when we run outta sand."

Eli put a milder spin on it. "Randy said he'd use us if we ever get the trucks together."

"Randy from EnerVest?" I asked.

"Yep."

"Make a lot more money on those wells," Wallace proclaimed.

"Yeah, but we don't even have the money to finish what we started."

"Gotta have it," Wallace added, as if the matter was settled.

"For the bigger jobs," Eli added.

Abruptly, it had just become an absolute need, a damned certainty, in fact. Reliance wouldn't survive without a second and unbudgeted sand dump, a new and wholly unexpected $200,000 hole on top of the other hole, what would be the blender overruns. Those two holes—$125,000 and $200,000—were now one $325,000-deep hole.

Under normal circumstances, I'd be jumping for joy. EnerVest was the biggest operator in shallow Pennsylvania. Their supervisor, Randy, was also a friend of the Kanes.

But there was nothing more I could raise. I had nothing left to be leveraged. Even my house had a second on it. Now this insurmountable raise. There was no way, not without dilution. Who would even buy into this fire when everyone else was running out of it?

But this EnerVest thing. Jesus, the carrot and stick. EnerVest was big enough to keep a work schedule going right through a downturn. And they paid their bills. And they were friends with the Kanes. And they said they would use us.

I had to try. I'd try harder. I would do as told. But I needed to open my eyes, too. My little dream of setting up a business and fading back into my Pittsburgh office was done. I needed to take over. Being the passive and compliant good partner was ruining me. If this company crashed on takeoff, it would be at my hand, not theirs. If it was going to be crazy, I needed it to be my crazy. Not theirs.

I'd have to find a way to raise more money.

But where?

All the oil and gas investors had already been burned.

Chapter 19

STIM SOLUTIONS MANUFACTURING

Bristow, Oklahoma

Pennsylvania was beginning to freeze over as the 2008 Christmas season settled in. Already the ground was frozen, and in another month the freeze would penetrate three feet down as the winter solstice arrived and the Northern Hemisphere tilted away from the sun. After winding clocks back for daylight saving time, nightfall was arriving at 4:30 in the afternoon.

It was cold and quiet, and little was happening up on our barren hilltop, where no progress had been made on roads, or drilling, or anything needed to move us forward.

And then there was Andy.

He was becoming a concern. Again. A month had barely passed since the contemptible lunacy of my last visit, and I was beginning to think it was time for another look. Good progress was being made down in Texas. Douglas was sending pictures, and the pump truck was right on schedule.

Not so in Bristow, Oklahoma.

STIM SOLUTIONS Manufacturing, the phoenix that had risen from the ashes of STIM SOLUTIONS, Inc., was struggling to take flight. Requests for progress payments were running ahead of progress. Andy was not as available as he once was, nothing like his availability the month before, when he was pushing to make a second deal. Since then, phone calls had gone unanswered and unreturned. The fanaticism factor had ebbed.

As I talked over my concerns with the Kanes, Eli grew worried and Wallace incredulous. This whole mess had Wallace bent right out of shape. He wanted to give a black eye to the guy who had given one to me. That blindsided me, given the $200,000 sand dump he had just dropped on me. But now this reversal. Just like Woodstock, it was one man standing up for another. Confused by it or not, I was overwhelmingly grateful. What I couldn't accomplish, maybe he could. His sullen demeanor—a walking, talking, pissed-off malcontent—might go a long way in quelling Andy's blather. And then there was his size. Wallace was a big, big unflinching badass. His cold, despotic stare, the sense that he was a stranger to restraint, might move Andy more than my cheery, convivial bearing. So when he dropped his phobia of flying and said, "Let's go!," I was all in and quickly arranging flights.

I called Andy to let him know we were coming. Of course, I had to leave him a message, but it must have jarred him, because he returned my call within seconds.

"When are you coming?" he asked apprehensively.

"We're looking at day after tomorrow."

"That soon?"

"We won't take up much of your time. We just want to have a look around."

"Haven't you been getting my pictures?"

"Yeah, Andy. But Wallace wants to have a look, and it's already been a month since last time...."

After a long pause, Andy seemed to relent. "Day after tomorrow?"

"Yeah, our flight gets in early, so we'll see you about late morning."

A few days later, Wallace shrank himself into the airliner's cramped, claustrophobic cabin and off we went. Half a workday later we were in a rental car, rolling down Bristow's Main Street, past the police station and miniature Indian casino. When Andy's shop came into view, I pointed.

"That's it," I said.

"That?" Wallace asked, taking a good look. "That's it?"

"That's it," I said as I slowed to turn in.

"You gotta be kiddin' me. What a dump!" he exclaimed.

"I know," I said embarrassedly, as if Andy's shop were my own. "I know, I know."

"This his *new* shop? The improvement over the old one?"

"Yeah, I know."

"What the hell. This's way worse'n I expected." This coming from a guy who had spent a lifetime working in oil-field squalor. "What a fuckin' shithole."

"Yeah. I know."

I parked in front, alongside a handful of pickups and beat sedans. Wallace and I stepped out of our rental and started for a jimmied-open, rolling steel door. As his inexhaustible shithole commentary kept running, I ducked under the door for a cautious look, hoping to see Andy's parishioners working and not gathered for more doctrinal purposes, like an impromptu religious service or some sort of sacrificial offering.

Not able to see a thing in the darkness, I stood still and adjusted. That's when Wallace grabbed me by the arm and pulled me back away from the building.

"You sure we can't get our money back?"

Meant more as a comment than a question, Wallace followed me under the door, and we stepped right into the big, chromed-over grille of our blender.

Andy must have been keeping an uneasy eye out for us, because just as we entered, he emerged from his cobbled-together office and met us on the shop floor, grinning as was his way and shaking our hands like we were long-lost friends. This was his and Wallace's first meeting, so there was the usual banter about flights and Pennsylvania winters and the frost making its way all the way down to Oklahoma. As their how-do-you-do played out, I had a chance to look around and was relieved; four or five of his congregation were inside, working. Welders and pipefitters were huddled over what looked like a manifold. Others were cutting and grinding and giving me the impression that these guys were, at the very least, outwardly serious.

I wandered back to Wallace and Andy for the start of a tour Andy insisted on. Along the way, we met each of the capable crew, every one of them with a full-time job elsewhere. This included Bryson, whom I had already met. Quickly apparent was that he was the one running the show. Apparent, too, was that Andy wasn't always on hand, made obvious by him doing more listening than talking, receiving information rather than conveying it. When Andy wandered off to take a call, Bryson innocently let on that Andy was spending a lot of time on fab plans back home in Tulsa.

"So, Andy's getting tied up back home?" I innocently asked.

"Oh, he comes in, but a lotta the times it's just easier working outta his office at home. He sure stays busy, though. You know Andy, that mind-a his is always working."

"Yeah, that Andy," I conceded, keeping it friendly.

As we moved on, Wallace grabbed my arm and spun me around. "So who's building this truck, then?" he said quietly, restraining himself.

Andy's call ended, and we dropped it. But our guard was up, and everything we saw, we regarded suspiciously. When we asked to see the fittings that our last progress payment covered, Andy made a big point of proving his good word and showing them to us. One of his crew was just finishing them, spraying them with a can of black paint, something you might pick up at a Dollar General.

An effort with weld-ups had been made, but the hydraulics hadn't been worked out. Other purchases looked Mickey Mouse. Right away we rejected the fifty-five-gallon drums Andy was trying to pass off as high-dollar, stainless-steel chemical totes.

Corners looked like they were cut, and there were holes in the build, though most glaringly absent was the vortex blender pod Bill was to supply. Andy assured us it was coming, promising even to show us the paid invoice. Beyond all doubt, he told us, it was only a matter of time before his brother delivered it.

"Lickety-split," he added defensively. "Nothing to worry about. Bill really wants to see me succeed with this build. He's gonna get it all over here any day now. I keep thinking it's him every time my phone rings," Andy promised, holding up his phone.

Wallace and I politely acquiesced, but there was no doubt that the more we asked him, the less he knew.

Our tour came to an end back at his office. Wallace and I sat on an old car seat that was propped up on concrete blocks and let Andy talk. "Rest assured" was his default position, repeating it over and over again, sensing that we were having more than a few misgivings. He was one month into a three-month build-out, and it didn't look like he was going to make it. Either blind, or calculating, he ignored the obvious and labored on about the incredible progress his committed crew had made—how, if he would have had the two trucks to build, some of his crew could have been there full time.

"Then you'd see some real progress!" Andy postured.

If Andy's intent was to extract some sort of guilt, it failed. Wallace didn't care about Andy's feelings. He just wanted our blender. I didn't want to hear it, either, especially when Andy began pitching a new deal on progress payments. Would we be open to accelerating them? he wondered. Given the speed of work being completed, he was outrunning scheduled payments, or so his pitch went.

"It would really help me to push this along. It's really important to me I get this done on time."

"You think it's going to take you longer?" I asked.

"Well, no," Andy responded.

"Then I'd say we're satisfied with the way it is."

"We need that truck," Wallace leveled, imposingly standing up and signaling the end of our meeting.

"That's fine. Everything will be fine. I'll have it done on time, no problem," Andy promised, as though backed into a corner.

Though we all remained friendly enough as Andy walked us out, I knew I was on a new footing with him. He was withdrawing from his omnipresent enthusiasm, from me, maybe even from our project. But people were at work and there was some progress, and Wallace and I gave him the benefit of doubt. Maybe we were just being hard on Andy, maybe he'd prove us doubters wrong. Maybe he'd pick up steam as soon as he got the holidays behind him. Maybe, maybe, but privately I wondered how long it would be until I had to make another last-minute, unplanned trip to Bristow.

Chapter 20

MORE OF STIM SOLUTIONS

Bristow, Oklahoma

It took three weeks.

Only twenty-one days had passed since Wallace and I had visited. That's all it took for Andy to stop accepting my calls. Every call or email went unanswered.

But when he needed something—money—his emails had no difficulty reaching me. He'd attach a few random pictures of progress, obsequiously demonstrating he had hit the next marker. What was always missing, what I had paid for months back, what should have been attached by now, was the pod. That big mystery, the vortex blender pod, was as absent as was Andy's explanation of its whereabouts.

My first thought was to starve him out and hold back a small $10,000 progress payment that his latest email claimed was due. My second thought, the one I acted on, was to hand him the payment directly.

Delta Airlines had to be loving me—showing up at the last minute and paying whatever price they asked. They should have had a pricing algorithm named after me—the "impetuous sucker"—for the optionless, backed-into-the-corner crowd.

This time, though, I wouldn't be making a sweaty, sleep-deprived, middle-of-the-night rush to the Pittsburgh airport like the first time. This time, I was more accustomed to Andy. This time, the third time, it felt more routine. But there was still a sickening side to it, the unease and despair of finally acknowledging that I may just have been played.

Stepping out of the early-morning ticket line with my boarding pass, I made my way past the same gated newsstand but didn't bother to stop and read the End-of-Days headlines. Oil was down to forty-nine dollars, roughly a hundred-dollar drop from when I started. Natural gas was down another 25 percent. The housing bubble had popped, so why stop to remind myself? Instead, I stepped into another short line for a cup of coffee at McDonald's. Next to me, the Starbucks line was three or four times as long, packed with college kids heading back to school after the holidays. *That was the easy money*, I thought, their parents' money, spent five dollars at a time. I could buy four cups of coffee for one of theirs. That made me feel smart. I needed that, particularly as it dawned on me that maybe I was the dim-witted, gullible one after all, not the kids with all that disposable income.

As I ambled along the narrow airplane aisle toward my middle-row seat, it felt as though I'd been hit by some sort of historic tsunami.

Is there even a need to finish the trucks anymore, let alone a rush?

Should I just wait it out, wait on a recovery?

Customers—if there are any—wouldn't take a chance on a newbie when the established competition are cutting prices to the bone.

Capitulation was coming, and the best I could hope for was an empty seat next to me. Then the seats filled in around me and that was gone, too.

What was even the point?

A few hours later at the Tulsa airport, I stopped in front of the fifty-six-foot-long mural *Panorama of Petroleum* and, just for the hell of it, called Andy. As his phone rang, I scanned the mural for names and found Jedediah Dowell and Marcel and Conrad Schlumberger. Together, the companies they formed would merge decades later to become the biggest oil-field services company in the world. And there I stood, decades late to the party. When my call went to Andy's voicemail, I hung up and started for the rental-car counter with a gait that belied a gathering anger. The son of a bitch. That dismal son of a bitch. I hated myself almost as much as him.

I slid into my rental, a Chrysler Pacifica, and made the same, uncertain, hour-long trek out to Bristow, wondering along the way at what point I would break. At what point would I walk away from this guy? My decision to stick with him, because of the money paid out, was looking like more good money after bad.

But stopping now…I couldn't. I had to stay on my feet, no matter my problems or the world's. Even if Andy's shop was closed up and my truck parted out, I had to keep going.

That resolution is all that drove me as I turned into Bristow with a plan as simple as showing up and seeing what happened. I wouldn't have to worry about guns and knives with Andy. Finding him was more of the concern.

Then, ahead, thank God. "Thank God," I said aloud as I rolled into Andy's dirt parking lot. There were two pickups parked outside, neither of them Andy's, but at least someone was there, maybe even working. One I recognized as Bryson's, the other I wasn't sure, but there were people there, and that meant answers and maybe even progress.

I quietly crossed the lot and tried the door. It was unlocked. Breathing a sigh of relief, I pulled the door open and saw the sparks and strobe effect of a welder at work, the flash bright enough to flicker across my blender, exactly where I had seen it a few weeks back. Blinking and trying to catch my bearings, I caught something black, like a hole in the flashing light, approaching me. As it grew in size, I could see it was a familiar face that I recognized as Bryson, stopping in front of me with his hand held out.

"How're you, Mr. Doyle? I had no idea you were comin' by today," he said, happy to see me.

"Sorry no notice," I said. "I was in the area and thought I'd check in."

That made no sense, "in the area," but he didn't push it and I didn't offer anything more.

"Yes, sir. Well, it's good to see you, anyways."

I returned Bryson's smile, wondering if he knew that Andy had gone quiet. A glance around the shop told me that it was just two men to match the two trucks outside, a 66-percent decrease in the head count I had made a few weeks back.

"So, where's Andy?" I asked. "Not in today?"

Bryson laughed, an unamused, I-give-up kind of laugh. "Not sure. I haven't seen much-a him. But we're on the phone all-a the time," he rushed to add, covering for his boss and cohort parishioner.

"Let's call him," I suggested. "My phone's dead out in the car. You got a speaker on your phone?"

"Why sure. I just talked to him."

Bryson dialed without hesitation and—presto!—Andy was on the phone, chipper and starting in with a laugh that played out over Bryson's speakerphone.

"Hey, I just talked to you! Or am I going crazy?"

"Yeah, I know. We got us a surprise here, though. Dan Doyle is with me. He just walked in for a visit."

The phone went silent. Was Andy about to hang up? I didn't think so, because hanging up would have been tipping his hand, not to me—I already knew—but to his entire staff.

"Hello? Andy?" Bryson asked loudly. "I still got you?"

"How you doing, Andy?" I asked, leaning into Bryson's phone. "You coming into work today, or should I meet you back at your house?"

After a long pause, Andy peeped, "How are you, Dan? I wish I would've known you were coming down."

"You mind?" I asked Bryson as I took his phone and walked away with it. When I glanced back, Bryson was staring at me, intuitively sensing a problem.

"You really coming out, Andy?"

"I'll be there," he offered defeatedly. "I just have to finish some stuff up here."

"Then I'll come over in the meantime. I have your home address here with me."

"No, no, I'm coming right now. It can wait. I'm coming. Gimme an hour or so."

"Okay, Andy. Fair enough… But you really coming?"

"Yes, I'm coming," he answered, annoyed. "I promise I'm on my way."

When I handed Bryson his phone back, nothing more was said about Andy. Bryson was far too polite to ask about the call, being the kind of a man you would imagine lived in Oklahoma. Instead, we made a slow and discouraging lap around the truck. Granted, there was a Christmas and New Year's between my visits, but nothing was getting done, not with two part-timers that looked to be suffering from an early-onset lack of morale. If my last inspection was lackluster, this one was flat-out disappointing. The place looked more like a pastime than a business, like where you'd go to drink beer and throw darts, like old friends restoring a car on a Saturday night.

Absent, too, was my foremost worry, the fabled pod of the vortex blender. At first, I was surreptitiously glancing around for it, then I was outrightly searching for it.

"I don't see the pod anywhere, Bryson. You get it from Bill yet?"

"The pod?"

"Yeah. From Bill?"

"You're asking the wrong person about that pod. You're gonna have to ask Andy 'bout that."

"Bill hasn't brought it by yet?"

"Not yet," Bryson mumbled. "We sure could use it, though."

Not that it was hard to figure out, but I had just uncovered Andy's reason for growing cold. Whatever the reason—more money, revenge, or "Bill just being Bill"—I just discovered that Bill wasn't out of my life. Not yet. With Andy's imprimatur—"it's all good, Dan"—wearing thin, Andy simply defaulted to his current state of silence. Coming clean and answering my calls could have forced an end to his cash flow. I sensed, too, that there was some frustration with Andy in the shop. Coaxing it out of Bryson wasn't very difficult. Parts weren't getting delivered. Plans were spotty. There was no oversight, presence, or stewardship. In general, things weren't going well with an absentee owner.

"So, he's not around much?" I smiled, feigning innocence.

Bryson was honest, but he was also aware of his station. He had the predicament of filial obedience bludgeoned by dishonesty, the struggle between truth and employment. Gradually, though, as with all good people, the truth won out.

"Well, you know Andy," he grinned back at me.

"Yeah, that Andy," I said, then paused. "But what do you mean?"

"Well, you know, he likes that tech stuff."

"Oh yeah. I know. I know all-a that, but like what, though?"

"His website."

"What website?"

"You know, the one he's been workin' on. It's like an online buyer's guide for the oil business. He's buildin' it all on his own, writin' it all just on his own, the code an' all. He's pretty good with that tech stuff."

"Oh yeah, the online buyer's guide. That's where he's been, I guess?"

"I think so."

Rage wasn't my first reaction. It was my second. First was skepticism. But that didn't last long.

"Boy, that's a great idea," I seethed.

Apparently, as Bryson explained it, Andy's website—websites being all the rage in 2009—would bring buyers and sellers together globally. This was his *new* new thing, which had created a bit of a vacuum at his old new thing, STIM SOLUTIONS Manufacturing. The fallout was a cynical regard for his other business, the one I was standing in, the one likely seeding his new, stay-at-home web business.

"I don't know, though. Seems to me like he's got good-payin' work right here," Bryson postured.

As a builder of empires, Andy had handed the reins of STIM to Bryson but without telling him. Bryson, in turn, was doing his best to temper his frustration with the arrangement.

"It doesn't make much sense, does it?" I added sympathetically. As much as I wanted to punch Andy when he walked in—if he walked in—I kept cool. I saw that I needed to keep Bryson onboard. He had just become my last weak link to getting the truck done, and my best guess was that if he was even being paid, it wasn't much.

An hour later, Andy walked in.

Unlike our previous greetings, where we met and shook hands like old friends, this one was between two guys thoroughly sick of each other, pushed together by circumstances. All Andy said after hello was what he had already said earlier.

"I wish I knew you were coming down."

"If you answered your phone, I wouldn't have had to."

With Bryson watching, and the guy in the back looking up from under his welder's helmet, Andy suggested we talk in his office. I followed him inside so that we could hide the charade from the earshot of his skeleton crew.

"So how was your flight down?" Andy asked as he sat down at his filthy desk.

"Great, Andy. I really enjoyed it. So, tell me, what's going on down here?"

"Well, you know, Dan, gettin' 'er done, as they say."

"Where's the pod, Andy?"

Andy started in on another.

"He's not being very responsive. Bill, I mean," Andy conceded.

"Responsive to what?"

"Me."

Andy slouched over in that big coat with his hangdog expression. *Jesus*, I thought to myself. How was it that this made me feel bad, like I'd just kicked the beloved family dog? Bill goes dark on Andy, Andy goes dark on me, and I'm the one who feels bad about it.

I finally took a seat on the blocked-up car seat in front of him, choosing the side opposite to what looked like a shop dog or maybe a stray raccoon had been burrowing.

"Did you pay Bill for the parts, Andy? You give him the money I gave you?"

"Dan! I told you! Two months ago! I gave it all to him two months ago. Everything he wanted."

"And you can prove that?"

"Yes, I can prove that."

"Let's go get it, then. Let's drive over and get it. We could fit it right in the back of your pickup truck."

Andy went white. You'd think I'd just asked him to knock off the Kum & Go on a dare. When I made a move to stand up and go, Andy cracked.

"No, no, no, no—"

"Come on, Andy. You paid for it. Let's just take it."

"No. We can't. You don't under—"

"Why not? He's not going to use his gun. Christ, he doesn't even know where it is!"

"You don't understand!"

Andy looked to be recoiling, as though he might bolt right out of the room. This wasn't the approachable, smiley-faced guy, his post-golfing self, stuffed full of smoothies and good family fun out on the golf course. This was a different Andy, a bad-decision Andy, a fretting and full-of-dread Andy.

"This is the stuff lawsuits are made out of, Andy."

Dropping his voice to a near-whisper, Andy leaned into me. "You have to promise you'll never tell anyone. Okay? You gotta promise me if I tell you."

"Promise what? What're you talking about?"

"The vortex blender, Dan! Aren't you listening?"

Andy was straight-up unhinged, something scaring the hell out of him. Maybe he feared another childhood-style ass-beating from his big brother, or maybe a sharp rebuke from his wife, as in, "Get a regular job!" Whatever it was, Andy had gone cold with fear, so I did as he asked and listened as he unwrapped the story of the pod.

What I learned was that Bill and Andy had stolen it.

All along, the answer to the vortex-blender mystery was right under my nose. It was back at Bill's shop, rusting away in the weeds. It was the orange Dowell blender trucks, discarded and seemingly forgotten, that I had passed by a few times. You wouldn't know it with everything cut off, but they had once been vortex blenders. As Andy explained it, they were now living out a second useful life as donors. Bill had a deal with

Schlumberger to scrap their old trucks, but anything proprietary, like the pods, was to be torched into pieces. Only thing is, Bill didn't do that. Instead, he carefully unbolted the pods, sanded the rough edges, then sold them as his own.

It all made sense, like finding the place for the last piece of a puzzle. I now understood why they had nothing on paper, no cut sheets, plans, or schematics. That would have been self-incriminating. Yet I had believed what I was told, that Bill had designed a variation of the tried-and-true vortex blender. I had believed them, so I had never checked for myself. I had failed to undertake the most elemental part of any deal. I had substituted blind trust for due diligence.

Andy rolled on, nearly levitating as he rid himself of his burdens. I kept listening, becoming more and more convinced that I was finally and utterly screwed, like I had just handed this guy a hammer to nail my own coffin shut.

"Andy, are the pods patent-protected? Does Schlumberger have a patent on them?"

"No. Absolutely not. You think I would— No."

"Well, great, then at least we're not in trouble with Schlumberger. Right?"

"We're not in any trouble. How can we be in trouble? The patent's expired."

"You just said there *was* no patent!"

"I just said it's expired!"

"When? When did it expire?"

"It's expired. I don't know. But I'm pretty sure recently."

"Holy shit, Andy. You don't think that's a problem? With Schlumberger? You don't think they're gonna have a problem with this, especially if you guys were supposed to be cutting up those pods?"

"Bill was, not me. He was—"

"You knew, Andy. Come on, don't act like you weren't part of this."

"Dan. The patent ran out. We have every right to sell those parts."

"Really? You cleared that with your patent lawyer? This is Schlumberger you're talking about."

"Well, they don't know. How they going to know?"

"You're kidding me, right?"

"I just don't think it's that big a deal. It's been over twenty years. You can't hold a patent in the United States for over twenty years. This is America, Dan! America! You get it? You can't do that!"

"You're kidding me, right? What if I need parts? I gotta call Schlumberger for them? Tell them they're for a pod we cut off the back of one of their old blenders? This is crazy."

Andy shrugged.

"All the bullshit so far, and now I gotta fight Schlumberger, too? You know how many lawyers they have on staff? I'm sure it's a whole department of lawyers, all over the world. Probably looking for guys just like you. Why didn't you tell me all this? I've got all this money into a crazy-ass vortex blender. Bryson out there is ready for the pod, and there's no pod, and if you'd been truthful, we could've just built a conventional blender, instead."

Andy chirped up, "You want a conventional blender?"

"You'd be done by now."

"I'd have to start over. That's a whole different blender."

I lost. Right there. I lost. It was like I was talking to a different species without the benefit of reason or accountability.

"No. No more deals."

"I could build that blender."

"No more deals, Andy. Same deal. Get my money from Bill. Go get it, or get the pod and all the approvals. One or the other. Right now."

Andy stood and walked across his office. That was it, I thought. I had pushed him too far. Him and all my money were bee-lining for the door. Should I grab him? Is that how this was going to play out? Then he stopped at a shelf for a piece of paper. He returned to his desk, his breath like a contrail behind him, and wrote something down in silence. When he was done, he folded up the paper into his fist and held it out to me.

"You have to swear on your life. If I show this to you, you have to swear on your life that you won't tell him where you got this number."

"Who's him?"

"Bill!"

"No, the paper, Andy!" I nearly shouted, pointing at his hand.

He uncupped his fist, exposing the secret in it, holding it close enough to his chest to keep me from snatching it away.

"You have to swear first."

"Not a chance.... What do you have in your hand?"

"It's a friend of Bill's." Andy shook the wad of paper in his hand. "He has your pod."

I was flummoxed. What was he talking about? "Bill has the pod—"

"No, Bill sent it to this guy to rebuild it. He has a shop where he can rebuild them. He can sell you parts, too."

"What the hell, Andy? Who is this guy?"

"You have to swear on your life."

"No, I'm not swearing on my life. I paid for the pod. Just give me his number."

"My life could be in danger. I can't," Andy cried.

"Keep it, then. I don't want it. This is...this is...I don't know. This is...I'm not going to help you defraud Schlumberger."

He held out his fist a little closer. "You don't want it, then?"

"No, I don't want it. You keep it, Andy. I'd hate to see you get murdered over it."

Crestfallen, Andy dropped his hand and the secret I had sought inside his palm. It was all just too ridiculous, cozying up to Bill's network of black marketeers. I'd be complicit if I took the number. Likely, too, the Brothers Brennan hadn't paid the guy for rebuilding it. Why else wasn't he releasing the pod? Paying twice for a stolen part held no appeal for me, nor did the thought that someone might just drop a dime on me after I paid up. I didn't need that, either, a cease and desist from Schlumberger's covey of lawyers.

"Andy, who built these trucks for Schlumberger?" I started back in quietly. "Who built the pod? Your guy there?" I asked, indicating the paper in his hand.

"Schlumberger designed it, I told you."

"No. Did they build it, too? Who built it for them? Did they actually, you know, fabricate it, or just design it?"

"Serva built it."

"Who's Serva?"

"You don't know Serva?"

"No, I'm a dumbass. But, boy, do I wish I did!"

"They're a competitor."

"To who? You?" I asked, trying not to sneer as I pulled out my phone and searched for Serva.

Andy shifted nervously. "Who you calling?"

"Serva. Where are they?"

"In Texas."

"Where in Texas?"

"You going to talk to them?" Andy asked, his panic morphing into self-preservation, another trait of his.

"Yeah. That's a good idea, don't you think?"

"What about me and Bill? You going to tell them about me and Bill?"

"I don't know what I'm going to tell them. But whatever it is, it'll be the truth. Here it is," I said, having found the Serva website. "They're in Wichita Falls, Texas. How far is that?"

"You going there?"

"I'm thinking I better. You want to go with me?"

"Go to Wichita Falls?"

"Yeah. If there's no patent protection—you said it expired. So let's go and buy a pod off of them."

I mapped it—only a three-hour drive from where I stood.

"You're serious?"

"Yeah, we can drive out Sunday and show up Monday morning. Or leave at four or five Monday. We could walk in first thing in the morning."

I said it for its shock value, but then, watching Andy squirm, I took a grotesque pleasure in it. That's exactly what I needed to do. I needed to go to Wichita Falls. Right away. Maybe I could reason with them, explain my situation. If the patent was truly expired, I intended to find out. If so, maybe they'd sell me one.

"Let's go get this done."

"Who's going to pay for it?"

"Bill is. You're going to get my money back from him."

"Dan," Andy pleaded. "You can't go out there, to Serva. Bill will come through. Just give him a little more time."

"Bill's not giving you the pod, Andy. That part's over. If he won't give you the money, you'll have to pay for it. I'm sorry, but I'm not paying for it. Paying once is enough, right? Think about it, Andy. You think Bill wants Serva or Schlumberger to know what he's up to?"

"No," Andy replied weakly.

I stood up. The meeting was over. Whatever he built, as long as it was something, I'd fix it back up in Pennsylvania. Just get the parts, I was thinking. Get the major components bolted down—the pod, the hydraulics, the data acquisition system, the manifolds—get all of it, and get the hell out of town.

"What am I going to do all weekend?" I openly wondered, hardly aware I'd said it aloud.

Andy brightened up. "You could come to church with me and my family," he offered. "We have a great Sunday service. You could come and pray together with me and my family."

I go to church regularly, but normally not with people that have a knife in my back. Maybe this was some form of apostolic test of a higher order, a test of the Christian construct of forgiveness. Whatever it was, Andy's hopelessly simple-minded disconnect actually added some perspective. I finally saw that he was the crazy one, not me.

"Thanks, but I'll be fine, Andy." I started for the door. "If you're up for it, maybe it's just easier to leave early Monday. If we walked in at eight, I could pick you up at, what, say four or so?"

"I can't go, Dan. I have things I need to do. I'm all tied up this weekend."

I wasn't surprised. I didn't press it, either. I really didn't want to spend all that time in the car with him, not on what was likely a long shot. The ride back would be a killer.

"Yeah, okay. I guess you got your website to work on."

Andy didn't pick it up, and I didn't press it any further.

"I'll call you from Serva when I get there Monday morning," I said as I stepped out of his office. "Pick up my call. Okay, Andy?"

Chapter 21

SERVA CORPORATION

Wichita Falls, Texas

According to primatologist Frans de Waal's 1982 book, *Chimpanzee Politics*, human liars and chimp liars share a duplicitous commonality. De Waal called it Machiavellian Intelligence.

> Humans are one of the few species on earth who display deceit and violence so that they can maximize their gene potential. The only other species is our near cousin, the chimp. Humans did not learn to be manipulative of one another at a particular point in history; instead, they have always been that way.... If humans were not innately manipulative, they would have evolved to be completely reliant on physical strength; yet, that is not the micro-evolutionary path humans took. Physical dominance was not the only indication of leadership and power. Leadership also depended on coalitions and acquiescence by those who are being dominated. In the case of chimps, it was not always the most physically fit chimp who was the alpha male; rather, it was the best deceiver of the group.

There it was. The best metaphor for my evolving charade of a start-up was chimpanzee life out on the Serengeti. Worse was that I wasn't the alpha chimp. I was the acquiescent chimp, trustful and tolerant, the unwitting rube chimp who kept getting run over by the deceitful alphas.

By association, Andy's duplicitousness had become mine, the two of us cojoined in our harebrained foolishness, in a death spiral that was sooner or later going to hit the ground, the blender, the website, all of it. Again. All over again, these two brothers, these liars, these deceivers, and their toppling pile of horseshit.

My latest misstep was giving Andy the $10,000 check I swore to myself I wouldn't give him. I had promised myself that under no circumstance would I hand the check over to Andy without first seeing the pod. It had to be there, in Andy's shop, under his complete control, before I made another progress payment. Over my dead body, no pod, no check. Period. Then I handed it over to him, anyway.

Jesus.

"What about the payment?" Andy had asked me back when we were in his office.

"What payment, Andy? You got me paying for things that aren't even here. I paid for the pod and it's not even here. It should be here."

"If I don't have that ten thousand dollars in my bank by Monday, I won't be able to pay my crew."

That stopped me. "You're shitting me?"

"And I had a bunch of bills, too. I even already mailed the checks."

"If you didn't have the money, why did you mail the checks?"

"Because they were due. And there's late penalties. All this pressure I'm under."

Stricken by the need to remain above the fray, to move forward, even as I was pushed up against a wall, I acquiesced and gave Andy the check.

"Don't cash it until you hear from me. Right? You agree, right? Andy...you agree, right?"

"I swear I won't cash it until you say it's okay."

"Don't cash it, Andy."

"It's safe in my hands."

"I've got your word. If this deal looks dead after Serva, you're giving it back to me."

"Dan, you have my word as a Christian. Only if you say it's okay."

As I drove away from Andy's shop, I chanted over and over, "What's wrong with me? What's wrong with me? What's wrong with me?" Try saying something out loud to yourself. If it sounds like an accusation, you better listen.

Over my weekend stay in Tulsa, I thought I'd sleep but didn't. Besides Reliance-induced insomnia, I was onto something new in the pantheon of human disorders. This newest disorder of mine was night terrors, a condition I had developed where I'd snap up out of a restless sleep and hover over our little girls in their cribs, poking and listening, waking them if I couldn't hear their little breaths. So great was my fear of SIDS.

No one was spared. Mary was constantly awakened by my back-and-forth to the nursery, waking our babies whom I tormented with my unstrung perturbation. Being a thousand miles away in a Tulsa hotel should have spared everyone, but it still wasn't near far enough.

"You check the locks?" I asked Mary for the third or fourth time over the phone.

"Yes. Front door and back."

"Side door?"

"Checked it. It's locked. Now go to sleep."

"You leave the outside lights on?"

"Yes. Go to sleep."

"You have any windows open during the day?"

"It's winter! No. Go to sleep right now! You're waking me up."

"Okay. Okay. I know. I'm going nuts."

"Me, too. Good night!"

"Hold on. If Elena wants to be rocked, careful of her fingers with the glider, okay?"

"I'm going to kill you if you don't shut up and go to sleep!"

Then there was nothing. Not even a dial tone. Mary had hung up.

"You there?" I mouthed, knowing that she wasn't. I sat down on the hotel bed, wondering what to do next. I hadn't eaten, so I thought I'd eat. I wandered downstairs to a quiet restaurant off the lobby, where I ate dinner with both hands, not just one, as such was becoming my way, driving with one hand and eating with the other.

Afterward, I made my way back upstairs and found some ease in a text Mary had sent. "Night. Love you. Go to sleep. Don't text back. I'm sleeping."

I lay down in my hotel room bed thinking I'd better sleep. I closed my eyes and waited. Five minutes, ten minutes, going on fifteen minutes I waited, with my mind racing from what I had to do, to what I couldn't do, to the little money I had on hand, to what Andy was promising, to what he wasn't delivering, to Elena's fingers, to Maria's blanket in her crib, to it covering her face, to SIDS, to global annihilation.

All of it had me wide awake, and sweating. I noticed it when I noticed my heart. It was pounding, though I was absolutely still. A heart attack? Is this how it went, a racing heart and a line of sweat around my scalp? My God, should I call Mary, or the lobby, or 911? I grabbed my cell phone and counted. I'd see how I felt when I got to sixty—no, thirty. Get to thirty, see how I felt there, first.

I made it to thirty. Then I made it to sixty and sat up in bed, seeing if I got dizzy or stayed clear. I was fine, good enough to stand. Standing, I was good enough to walk. I started walking, pacing from wall to wall, sucking in air and holding it for short counts, trying to get ahead of my racing heart. This was just stress, I thought, maybe even an anxiety attack, but not my heart.

When my pulse quieted and the sweat dried up, I climbed back into bed. Maybe an hour or so later, maybe fifteen minutes, I finally fell into a high-cotton kind of sleep. Not a care in the world.

Until it came to a crashing end.

Bang! Bang!! Bang!!!

I snapped straight up and jumped out of bed, looking to see if someone was in my room, bracing myself for some unseen rushing attack—a gun, no, a knife.

"You ruined my life!"

"Fuuuuucckkkkk youuuuuuu—"

From the hallway: *Bang!*

No. My God, it was from my door, the hit so loud I could feel it. I ran to brace myself against it.

"Ouuuuuwwww!" a man screamed.

Through my peephole, I saw it—a booze-soaked man with his fingers trapped in the door across the narrow hallway, shouldering so hard into it that he pushed right out of one of his sneakers. Inside the room was an equally sloshed woman throwing her weight against the door and the man's trapped fingers.

"Ouuuuuuwwwww! My fingers! My fingers! Ouuuuuuwwwww!"

"Let go, you fucking asshole!"

I hurriedly double-checked the chain on the door to my fleeting little sanctuary—check-check-double-check. Unutterably deranged, it only got worse, with more voices and more screaming.

"Hey! Hey, you! You two! Stop it! Right there, stop! Get away from that door, both-a you!!"

A radio crackled and I could hear a rush of footsteps closing in, something jingling, too. It was the Popo, two of them, bearing down on the damaged man and his ensconced paramour.

"Hold it right there! Right now! The two of you!"

"The police! Thank God, the police! Lookit she did to me!" the drunken man shouted, holding up his bleeding hand. *"Fuck you! Fuck you! I wanna press charges!"*

There wasn't a single wasted movement in the way the police separated the shit-faced couple, one cop on each. I told myself to turn away from it, shaming myself for watching this bit of reality TV; but I waited it out, wanting to see what happened next, watching as a small Indian man arrived and hovered just far enough away.

"Sir, sir, sir!" the clerk pleaded to the howling man. *"There are sleeping guests to consider!"*

"Sleepin' guests? You kiddin' me? Fuck yer sleepy li'l guests. Lookit my fingers!" he cried, holding up his bloody fingers like a withered crow's claw as the police frog-marched him away and pushed the woman back into her room. Scratching my behind, I kept watching even after the hallway emptied, a million miles from sleep. Thinking I should call Mary and tell her all about it. Then thinking I shouldn't.

When Sunday finally came, my ride to Wichita Falls was less eventful simply another unanticipated run to a town I couldn't have located on a map a few days before. Another distant town that held an invisible key to my family's future. It was a short 250-mile drive, west by southwest through Oklahoma and over the Red River uplift where 300 million years ago, during the Pennsylvanian period, a colossal, slow-motion continental collision occurred. To a preoccupied motorist trying to make good time, there were no conspicuous signs of plate tectonics and landmass pileups. Nothing jumped out to suggest chaos and the mélange of crushed continental edges and a onetime ocean that had overlain the area. It was just a dry landscape punctuated by live oaks and prickly pears, cut by fluvial erosion softening the ridgelines sloping down into the Red River.

It was dark by the time I drove into Wichita Falls in North Central Texas. I found Serva out on the edge of town, and satisfied I could find it again in the morning, I checked into a hotel. After that I found a Mexican restaurant in a long, low strip plaza, like you see anywhere in America these days. I sat down and ate and made notes for what would be my unannounced meeting in the morning, when I walked in their door and hoped for the best. Because Serva was also a frack-truck builder, I knew they would talk to me. They would want my business. Calculating that I'd be welcomed took a little of the edge off.

When morning came, I was already sitting in Serva's parking lot waiting for some sign of life to appeal to. At a little before eight, the lot began filling in around me. With nothing left to hold me back, I stepped out of my Pacifica and started for the front-office door, hoping to catch the right person before they got too busy, before Monday morning's stupor wore off and everyone remembered where they left off Friday afternoon. Inside the doors, I found a few people talking about their weekends in a hallway. Standing a little too close to anyone is always unnerving, so that's what I did. When they paused their conversation and politely turned my way, I started in.

"Who's in charge?"

That drew a laugh, as it was meant to. It was silly and nonthreatening, and right away I was escorted down the hallway to the office of the guy in charge. That's where I was left, with a laugh and a pat on the back.

Sitting at his desk and hunched over his first cup of coffee of the day was a genuinely decent middle-aged man, as caught off guard by me as his coworkers were out front. I was announced as a guy "looking to talk to the big man," and there he was, politely wondering who I was and why I was darkening his doorway. So I got right into it.

"I'm having trouble with a blender I'm building, and I was hoping you could help."

The Serva man pushed his coffee aside and stood up and shook my hand, as I expected he might. "Well, you've come to the right place, then."

It didn't matter to him that these kinds of conversations generally started over the phone or at industry events with booths and salespeople in coded colors. His was a business-to-business model, but these were odd times, and there were bound to be oddballs.

After taking him up on his invitation to sit, I began my simple-minded strategy: spill my guts and explain my tortured path. Look for any sign of sympathy, then beg. Having done a piss-poor job of rehearsing, though, I saw that I was losing him. Adjusting, I culled my story down to the essentials, keeping it to all the stolen parts that had gone missing. At that, the kind man nodded in a sympathetic gesture and stood up.

"You should have started here," he said with a small, measured laugh. "Let me show you around," he added, giving me the feeling that he had seen it all.

From shop bay to shop bay, one after another, he showed me blenders and pumps and specialized trucks and equipment skids in various stages of construction. As much as I had been impressed with Tribute down in Granbury, I was awed by Serva. They were big and diverse, and they built everything, even proprietary components under their own design and on behalf of others, like Schlumberger.

In short, they were real, and I felt stupid, over and over again, for not having ferreted them out in the first place. A simple internet search would have found them. Instead, there I was, amongst competence but unable to grasp it, in another dispiriting blow.

Serva was out of reach, because I was joined to Andy by a noose that was choking the life out of me. When I asked the man if he had ever heard of STIM or the Brennans, he drew a blank. He only knew that the pods were born at Serva but had no idea where they went to die.

Our last stop was a small storage room in a dark, forgotten area of the shop. We might have landed there last because my tour guide planned it that way—a last stop at the Serva graveyard, the place where obsolescence came to rest. Whichever it was, his underlying disdain for the room was clear. It meant absolutely nothing to him.

As my eyes adjusted to the piddling, rayless room, they landed on a rounded cast-iron object, strapped to a pallet on steel shelving running along a back wall. The Serva man held his hand out toward it, like a game-show host pointing to third prize. And there, a few steps away, in a hopeless little corner of a building somewhere outside of Wichita Falls, Texas, was the absolute center of my universe. Like walking into the Lost City of Gold, there it was—*The Pod*—the almighty pod, the very heartbeat of the vortex blender, dumped onto a dusty shelf, with no more significance than a tub of mismatched bolts.

I looked to my new best friend and pleaded, "Can I buy it?"

"I can't sell that one. It's Schlumberger's. I gotta keep one on the shelf for 'em."

"Can you make me one—or how about you sell me that one, and you can make them a brand-new one?"

The guy laughed. "Sure, but you'd have to ask Schlumberger first. We just build 'em. It's their design."

"What if the patent's expired? I think the patent's expired."

My friend had another laugh. "That may be, but I'm not about to get sideways with Schlumberger."

"You think they'd care?"

"Absolutely they'd care."

"This pod, really?" I said, pointing at it incredulously. "How could they care?"

The man shrugged. "Because they're Schlumberger."

As I stood there, premeditatedly staring at the volute, a massive bowl-like casting on the pod, the man switched on a light that I hadn't been aware of.

"Dan?"

"Yeah?"

"Why don't you let me build you a blender that'll work?"

Jesus, I thought. *He just stated the obvious, and I've only known him twenty minutes.*

"I can't," I confessed to the Serva man. "I wish I could, but right now I just can't.

"You like those pod blenders, huh?"

"Honestly, I hate everything about them."

"Well, you're not getting an argument from me there," he said, confirming my fears. "I'll tell you what, though, we'd love to sell some of these things," the man said with a dismissive wave toward the pod. "You get Schlumberger's permission, and I'll build you one."

That was a start and was good enough.

"Who do I talk to?"

"I'll get you the guy's number. Guy named Lionel Fah at Schlumberger down in Sugar Land. We need to have an understanding here, though, Dan. You need to tell Lionel I wouldn't sell it to you without his written permission."

"You think he'll let you sell it?"

"I doubt it. But what's the harm in asking? It's Schlumberger," he added a second time.

"All right. Understood. I'll tell him anything you tell me to."

A few minutes later I thanked the man endlessly as he handed me Lionel's name and number on a folded-up piece of paper, a legitimate piece of folded-up paper. "Serva will be here for you," was the last thing I heard on my way out the door.

Chapter 22

H. R. STASNEY & SONS, LTD.

Albany, Texas

I sat dead still, like a cold stone in my Chrysler Pacifica. I wasn't resting or feeling sorry for myself or sobbing over not making a deal. I was thinking that I didn't know what to do next. My three-day-old fantasy of showing up, writing a check, and driving off with my dreams intact had just come to an unequivocal end. Other than that, there was no hierarchy of tasks, no incremental plan forward, no direction.

All that had come from my Serva meeting was another phone number written on a piece of paper. The other piece of paper with a phone number, the one I'd refused from Andy back at his shop, had me thinking otherwise. Maybe I should have taken the phone number he offered, the one I was sworn to secrecy over. It was my direct path to Bill's go-to guy, the black marketeer who traded in pods like dope or explosives or body parts on the dark web. Now it seemed stupidly gullible, me digging in and not calling him, letting ethics get in the way of expedition. Now I had another phone number in its place, this one from a legitimate guy at Serva, a legitimate company, leading to a guy named Lionel at, legitimately, the biggest oil-field services company in the world.

Lost in a fog, I didn't realize I was moving until I exited the parking lot and found myself in traffic. A few minutes later I was back at the Hampton Inn I had stayed at the night before. But I had already checked out. I was there only because it was familiar. Wondering what in the hell was wrong with me, I spun around and drove on in another direction without reason. What in the hell was I doing?

I was thinking, thinking that maybe I should drive to Sugar Land, Texas—Schlumberger's US headquarters—even though better sense told me it wouldn't do me a damn bit of good. It didn't matter that Sugar Land was just outside of Houston, on the southeast side of the state. I could be there by night and walk in the next morning, just like I did at Serva, leading with compliments and a box of donuts. That might work. People like people who bring donuts. In person, I could make a humanitarian appeal, a play for simple human decency because, other than donuts, that's all I'd have. But walking into Serva was entirely different than walking into Schlumberger. Getting inside the world's largest oil and gas services company would require a meeting, which would require a phone call, which would require a confessional, which could shut me down as the cold end of a nuisance call. Fearing Lionel would say no or maybe or anything other than yes was what stopped me from making the call.

But what if? What if he said, "Okay with me. The patent expired; do with it what you want." Or, "Sure, I'll send a release to Serva."

"Shit in one hand and wish in the other, see which one fills up first," is what my dad would have said if he were sitting with me, listening to his kid fantasizing about a bad deal gone good. After surviving a mine blast and a few bullet holes in Korea, he had a unique take on risk. To him, risk wasn't the barrier; it was effort. Risk was just a breakable roadblock.

"Keep pushing," he'd say. "Eventually something will break."

He knew, because he had gone through his own start-up. He, too, had a story about a guy with a gun, a bully just like mine. His was an ironworker looking for a kickback years before, when me and my six brothers and sisters were just little kids. He knew...

I pulled the paper out of my pocket and dialed the number. This would tie my fate to Serva and Schlumberger. It would be me spilling the beans on Bill, Andy, and myself. The genie would be let out of the bottle. There would be no going back. If Schlumberger said no, patent-protected or not, I'd be starting over from scratch—another way of saying every advance I'd given to Andy was gone.

I dialed the number.

But what if he said no? Or what if he said maybe. Maybe could be worse than no. A mid-level guy at a big company wasn't going to stick his neck out. He'd need to get someone senior involved. Schlumberger was a French company. Would a decision have to come out of France? France is a long way away. They speak a different language there. How long would that take when there was nothing in it for them?

I hung up.

I wasn't ready—not for the truth, anyway.

I started driving east, only because that's where familiarity was pulling me—toward home. By the time I cleared the shopping centers that act as demarcations around most towns, I knew where I was going. Not to Schlumberger; that was a phone call I needed to think about. I decided to do what I should have done six months before: I'd do some due diligence. I'd go to Albany, Texas, barely two hours away, and take Andy up on an offer he had made a while back, right around the time when our conversations had turned into confessions.

Before Andy's masterstroke of forming STIM SOLUTIONS, Bill had built a vortex blender for another customer through his wholly owned Sooner Fleet Service. Neither of them ever mentioned it to me until I found a few promotional pieces about it on the internet. When I brought it up, Andy instantly ducked it as a Bill project. That was before him and STIM, he stated defensively. But if I really thought it was necessary, he'd be happy to make an introduction…if I really thought it was necessary.

"There were some problems there, but it's all good now. I mean, from what I heard about it from Bill," Andy added, placing plenty of light between himself and Bill's stand-alone build.

My mood lightened along the way, now that I had some direction and purpose. I was heading in the direction I should have started, not ended. Heading east by southeast, I figured I'd just show up and see what happened, my new go-to move.

Two hours later, I was driving down the main drag of Albany, Texas, getting the feeling of being lost in time. It was as though I had driven into an old-world western cow town. When I found H. R. Stasney & Sons, Ltd., I was all the more certain that I had gone back in time. It was a single-level, adobe-style building with a posted porch roof. When I stepped inside, it was like stepping into an oil-field museum. Sample jars of drill cuttings lined the walls, and old lease and topographic maps were laid out on a timeworn desk. You couldn't have made the place more authentic. Apparent, too, was a sense of quiet stability, a steadfast, old-money look in this little oil company that looked to be printing money.

I saw a woman at a desk and wandered over.

"Hiya, is Lance around?"

"I could check. Who's askin'?"

"Nobody, really. My name's Dan Doyle. I don't know Lance, but I got his name from Andy Brennan, over at STIM SOLUTIONS, in Bristow. I thought I should stop in and say hi."

"Say hi about what?" she smiled.

"Vortex blenders, ma'am."

She asked me to wait while she checked to see if Lance was in. When she returned, she waved me toward his office.

"He's all yours. Keep him as long as you want."

We shared a smile, and I stepped into the threshold of Lance's office and met a gregarious, honest, well-intentioned man. After a few comments about what a rustic, old-timey town he lived in, and a little about where I came from, I got into a carefully worded explanation as to why I had chosen to interrupt his day. Not only did he have a sympathetic interest—as a fellow member of the vortex-blender club—but, as it turned out, he had a few Brennan stories of his own. Just like me, he had his own share of problems, misrepresentations, and delays. But by the end, we shared a laugh over the emerging fact that I was the runaway winner in the Brennan family customer service department.

"Don't worry, Dan, you're not the son of a bitch in your story. Sounds like Bill and Andy got that covered pretty well."

That kept the laughs going in a shared collegiality. Funnier even for Lance was that he had come out of the Brennan brothers' hazing in far better shape than me. At least he had his vortex blender.

"You want to have a look at it?" Lance suggested as he stood, waving at his door with a bit of showmanship. "It's right outside."

"It's here?" I asked, jumping up.

"Yeah. Come on, I'll show it to you. The guys are trying to get it running. But that's an everyday event around here."

I followed him out a back door and into a wall of blinding sunlight typical of a cold North Texas day. Unseen from the road, but now spreading out in front of me, was a long and low vista of dirt and rocks, prickly pear bushes and mesquites, punctuated in the foreground by a group of men bitching and moaning about the "cheap-ass piece-a junk" bedeviling them. What they were referring to was the ugliest piece of oil-field equipment I had ever seen. It was a blender, *the vortex blender*, surrounded by three men trying to roll out for a frack job. They couldn't get the pod impellor to turn and had a fix in mind, but I could hear one of them talking about calling Bill anyway.

Transfixed, I couldn't stop staring at the blender's unremarkable, unfinished, and patched-together look. It was dingy brown, with a sullen, brokeback posture. Every bit of it looked like someone's first attempt, like an endoskeleton missing its skin. Piping, manifolds, and a bird's nest of hydraulic lines ran like tendrils out of the dark underbelly rearward toward the pod, like snakes slithering out from Medusa's head. What I was seeing was an abomination of forethought and an absolute lack of grace or any appreciation—at all—for aesthetics.

Stepping in closer, wanting to see for myself what the problem was, I kept hearing the crew's favorite refrain.

"—cheap-ass piece-a junk—"

One of the three men circling the blender acted like a supervisor, mostly because he was the one telling the other guys what to do. He was also the one who looked to be the most agitated.

"You mind if I talk to them?" I asked Lance.

"Not at all."

Lance led me over to the supervisor and introduced us.

"Dan has a few questions about your blender there."

"*My* blender?" The man nearly spit.

Lance laughed and gave me a "go ahead" nod.

"Not working, huh?" I asked. Stupidly.

"Some-a the times it works, and some-a the times it don't.... Mostly don't."

"What's wrong?"

"Ya mean what's *not*."

The supervisor didn't suffer fools, particularly not this one, not with my ridiculous questions, but he was forced to slow down and answer them only because his boss had said so.

"I'll let you get back to work. But let me just ask, when you get it running, how's it run? You like it, with the pod and all?"

"It's okay. It pushes sand and water pretty good, so it's okay."

"You think a vortex blender is better than a conventional?"

The supervisor glanced at Lance. "I don't know. Maybe. Lot of problems... But you ask me, probably not."

"Why'd you build one, then?"

"Probably 'cause it was cheap," the supervisor said, staring at Lance with a smirk.

Lance grinned and shrugged. "We better let these guys get back to work," he said, letting the supervisor return to the blender.

The man nodded to me, then shouted to his crew, "You get ahold-a Bill yet?"

One of his crew already had his phone to his ear and waved that he had. Apparently, it was that easy to get ahold of Bill—not a matter of raising the dead, as it was for me. Oddly, that stung, like I'd been cheated on. Funny, given that I was doing everything I could to get away from him.

Chapter 23
SCHLUMBERGER

Sugar Land, Texas

I settled into my Pacifica and for the second time that day didn't know what to do next. The vaunted vortex blender, our go-to signature piece of equipment—the rising tide that would float us above all others—was a bona fide piece of cheap-ass junk. Parts and permissions aside, no one up in my basin was going to use a new frack company with sketchy equipment. Even if we rounded up all the permissions we needed, even if Andy actually got it built, we still wouldn't stand a snowball's chance in hell with a vortex blender. Before, my worry was getting a vortex blender built. Now, it would be owning one.

Over a cup of coffee and a late breakfast at a little Mexican joint down the street from Stasney, I watched the clock count down to when I would call Schlumberger. I still had to call Andy, too, but I would do that later, after I closed the pod matter one way or another with Schlumberger.

When the server poured me another cup of coffee, I never noticed until I lifted the cup and burned my tongue. I sipped it anyway, barely noticing it, thinking over the dirt-poor regard the Stasney crew had for their blender as I slipped back into an uneasy and edgy state.

Would the blender work if Andy built it?

Could we make it work back up in Pennsylvania?

Should I fess up to Schlumberger?

Would this risk more money?

Would Schlumberger care?

Would they give me a pass?

Would they sue?

Should I leverage Schlumberger to scare Bill?

Would that make Bill release the pod?

Would he give my pod money back?

Would Andy?

What would my partners in Pennsylvania say?

Should I tell them no one cared what kind of blender we had?

That they only cared if it worked?

Should I pull the plug?

Take the losses?

Dilute?

Sell out?

Run?

Hide?

Where?

Half an hour later, I was parked at an abandoned gas station, a stuccoed relic covered in ivy and collapsing in on itself. I sat still in my Pacifica, admiring the building's Mission Revival beauty, wondering why it hadn't been restored and repurposed, wondering about anything other than Schlumberger.

Just do it, I resignedly told myself. A few difficult minutes later, I dialed the number on the piece of paper, then stiffened up and readied myself. Two rings in and I had Lionel Fah on the line. After that, it went quickly, but not well.

I unloaded as fast and as clear as I could—time was of the essence—telling him what a great company he worked for, best service company in the world, how much I loved the vortex blender, wanted to build one, me a nobody from up in Pennsylvania, would never cross paths with Schlumberger trucks, anywhere, ever.

"You're a frack company?" Fah asked.

I drew another breath. Barely a minute in, and he had just driven a stake into the heart of the matter.

"More like I'm starting one."

"Uh-huh."

"Just one pump and a blender. Tiny, really. Little Pennsylvania wells, is all. Some of them just for myself."

"Dan, is it?"

"Yes, sir."

"It sounds to me like you're a competitor."

"Me, sir? No…hardly…I'm just…I guess you could say…but I'm doing this in an area Schlumberger's not even working."

I was losing him. He was going to cut me off. I needed to stop that. I would have to tell him the truth, every ugly bit of it. Surely that would generate some pity. I took in a gulp of air and told Lionel Fah my story. I told him of my partners in Pennsylvania and their hardships, of my past and my current and all of my frack company missteps, of Bill's miserable trip up to the Pennsylvania frack job, of the pods lying in the weeds behind his place, of his deal with Schlumberger, the one where we were supposed to scrap the pods. I told him about everything outside of Lance's pod blender, omitting it so as not to victimize another victim.

It was a rambling, pathetic admission, punctuated only by the man's interest in Bill and what the hell he was doing with Schlumberger pods. I played up my promise to stay out of his way, that I just needed to get this one done, after that there would never be another pod blender for me. I had already sunk a fortune into it—you can understand that, sir—but by the end of my imploration, nothing stuck. My counterpart, Lionel, had tired of my diatribe. Politely, but firmly, he dropped his foot right on me.

"It sounds like you've had a tough time, but there's nothing I can do here. We don't support our competitors. I cannot agree to your use of our patent."

I was devastated. But after a pause—wobbly but trying to right myself—I took my last shot. A Hail Mary.

"But the patent has expired, right?"

"I don't know. Maybe. What did you say the name of your company was?"

That was the end. That put a nail in it. I was about to put myself and my little start-up on Schlumberger's radar. He could have just said, "What difference would that make? We're Schlumberger. We'll sue you into oblivion," and it would have been the same. I had nothing left to stand on. Nothing. There was no counterargument left.

I heard something along the lines of "Best of luck and sorry again you had to go through this, Mr. Doyle—Daniel Doyle from Reliance it is, right?" and that was it. The phone call was over, and for the third time that day, I was stupefied. I didn't have a clue what to do or where to go next.

A dog could have bitten me, I could have been struck by lightning, and I wouldn't have known.

Driving, just driving—something about losing myself behind a steering wheel, as stupidly dangerous as that sounds—made me pull out of the lot and onto Albany's quiet streets. Five minutes later I was back at the abandoned gas station, weirdly back to another familiar spot. I found myself dialing Andy's number, because it was the only thing I knew to do in the moment, and only because I had promised.

This time Andy actually answered, haltingly wanting to know how it went. I told him about Lance and where we stood with Serva and then all about my call with Schlumberger.

"What did you tell them? You didn't mention my name?"

"I told them the truth."

"You told them the truth, what truth?"

"The *truth* truth."

"About who?"

"About everything, Andy. Everyone!"

I could hear Andy's sigh right through the phone.

"Dan, you don't understand. You didn't need to do that. I actually have a really exciting development. I was saving this, but now's as good a time as any. We're getting our pod, Dan. Bill and I just had a great call, and he's absolutely one hundred percent. We have our pod. We have it! I was just going to call you, but Bill's going to deliver it this week. No kidding, he swore to it. I made him swear over the Bible, like an imaginary one, but he swore over it, right over the phone. He's going to deliver the pod!"

"Andy, we got to talk about that check—"

"You going out to Serva, he was pretty angry about that. But that sure got to him. Then Schlumberger, and Lance, that kinda—Bill kinda swore about all that, nothing real bad, just Bill, you know. But I think he's going to come through. I mean, I know he is. Tomorrow he's going to deliver it. Wednesday at the latest. My hand to God, Dan. Honestly, we're almost through this."

"Andy, we got to talk about that check. I need that check back."

"What do you mean, 'need the check back'?"

"The check I gave you. The ten-thousand-dollar check."

Radio silence.

"Did you cash the check? You didn't cash the check, right?" I asked.

"Well, I told you I was short on payroll. I had bills to pay. You remember me telling you I already mailed checks."

"Did you cash the check?"

"Yes. I cashed the check. I had to. I told you."

"You kidding me, Andy? You gave me your word. You gotta be. Tell me you're kidding me; you didn't really cash the check."

"It was owed to me. You know it was due. Plus, Bill's getting the—"

"You're full of it, you know that? You're selling stolen parts and lying to me. I'm a customer, for God's sake! *And I gotta drive to Texas to find all this out on my own! After five months of your bullshit!*"

I was panting. Outraged. Ready to punch out the car window and choke him to death.

When Andy finally spoke up, his delivery was octaves lower than mine, playing the calm, reasonable guy in the conversation.

"I mean, we have a deal, after all. I have to keep my guys going, you know that. I stop paying them, I'll never get them back."

My first thought was to call my bank and have them place a stop order on the check. But if I did, I'd never get my chassis out of STIM Manufacturing, not without a few high-priced lawyers and a sympathetic judge. In the meantime, Andy would lock the place up and go dark…again. That meant I had to stay in so I could get out. I had to cool down. I needed to take a few breaths and change my tune and put the $10,000 behind me.

"We're going to be okay," Andy continued. "Momentum is on our side. I'm as sure of getting this truck built as I'm sure the sun will rise tomorrow. My word is my bond, Dan. Bill's on our side now. You can count on it."

"Well, if you think so, Andy," I acquiesced. "Whatever you think."

I was done. It was over. As much as I wanted to puke it all up, I'd have to let him keep the $10,000 and then find a way to get my truck out.

Andy asked if I was coming back or what my plans were. I surprised myself by telling him I had to head on down to Granbury and check on the pump progress. That one had to have come from my subconscious, because my cerebral cortex, where most high-order brain functions occur, was not yet aware of it. Somewhere deep down, I knew that Douglas had found a way to get me out of my pump predicament, and maybe he'd do the same with the blender.

"Well, have a good trip. Let me know if you're going to need help on that pump, if they're screwing it up, you know? I'd really love to get that pump back, Dan. That would really help all of us along."

"Yeah, sure, Andy. I'll let you know."

I shifted into drive and turned east for Granbury. I knew Douglas would want to see me, especially about the blender. And if he were to price out a blender on the cheap, something scaled down and just good enough, I might still make it to the starting line.

Chapter 24

TRIBUTE OILFIELD SOLUTIONS

Granbury, Texas

"I don't know when I'll be home. Maybe tomorrow, maybe day after, maybe longer if I have to go back up to Bristow," I told Mary when I called to check in on her and Maria and Elena.

"It's okay. We're all good here. My mom and dad are loving it. Colly's helping out. It's all good," Mary said from her parents' house, where she was happily waiting it out with her sister, our girls, and little dog, Elroy.

"I'm really sorry."

"You kidding me? This is great. Stay as long as you want."

"As in, don't come home?"

"Just kidding. Hurry back, but finish it once and for all down there. Just get it done. Then we'll all see you at home."

Home was our house, a good sign, Mary turning my failure into a win.

Next, I called Douglas and told him I'd like to come down and see him.

"When you thinkin'?"

"Few hours. You around?"

"Few hours? Hey, hell yeah. Come on down!"

"Great, I'll see you in a little bit, then."

"That be good. Zahir's here, too. Probably out sleeping in that RV of his."

After we hung up, I was beginning to feel that I had made the right decision. This trip had all the uncertainty of the last trip down, but this time I was more settled, more accustomed to it. My speedometer never touched ninety. This time, I was even looking forward to it.

By late afternoon, I was at Douglas's door. When I walked in, it was like I was walking in on family. Everyone—Douglas, Clayton, Lisa, and the usually dour Zahir—met me with handshakes and coffee and a welcome-home-son kind of feel. They had a lot to show me and wanted to get on with it.

"Let's have a look, why don't we? I think you're going to be real happy with the progress we've made here, Dan," Douglas said as we headed for the door to his shop. This time we skipped the view from the raised platform and headed right down the steps for my truck. Along the way, we passed the same workers as before, 100 percent of them, not like the 33.33 percent at Andy's place. All of them said hello, happy to see me, each wanting to see my reaction to the truck.

And then, there it was. I was stupefied as I came alongside it. Absolutely colossal in size, it was forty feet long and over thirteen feet tall to the top of the exhaust stacks that two men on scaffolding were installing over the engine skid. The major components, the engine, transmission, and pump, were sitting on the chassis, with minor components beginning to fill in the space between.

When Douglas leaned in and asked in a low voice, "Whatdya think?" I was swooning. The last I'd seen the pump truck, bare and just a backbone, was with Woodstock behind the wheel up in Oklahoma. He was laying on the air horn and pumping his fist out the window as he pulled away onto I-44, his hair blowing back from under an Adidas bandana, a gallows grin lighting up his face.

Now, bumpers were being welded-up off to the side. A driveshaft between the deck transmission and rear-end triplex pump was being fitted. It was all legitimate, and I was enthralled. No dust had settled on it; the truck wasn't parked out in the weeds. It was coming together. After nearly five months of trying to get something built, and seven months since hatching my frack business embryo—after all the craziness, from oil prices crashing to my build dollars disappearing—it was a momentous feeling of accomplishment.

"It looks like a frack truck," was all I added. That must have been good enough because Douglas and Clayton were right away rolling out a set of CAD drawings on a plasma table next to the truck, showing me all the cuts and welds and care they had taken to balance the truck and its four axles and make it road- and bridge-legal in Pennsylvania.

"We're gonna be done with that pump in fairly short order, you know. It's gonna need some company," Douglas leveled. "How's it going for you up in Bristow?"

Zahir and Clayton turned to me and waited. They had to have known, I thought. Everyone talks in the oil business. It's like an old-fashioned sewing circle. Everybody knows everybody else's business.

When Douglas suggested we grab a cup of coffee upstairs and see where things stood, I knew it would be about the blender and not the pump. The pump was right in front of us. Why leave it behind just so that we could talk about it upstairs?

"Dan, did Bill deliver the pod?" Zahir asked the second we sat down around the conference table.

"I was told tomorrow. Day after at the latest," I mumbled, realizing my suspicions were correct. They all knew. I'd have no bargaining power.

"I talked to Andy this morning. He didn't mention to me Bill was dropping the pod off."

"Any day now, is what I heard," I said.

"I've been hearing that, too, for two months now!" Zahir snickered. "You can't count on Andy, Dan. You know this. Andy's—you know how Andy is."

I shrugged.

Douglas smiled ruefully at me. "You'll get it. You're gonna be okay there. If your Andy up there said he was gonna get it done, he's gonna get it done, right?"

"Andy couldn't get out of the right side of the bed if his own wife pushed him out of it. He is a certifiable idiot!" Zahir spit through his Egyptian-Arabic accent.

Douglas and Clayton and I laughed. Zahir didn't. He was having none of it, because—as I came to learn—he was the guy in the room who hadn't been paid. He'd already built Andy a computer but was holding it on a prepay. One way or another, he wanted his money, and right then I was his last train out of the station.

"Zahir, I don't think you heard. Dan said Andy's gonna build that truck." Douglas turned to me. "Didn't you?"

"You can build Dan a blender," Zahir blurted out to Douglas. "Build Dan his blender, Douglas. Please!"

"Zahir," I calmly protested. "I know Douglas can build me a blender. But listen, I still have a deal with Andy. I've got all this money invested. I'd be losing a fortune if I pulled the blender away from Andy. I don't have the money to start over."

"You're going to lose it all, you don't stop it now," Zahir insisted. Undeterred, he turned to Douglas. "These are low-rate jobs Dan is doing," he said. Then to me, "What, twenty barrels a minute, no more?"

"About that. Twenty's at the higher end."

"Twenty barrels a minute is all. You don't need two or three screws. Just one. Small hopper, one screw, that's all. Douglas, think of all the hydraulics you could cut out. If Dan could get some of the parts from Andy—the manifolds he built, hoses, flanges, whatever—some of what he has already paid for. Think how easy it would be. You could build Dan that blender. It would be in his price range."

Now Zahir knew my price range, as well. I could have stopped and asked him what color socks I was wearing—certain that he knew that, too—but things had turned my way, so I didn't say a damn thing.

Douglas tried on a taciturn posture against Zahir's invasive practicality, acting as though he was mulling it over for the first time. Sales tactics, pressure tactics, good cop, bad cop, it was all just a sham. The oil rout was worsening. Orders were being cancelled. A few minutes before, I caught a glance of Douglas's backyard. A month back, there were trucks and trailers waiting their turn. Now, it was mostly a vacant, dusty, fenced-in lot.

"Never built a single-screw," Douglas said when he finally spoke up.

"We could work on that, Douglas. We could come up with a price," Zahir said. Then he turned to me. "Dan, you signed a deal with Andy that Andy can't keep. He's not getting that pod, and even if he did, his blender will never work. It will be a disaster for you. You know that."

"I don't know that, not for sure," I lied.

"Been a rough ride for you with those fellows. That's for sure," Douglas added.

"I could work on it?" Clayton said, inserting himself.

"You guys want to come up with a price, fine, great, but I don't have the money," I said.

"We shall see, Dan," Zahir said, as though he was an authority on my money.

"Listen, let us think about this. How long you gonna be around?" Douglas asked.

"I was heading back up to Bristow. But you guys want to work on something, I can stick around some. How long you need?"

"Can I have till tomorrow?"

"Tomorrow?"

"I know that's an imposition. But it be a lot easier in person, we have any questions."

"Sure. Okay. That's fine," I said. "I have a few people in Dallas I've been meaning to stop in on. I'll stick around. Noon or so give you enough time?"

"That be fine, Dan. I appreciate that."

That was it. The meeting was over. Douglas walked me to the door and told me he'd be looking forward to seeing me tomorrow, and I mentioned the same. Zahir and Clayton never looked up, already immersed in scratching something out on a blank sheet of paper.

I never thought about it until I settled into my Pacifica, but what was I going to tell the Kanes? I never asked them for their blessing to dump their dream, the whole vortex-blender idea, in favor of something conventional, something that would get built and would work. They weren't there, though, and I was. So, I decided I'd tell them instead of asking them.

That whole disease-to-please thing; I was done with that, too.

Chapter 25

BARNETT SHALE

Fort Worth, Texas

One hundred million years ago, back in the Cretaceous Period, a warm-water inland sea covered the bone-dry roads I was driving along after leaving Douglas's place. Sediment from the ongoing erosion of the nearby Ouachita Mountains was carried by water and wind to the inland sea, where it settled better than a mile below me, overlain by three hundred million years of additional deposition filling the stratigraphic column right up to the surface and the Dallas–Fort Worth metroplex.

This was the heart of the layered and organically rich Barnett Shale, where the shale boom got its start, not by accident or folly, or by big-government grease or mandates, but in a typically American way—by exhaustively hard work, risk, and ingenuity. It was where George Mitchell, a Greek immigrant's son and a lifelong Democrat, spent tens of millions of dollars of his and his company's money, and years of his life, to be the first to figure out how to extract gas from low-porosity, low-permeability shale in horizontal wells. When he finally succeeded, he changed the world. Wars and alignments with dictators and despots would no longer be necessary. World order wouldn't have to revolve around energy needs. The expatriation of billions of dollars a year—keeping it out of our own labor's reach—could finally stop. All this from an immigrant's son just out to prove a hunch.

That should have earned the now-deceased Mitchell a Nobel Peace Prize. Like most other things, though, the Prize is reserved for those who fit in an ideologically approved box. But by all rights, a guy who ushered in affordable energy for the middle class and the poor deserves something more than a footnote in the development of shale extraction. The fact, too, that a first-generation American did it on his own dime makes the story even richer.

I was driving just to be driving, killing time, and spending the day looking for drill sites and frack jobs in the Barnett Shale, like a sportsman spotting for deer. There was no reason to go to Dallas. I fibbed to Douglas about that. I didn't know a soul there. Instead, I was winding my way around country roads and past weathered wooden posts holding up long-running, rusted strings of barbwire. When I came upon a Chesapeake Energy drill site, I stopped and stared. Just off the road was a security hut with an older woman in a uniform staring back at me. Behind her, and towering up like a rocket launcher, was a late-model, top-drive drilling rig. Surrounding it were concrete sound-attenuating panels, office and storage trailers, cement silos, pipe boats, and a few drop-deck trailers. Most noticeable though, stuck right beside the dusty caliche entrance, was a sign put up by what I could only imagine was a ticked-off landowner.

Chesapeake is a bunch of liars and thieves,
not the hard-working men and women doing the real work,
just the no-good thieving liars in Oklahoma City (Chesapeake's HQ).

Ha! On and off, I laughed about that for the rest of the day. A land rush was on, and Chesapeake was notoriously aggressive about picking up leases. Someone obviously got elbowed in the scrum, where old-lease bonus rates to landowners may have been less than $100 per acre. A few years later, once the Barnett rush was on, a neighbor's unleased land could easily capture $20,000 an acre or more. The salve, though, was that early to lease or late, both landowners would earn a minimum 12.5 percent royalty override (much higher now), which meant they were carried for an eighth of a well. So, if an $8 million well paid out in a few years, the landowner kept a million, free of costs other than taxes. If a driller didn't get to the well in five years, another bonus payment came due. It was a good place to be for a landowner, and it was purely American. In most countries, the minerals belong to the state.

After taking a long walk down a county road, I got back in my Pacifica and turned toward Fort Worth. I was looking for the Stockyards, a historic part of town, to spend the night. I was certain I'd found it when I passed a longhorn steer tied off to the front of a place called the Stockyards Hotel. That was enough to catch me, so I parked and gave the steer plenty of room as I walked into a lobby stuffed full of leather-covered furniture, frontier antiques, Old West oil paintings, and dusty head mounts.

As I checked in, the clerk told me of the hotel's roster of famous guests, including Bonnie and Clyde, who, rumor had it, were spying on a bank across the street. Whatever it was, it was time to call Andy. Once I was in my room, I did, but after a number of rings it went to voicemail. Hoping it wasn't the start of another pattern, I figured I'd wait an hour and try again.

I stepped out for a look around and stopped in a small shop that made custom cowboy boots. For $2,000, the proprietor offered to make me a pair with the Pittsburgh Steelers logo emblazoned on the toes. I confessed that I didn't have the money, and he admitted he didn't either, until recently, anyway, when he leased the minerals under his church and some land of his own for $22,000 an acre to a Barnett gas driller. That was tenfold his entire land cost just a few years back, when shale was just the crumbling rock showing up in road cuts. Boots didn't matter so much to the bootmaker anymore. I got the feeling they were just his hobby.

Down the street, I caught a sign on the facade of a saloon claiming it was the world's biggest honky-tonk. That made it a must-see, so I poked my head inside. It was definitely big, but I didn't bother hanging around, not with anything inside to make my situation any better.

On my walk back to the hotel, I called Andy again.

He didn't answer then, either.

Chapter 26

THE STOCKYARDS

Fort Worth, Texas

Tuesday morning came, and I grabbed a cup of free coffee in the hotel lobby and sank into a big red-leather couch and called Andy again. It rang then stopped short and went to voicemail. He was blocking me, pissing me off all the more. I immediately dialed him back and heard his voicemail after only a single ring.

In a few hours, Douglas would be presenting me with a bid that he and Zahir and Clayton had likely worked on deep into the night. I needed to be able to give them a yes or a no. But I had partners, and it was only right to tell the Kanes I was about to kill their whole vortex-blender fantasy. Surely they had to have seen this coming. "How hard does this have to be?" was my ongoing mantra with them. But still, it was their dream to have that blender and mine to keep us together. This was before three-way cellular calling, so I called Wallace first and figured I'd call Eli right after, because it was Wallace who would have to come around the most. Eli just wanted whatever worked, since he'd be the one working on it. Not Wallace. Wallace didn't turn wrenches much. He was the one who'd be out talking to operators, and he wanted to make a statement, something about technical superiority. Unfortunately, he had already started talking up the vortex blender, and that's why talking him out of it was going to be a challenge.

"I'm in Fort Worth. In this old western hotel," I said when Wallace answered his phone. "They've got a steer tied up out front."

"A steer?"

"Yeah. A steer. With the big horns. Like a longhorn steer."

"Makes sense. Steers and queers, that's Texas."

"Yeah. Nice place, though. Real western. You'd like it."

Wallace grunted something indecipherable. I let it go. I wanted to keep things moving along.

"Where you say you are, down in Fort Worth?"

"Yeah."

"You shoulda told me."

"Yeah. Sorry. It was an impulse thing. Not that you don't already know, but we've been having trouble with Andy. More of it, I mean."

"More of his shit? That's a big surprise."

"Yeah. Listen, Wallace, I been thinking. This vortex blender—Andy's not answering my calls again. It's not…I don't know…it's just like before, when he went dark."

"He not answering his phone again?"

"Yeah. It's back to that. Remember I told you about Bill building a vortex blender for a guy in Texas?"

"Yeah. I remember about it."

"I went and saw it yesterday. It was in Albany, Texas, a few hours from here."

"Hold it. You saw one? A vortex blender?"

"Bill built it a year or two ago for him. And guess what?"

"What?"

"It doesn't work."

"It doesn't work?"

"Yeah. I mean no. They couldn't get it to run when I was there. Something with the hydraulics not turning the pod pump. Guy had to get Bill on the phone. Told me they got Bill's number memorized, they call it so much."

"What do you mean, 'it doesn't work'?" Wallace defensively demanded.

"I don't know. It doesn't work. Always something, they told me."

"Well fuck me! They used to work when Dowell had 'em."

"Yeah, maybe when Dowell had them." I didn't add that Serva wasn't building them for Schlumberger anymore, and there was a good reason for it.

Wallace seemed to be mulling that over. "So, what are you saying?" he finally asked.

"I'm saying we're gonna have a pretty hard time with that blender, even if Andy ever gets it built. The guys in Albany, when I was watching them work on it, the whole time they're calling it a cheap-ass piece-a junk."

"Jesus Christ."

"Yeah."

"It really doesn't work?"

"No. Never really has."

"And now Andy's not calling you back again?"

"Nope."

Wallace went silent for a moment. "None-a this makes any goddamn sense."

"Well, here's the other part. It kinda does make some sense. I started poking around and I talked to a guy at Schlumberger, this guy named Lionel."

"Lionel?"

"Yeah, Lionel. And here's the truth—the truth is we can't build that blender."

"What do you mean we can't build it? We're building it."

"Yeah. Maybe not, though. Remember the old Dowell trucks out in the back of Bill's shop? Out lying in the weeds?"

Wallace grunted that he did.

"That's where Bill got the parts. He was supposed to cut them up, but he didn't. He cut our pod off the back of one of those Dowell trucks. Least that's what I think. He didn't design it. He didn't do shit but maybe sell it to Andy, and then stiffed him on delivering it. Or maybe Andy's in on it, too, and they're both stiffing us. I don't know. But he didn't design it."

"He didn't design that pod?"

"No. Schlumberger did. Serva built it, but off-a Schlumberger's design. And Serva's not selling us one, not even parts, without Schlumberger's blessing. And no way Schlum—"

"How the fuck did Schlumberger find out?"

"I told them."

"You did?"

"Yeah. I did. I don't want to get sued, Wallace. Not by Schlumberger, anyway. We ever even get the blender built, we'll end up giving it right back to them. You understand what I'm saying, right?"

"That fuckin' cocksucker."

"We can't give Andy any more money. It's a black hole in Bristow, Wallace. And it's not going to work, even if he does build it. And no one else builds them."

"And they knew this? Bill and Andy knew this?"

"Well, yeah."

"You serious? Those fuckin'…those fuckin' pissant assholes. All along they did this! *They knew! Andy!*"

Wallace screamed it so loud that I had to hold the phone away from my ear, broadcasting him throughout the hotel lobby.

"I know," I said quietly, keeping it down.

"What about all the money you gave that asshole son of a bitch? What about all-a that?"

"I'll try to get it back, but the truth is he's not going to give it back. We been had, is the truth. Maybe we'll sue him, but that wouldn't do anything but get us into a hole with a bunch of lawyers. He probably doesn't have anything, anyway. Probably be blood out of a stone."

"That lowlife piece-a-shit asshole—"

"Yeah. I know, know," I interrupted. "Here's the deal, though. Douglas and Zahir are quoting us a conventional blender. I saw them yesterday. I saw a lotta people yesterday. I'm heading back over there in a few hours to see what they're thinking."

"A conventional blender. You mean a screw blender?"

"Yeah. Just a screw, like everyone else uses. They give us a good price, I think we gotta take it. We do a good job with it—all we gotta do is outperform the other guys. Or be cheaper. That's all anyone's gonna want. But this whole vortex-blender thing—"

"Jesus Christ—"

"Andy's not gonna build it, Wallace. He can't. Even if he could… If the price is right, let's have Douglas build this. He dropped his price on the pump. Maybe he'll come in cheap on this, too. Plus, Andy's got some parts lying around. A few hydraulic pumps, manifolds, some valves. You saw them. Douglas says if he can use them, it'll save us some money." I stopped because I thought Wallace was about to protest, but when he didn't, I kept on. "It's also the same controls as the pump. Both will have Quantum controls on them. It would be a single-screw blender. Little over twenty barrels a minute, but that'll work. It'll be simple, and it'll work for what we're doing. That pod blender probably worked when Dowell built them, but not with these guys."

Wallace was silent for a few moments. "I wish I woulda never seen their ad."

"Yeah, that's all right. No one's to blame. But we gotta move on, Wallace. We might get a good deal. These fab guys are really getting hit with the downturn."

"That no-good piece-a shit," he added, returning to our earlier Andy theme.

"Yeah, no kidding, huh?"

"Listen, though, I been thinkin'…"

"Uh-huh," I replied, wearily.

"I been talking to people, an' we better start thinkin' about gettin' a van, too. We can't be runnin' jobs without a van. These kinda people need a place to sit."

"What do you mean, a 'van'? I thought we were skipping that."

"Yeah, I know, but I don't see how we can't have a van. Everyone I'm talking to wants a place to sit. They're not gonna take us serious, they don't have a place to sit."

"We all thought we could frack right off the blender controls."

"Yeah, but the customer can't see the job off-a the blender. We got nothin' to record it off-a the blender. Everyone I been talkin' to—they all gotta have all-a that digital crap with all the graphs now. And they gotta have a place to sit. I never needed it before, but now everyone is used to all-a that crap."

"I know. But, Wallace, that's like another fifty thousand dollars, just for the van part. Minimum. We don't have the money."

"Think-a all the money they're laying out for a frack job. No one's gonna take us serious."

"That's like software, plus the van. I thought we were going to wait. We get some jobs in, we can buy one, like we agreed.

"Won't be any jobs without a van."

I set my coffee down and cupped my head in my hands, every bit as stupefied as I was after a typical conversation with Andy.

We were going to be the economically minded service company that let operators watch a job from the field or alongside us on the blender. They'd watch the analog gauges and nod to us over the noise that everything was all right. That was what we talked about over and over again. Now, with just a few words, we needed another $50,000 for a van, and God knows what for an unbudgeted frack operator to sit with customers, and then the cost of the software needed to process streaming data into neat graphs and charts. Adding it all up, hard costs and soft, it was all red.

"Okay, Wallace. Why don't, for now—let's just focus on the blender."

I politely hung up instead of asking Wallace if he was a sadist. But I had just gotten his consent to build a conventional blender, and that was enough of a win. We were moving on. No longer was I locked into working with the one guy in America still building vortex blenders out of stolen parts.

It would take a good price out of Douglas, though. If I didn't get it, I'd stay in Texas and drive around until I found someone else. As to the van, who knew? But my partnership with Wallace was still intact, and I had hope. That was good enough.

It was time to head back to Douglas's. That's when I got the email. From Andy. There, amongst the junk.

> Dan: This is for you [sic] knowledge only. The patent has expired, but if you take this any further, you will be opening a big can of worms. It would kill STIM, Serva, Sooner Fleet and Reliance. I think that Schlumberger has the power to do this.

I smiled. Andy was right; it would kill Reliance. But screw him. I made a beeline for Douglas's Tribute Oilfield Solutions.

I couldn't get there fast enough.

Chapter 27

TRIBUTE OILFIELD SOLUTIONS

Granbury, Texas

"Howdy, Dan. I'm so sorry I missed you yesterday," said Lisa, Douglas's AA, as I walked in the door. "Douglas gave me the afternoon off yesterday, so I'm sorry I didn't get to say goodbye. I had to take care of some personal matters, but I'm so glad to see you today."

Lisa was holding the open door for me, smiling in her authentically kind manner.

"You too, Lisa. Good to see you."

"I saw you coming and told Douglas and Clayton and Zahir. They promised me they'd be right out." She lowered her voice conspiratorially and added, "They been working in there forever." She threw a thumb toward Douglas's closed office door as she steered me to the conference room.

"I figured you-all'd want a fresh pot a coffee, so I made us one. I'll be right back."

Lisa shot off down the hallway and was back with two cups of coffee before I'd even taken a seat.

"Little bit-a creamer, right?"

"Pretty good memory, Lisa," I said as we sat. "How was your day off? You in Fort Worth shopping for prom dresses again?"

"Aww," Lisa smiled. "I wish. We're still lookin', though. We ended up spendin' the whole day at the hospital."

"The hospital," I erupted, too loud and too surprised.

"It was nothin', Dan. Just somethin'—"

"You okay?" I asked.

"I'm fine, thanks. It was just nothin'. God looks after me and mine. I couldn't ask for any more out of this life-a mine." Lisa said, dodging me, having let too much slip and embarrassed about it.

"Okay, Lisa. I hope you're okay, anyway."

That left us with an awkward gap that Lisa finally filled. "Well, you see," she started. "Well, I always get flustered with this, but I shouldn't. You see, my daughter has AIDS."

"AIDS? Oh," I replied, my intonation absolutely wrong, too shocked, too much of a recoil.

"Yes, she has AIDs. You see, she's a hemophiliac, she has hemophilia, and all the blood transfusions and all. You see, the blood supply was tainted. Nobody knew back then. She picked up HIV and then, well, AIDS developed."

"Lisa, I am so sorry."

Lisa was used to handling people like me who didn't know what to say. She tamped down my disquiet with a calming smile.

"She's just a normal little girl with a boyfriend who loves her, Dan. He knows about her condition, and his parents know, and God bless them, the way they've opened up their hearts to us. It's been really wonderful. We're blessed. She's just an average little girl from Granbury, Texas. But we're okay, and we got a big prom comin', and you can bet, Dan, we're gonna find that absolutely perfect dress. It's out there just waiting for us!"

This was in early 2009. Over one million people had died of AIDS the year before.

How Lisa could smile. It was a gift. Her unconditional belief in God's guiding hand. She was so sure of it, already having accepted all the possible outcomes, the good and the bad, the horror that just might darken her doorway.

I hardly noticed when Douglas appeared.

"How you doing there, Dan? We're almost done in there, but I need to borrow Lisa. Lisa, you think you could type somethin' up for me?"

"Sure thing. Just was keepin' Dan some company."

"Sorry about this. Just a couple more minutes," Douglas said to me before walking back to his office.

Lisa rose from her seat and followed Douglas out, stopping for just a moment to place a hand on my shoulder and whisper, "God is watching out for us, Dan. Don't you worry about us. He's guiding us, and it's gonna be just fine. It'll be just like He wants it."

Lisa stepped into Douglas's office and closed the door behind her.

I immediately walked out of the building into the front parking lot and turned away from where I thought people might be. I was just tired. Too susceptible, vulnerable. But I found a hidden spot, anyway, and did everything I could to keep my eyes from flooding. The randomness of it all, the way life unfolds. Trying to make sense of Lisa's little girl, and seeing the world differently since I had my own children, both of them back home and safe; but God only knew what might be coming for all of us. How little my problems were, how insignificant, compared to this wonderful woman whose husband had left a long time ago, leaving her alone to wage a battle that could kill an army. It was all just too damned much for a few minutes, too close to home, too pointless. This wasn't people trying to rip me off. This was the terminus.

Finally, I stood and stepped out of it and back into the trajectory of getting trucks built, and putting away things that got in the way. It's easier that way. Self-preservation is easier. It's the subconscious fallback you make when the cataclysm gets too close.

I returned to the conference room and sat, wondering what in the hell was coming next. That question was answered when Douglas stepped in and abruptly dropped two contracts on the table. He, Clayton, and Zahir filled in the seats around me.

"It'll be a single-screw, twenty-barrel-a-minute blender," Douglas said, making it sound simple. "You got any head pressure, you might see twenty-two, twenty-three barrels out of it, but that's about it."

"With Quantum controls. Precisely the way you wanted it, Dan," Zahir added. "Douglas's and Clayton's blender will talk perfectly with the pump. And it will work."

I turned to Douglas. "Can I have a look?" I asked, reaching for the contract.

"Please do. That's what they're there for."

I scanned the agreement as Douglas and Zahir went on about hydraulics and Quantum controls. Clayton added something about technicians and the installation. I nodded but wasn't listening to a bit of it as I flipped pages, searching for the price, trying to look as though I had some control over myself.

I stopped. There it was. I fixed my stare.

Douglas saw I had found his number and spoke up. "We can do a li'l better if Andy up there's got anything we can use. That price is me starting from scratch."

It was $185,000. I thought it would be twice that. In my disbelief, I read on and looked for adders and omissions, like I did with the pump contract, but again, found none.

At $185,000, I'd go underwater some on my blender budget, but not much. It was salvation in front of me, and I knew I'd take it.

"I'm just supplying the chassis and what we talked about?" I asked, trying to contain my joy.

"That's right. It's all in there."

I looked up from the agreement to find Douglas staring at me. In just that short moment, I saw it. All his swagger and confidence were gone. He was nothing like he was a month back. This time he looked withered and slight, looking down the same barrel of the gun as me, and every bit as scared. He was prepared to build a blender at cost or, judging from his price, below it. I could only think he planned to use his existing inventory for my build, turning it into revenues rather than letting it sit on a shelf. I saw something similar in Zahir. He, too, was feeling the pressure of the falling sky.

"Need about four months to get it done. Never built a blender in four months, but this one I think we could."

I thought about Douglas's empty yard out back, and the few open slots I saw on his shop floor. I wondered if he'd be open for another four months. I wondered, too, if he suspected the same about me.

"I'd say we had a deal, but I gotta see Andy first."

Zahir scoffed, "This is the deal of a lifetime, Dan. Take it before it goes away."

"I got a contract with another guy, Zahir. I'd love to sign this one, but I can't have two contracts for the same truck. I gotta go up and see Andy. I wish I had a choice, but I have to go see him and see what I can do. He still has everything."

Douglas smiled. "It's okay. Go make sure for yourself. I don't wanna keep you around for just these two trucks. I want all your trucks. You take a couple-a days, Dan. That deal," he nodded at the contact, "isn't goin' anywhere. In fact, I'll sign my side of it right now."

Douglas reached for the contracts and signed both copies.

"You take them with you and bring them back signed," he smiled. "I'll keep one an' you keep the other."

I smiled back. Two peas in a pod. I had my deal and pushed away from the table, wanting nothing more than to get to Bristow, Oklahoma, and end my deal there.

I found Lisa and hugged her goodbye and headed for the door, waving goodbye to all and promising I'd be in touch as soon as I could.

Stepping out into the warm sun made me feel reborn. The oil and gas industry may have collapsed in around me, but I was ecstatic in its rubble. The contract I carried in my hand lifted the weight of failure from my chest. I felt free and, just for a few minutes, I felt grace. And that was enough.

Chapter 28

STIM SOLUTIONS MANUFACTURING

Bristow, Oklahoma

Tuesday afternoon. 2:00 p.m.

My well-worn path to Bristow and the drive there came easily. North toward the Texas Motor Speedway and the Dallas Cowboys' stadium, crossing the Red River along the Oklahoma-Texas line, passing the WinStar World Casino on the east side of I-35, and the two-story-high pumpjacks south of Oklahoma City, then a turn to the east and into the hillier parts of Oklahoma, to Bristow.

Along the way, I called my partners and told them Douglas had come through on the blender price. We could save the company with Douglas's contract, I told them. We'd still be above budget, and we'd be late to the starting line, but at least we'd get there. Of course, it wouldn't be with a vortex blender. It was just a plain old screw-type, but we could get it in four months and be on our way.

That made them happy enough, until I told them I didn't take Douglas's deal.

"Whatdya mean you didn't take his deal?" Wallace asked roughly.

"I can't."

"Whatdya mean ya can't? We gotta have a blender."

"We got a problem."

"What problem?" Eli chimed in.

"Andy's got our truck. We still have a deal with him."

Everyone went silent until Eli broke in. "You think that's gonna be a problem?"

"With the Brennans, there's always a problem," I responded.

Good moods are like bubbles. Eventually they pop. As I considered what might be, what lay ahead, the high I felt coming out of Douglas's place ebbed into cautious hope the closer I got to Bristow. That hope wilted into concerned worry. And then into loathsome fear.

What if Andy decided to keep my truck, and all my parts?

Barely catching the Bristow exit in the dark, I didn't immediately go to a hotel. Instead, I went to Andy's to see if anyone was around, maybe even drive my truck away right then and there. Not surprisingly, when I came upon the shop, there were no lights, no pickups, no one. I slipped out of my Pacifica anyway and tried the front door, but it was locked. I could have walked around the building and looked for a way in, but when it's dark and you don't belong, bad things will develop quickly. It was best to do this in the daylight, so I drove off and found a place off the highway to sleep.

Wednesday morning. 7:00 a.m.

I was out of bed early and checked out of my hotel room with the hope that I wouldn't be back. Eating breakfast off my lap, I rolled into Andy's shop. The first thing I noticed was that he wasn't there. There was no shiny black pickup with the ridiculously emblazoned STIM SOLUTIONS logo screaming of his bungled shot at entrepreneurism. I expected that, but missing, too, were all other signs of life. Not a single vehicle was parked out front. The only thing moving was a dust devil being blown about in the winter wind, sweeping across the gravel lot like a marauder looking for a fight.

I parked and snuck up on one of the holes in the walls where the sheeting had separated. Peeking inside, it was all just a shapeless black, too dark to see anything until my eyes adjusted and I saw the outline of my truck. I thought about breaking in and finding the keys and driving it away, but if I were caught, what then? Would it stop at a B&E charge, or would that be just the beginning? So far, I had the ethical edge. For the time being, I thought I should keep it.

I slipped back into my Pacifica and sat. What in the hell was I going to do now? I hadn't anticipated doing nothing, but that's what I did. I sat in the lot and waited for someone to show up, any sort of life-form, Andy or otherwise. After two hours, I started calling him. Four or five times I called. Each time except the last, I hung up when it went to voicemail. On the last call, I left a message.

"Andy. You alive? If you're alive, why don't you pick up? Be a lot easier if you'd talk. Gimme a call, all right? I just want to build a blender."

I hung up and threw my Pacifica into gear and drove into town, where I rolled slowly past the Kum & Go and an auto parts store where I thought Bryson and Andy might possibly be. After a few passes up and down Main Street, I started thinking the unthinkable—the long shot that maybe Andy and his crew were over at Bill's place, finally picking up the long-promised pod.

I headed over, and by the grace of God, neither Andy's nor Bryson's truck was there. No one was loading a pod onto a truck. No one was doing much of anything as I shot past Bill's debris field, accelerating with the thought that I might go unseen.

I returned to Andy's shop and waited, serving a penance for all my bad decisions. It was still morning, and my thought was that Andy's guys had regular full-time jobs. If they were first-shifters, they wouldn't be by until late in the afternoon. If they were second-shifters, they might still be sleeping. With that in mind, I sat still and waited and wondered just how in the hell I could smoke Andy out.

A few hours later, I grew bored and thought I'd amuse myself at Andy's expense. "Hey Andy," I said into my phone when my call went to voicemail, "I'm in Tulsa down at the hospital. I wanted to make sure you weren't hurt or something. But they didn't have any record of you. You maybe at another hospital? You okay? I'm worried about you. This is Dan. Did I say that? You know—Dan Doyle? Your customer? Gimme a call. Let me know you're all right. All right?"

I hung up and grinned, hoping he'd take my message about as well as I was taking sitting in his lot.

Then I got to thinking about my earlier trip to Bristow with Wallace. Andy had driven us out to one of his worker's homes, where the man was doing a little off-site flange welding. If I could retrace our tracks and find him, maybe he'd be willing to shed a little light on STIM SOLUTIONS Manufacturing. After an hour of poking around, I found his small trailer deep in the Oklahoma woods. I honked my horn and hung back by my car, well aware of Oklahoma gun laws and roaming dogs.

I may have had my share of troubles with Bill and Andy, but everyone else had been remarkably kind and hospitable. So when the welder approached me with a smile and an outstretched hand, I wasn't at all surprised. After apologizing to him for the horn honk, he sheepishly confessed that he was looking at taking a job pipelining up in the Marcellus.

"You're not sticking around to help Andy?"

"You didn't hear? He let us all go."

"I didn't hear that."

"Yeah. All-a us. Last Friday. Me and Bryson and all-a us. He just walked in an' asked us to set down our tools an' told us he was shuttin' it down."

"You're kidding me! Last Friday? He let all of you guys go last Friday?"

"He wrote us checks for what he owed us and said we was all done for now. Maybe later, but not now."

I was speechless, like words had been kicked right out of me. I was astonished, too (a smarter man wouldn't have been), but Andy had already shut down before I even walked in the door at Serva two mornings before, before his suggestion that we pray together at his church's Sunday service.

"I still got mine. Andy said not to cash it till he said so, an' so far, he ain't said so."

"It's good. Cash it. It may not stay that way very long. Cash it right away."

Duped and outwitted, I left the welder, but not before taking Bryson's cell phone number from him.

"Bryson knows a lot more 'bout how Andy's brain works than I do. You call Bryson, Dan. If anyone can help you out, he can. He don't have any problem helpin' out people that needs it."

I left the man waving after me from his dirt driveway, another one of God's creatures trying to do right in a world gone wrong. When I got back to Andy's front lot, I called Bryson, and right away got ahold of him and spilled my guts. I told him about the unaccounted-for dollars, about Serva and Schlumberger, about Andy claiming his own brother might just murder him.

Bryson was receptive and landed somewhere between bewildered and baffled, just like me. "Andy's got good-paying work right here," was his ongoing theme over the phone. "Why not focus on that an' make a business outta it?"

"Right."

"Good-paying work right here."

"Right," I responded again, with little else to say.

"A lotta us is pretty disappointed, all-a the work an' hope an' all. But it's his company, an' I guess he's got that right. I'm sorry to hear it didn't work out for you, either."

"Listen, Bryson, I don't mean to put you in the middle of it, but you still have a key to the building?"

"No, Dan. Andy took that, too."

Chapter 29

CROWE & DUNLEVY

Tulsa, Oklahoma

I was in over my head. I needed help.

The only option I had left was the one I had feared all along. I needed another lawyer. All along, it was out there on the horizon, but now that I had met the horizon, and Andy had jumped off of it, I was stranded without options.

I could drive back to Tulsa and walk up his driveway, but where would that get me, involving his wife and kids? Making it that personal invoked some kind of urbane, highbrow reluctance in me. I also thought it could get the police involved. Whose word would they take when I was standing on the homeowner's porch, raging over money and due dates, pods, Christians, and knives? Corner him like that, and I'd be the one getting hauled off and booked. Not the guy with my money.

So I'd beat him to it. I'd call the police first. I'd been thinking about the Bristow Police Department. The station over on Main Street I passed every time I was in town. Maybe if I called them, I'd find a sympathetic police officer, someone who would stand by while I broke into Andy's shop and drove my truck away.

Adam up at Lightspeed could fax down a registration card and proof that I owned the truck. It was another long shot, but a cheaper and faster scare tactic than hiring an attorney. So I dialed the police and a woman dispatcher answered. Not sure how to start the conversation, I asked if I could speak to her candidly about a business deal gone bad.

"You see, I paid a guy to do some work on a truck. The truck's titled in my company's name—I'm the owner—and I paid him all up to date and then some, quite a bit more, truthfully, but he disappeared and I need my truck back."

"Have you tried calling him?"

"Yes, I have."

"Do you want to file a missing person's report?

"No, no, I don't want to do that. He's not really missing. Just missing in action."

"Well, what exactly would you like me to do, sir?"

"Well, truthfully, I'd like you to send an officer over with me—it's only like a mile or so away—and help me get my truck out of his shop."

"Are you saying your truck is stolen, sir? Are you asking to file a stolen vehicle report?"

"Technically, I'm not really sure that it's been stolen, but—"

"If you don't know whether it's stolen or not, then I don't know what it is I can do for you."

"Well, how about, can I hire an off-duty policeman or policewoman to go out there with me?"

"To do what, sir?"

"To get my truck for me. You know, to keep it legal."

"Is the business open?"

"Really, it's not even a business. It's more like a junkyard, but no, I guess technically it's not open. Like I said, I've paid him up to date, way more, really. And this guy, Andy Brennan's his name, has been ripping me off forever. He's basically breaking the law."

"Sir, the scenario you're describing sounds to me like you are asking me to provide an officer so you can break into a business that is closed for business. Is that correct, sir?"

"Well…I'm not sure I'd put it just like that."

"Because if you are asking me to do so, I'm telling you that you are asking me to do something illegal. Is that what you are asking me to do?"

Jesus God, now she was angry at me. And that took all of a minute.

"Sir, you cannot walk into a closed business, whether it's unlocked or locked. And we're not going to do it for you. Why don't you wait until the business opens, is my advice. Or hire a lawyer. Lord knows there's plenty of those around."

"Understood, fine. You got a few criminals right here in town, though. Just thought you should know about it."

Man, that went bad.

But this congenital liar, this son of a bitch! My truck, all my parts, hostages in a hostage situation. Andy would hide while he claimed I was breaking our contract. He'd play the victim, and I'd be left to prove otherwise—in his home state, in Oklahoma, with all my possessions in his possession. No matter the circumstances, no matter his Christian principles, he'd hold out, and I'd be paying good money after bad to get them back. Because our laws allowed for it.

That got me to my last option, out on the edge of the horizon: calling a lawyer to back Andy down, handing over good money to capture bad.

Wednesday *evening. 7:30 p.m.*

Sitting and stewing and watching day turn to dusk, then dusk to nightfall, I drove off my perch in Andy's lot. If Andy wasn't coming out in the daylight hours, I doubted he'd come out at night. I wouldn't, either, if I were in his place. Why leave the comfort of home, with that clean toilet and stocked fridge, to drive out to a failed, filthy, and shuttered enterprise? Besides, who else might be looking for him? Who might confuse me for him?

Not wanting to be in the wrong place at the wrong time, I drove back to my roadside motel and checked in—again.

Sometime in the middle of the night, I gave up on sleep and started searching Tulsa attorneys on my phone. It would have to be a local lawyer, a transactional attorney, someone who could match Andy's behavior to the clauses in his contract. After an hour or so, I narrowed my search down to three law firms with a good number of lawyers each. As disinclined as I had been to involve one, I met my decision with some relief, but not much. Hiring a lawyer was a gamble. There's an implied threat when you put a lawyer between you and your problem. That helps, but once you involve lawyers, all communications with the other side cease. Lawyers want to control it all in their dot-the-i's and cross-the-t's approach. Nothing gets done. The ball doesn't move. Bills pile up. Then, when the pile becomes too tall, those who can't afford it topple first.

Thursday morning. 5:00 a.m.
As soon as it was early enough to find a cup of coffee somewhere, I got dressed and drove to Andy's shop. Maybe, as my hope went, something would develop before law offices began opening for the day.

Back in my front-lot perch, I expanded my search from shiny black pickups to every passing car and truck, suspiciously eyeing everyone, drivers and passengers, just in case Andy was riding shotgun, doing drive-bys as he waited for the stalker in his parking lot to get the hell off his property. Four hours I sat and watched, twisting in my seat to stave off rigor mortis. All for nothing. Clearly, my sedentary plan of action wasn't going to yield results, and with Andy's spotty record of showing up for work, it may not work at all.

Thursday morning. 9:00 a.m.
After the intermittent and spare Bristow rush-hour traffic ended, I called the first law firm on my list, Crowe & Dunleavy—and immediately hung up.

I wasn't ready—not for legal bills rolling in, in ten-minute increments, carrying along with them a go-nowhere outcome.

Ten minutes later, I gave in and called the law firm back. A receptionist answered, and I explained myself. After a long hold, I was patched through to the managing partner who, to my surprise, seemed to listen as I unloaded. I wasn't sure if my ten-minute rampage would be added to my bill, but I had a sympathetic, five-hundred-dollar-an-hour human actually paying attention as I heaved up all that had gone so outrageously wrong, breaking every tenet there is of attorney time management.

Eventually, the man cut through my blather with an offer of his condolences and a few assurances, promising me he'd assign it to a partner best suited for matters like this. Calmed a little from my unburdening, I asked how long it would be, and he promised it would be right away, that day certainly, given the gravity of the situation.

I hung up, relieved but worried about my extravagance. Never turn a lawyer into a therapist. Therapists are cheaper.

A few minutes later, I moved my Pacifica across the street into another empty lot. If Andy was trying to avoid me, why would he turn into a parking lot where I was sitting? I should have thought of that sooner, too.

Chapter 30

STIM SOLUTIONS ENTERPRISES

Bristow, Oklahoma

Thursday afternoon: 2:00 p.m.

I made a list. After five hours of watching for Andy and waiting for a phone call from an attorney, I was looking for diversions. The list wasn't comprehensive, not even complete, but it made its point.

1. Don't be stupid. Do what you know. Don't start a frack company when you haven't fracked a well in twenty years.
2. Don't be arrogant. Beware of arrogance traps, like starting a frack company when you haven't fracked a well in twenty years. (See #1).
3. Don't be self-delusional. Beware of any elevated sense of self. Delusion is a rickety platform. It hurts when you fall off it.
4. Don't pass on due diligence. Sloppy on the way in, sloppy on the way out.
5. Don't put up 100 percent of the money for a 50 percent interest. See #1 above: "Don't be stupid." Skin in the game works. Free doesn't. Ever.
6. Don't be impetuous. That is the sixth form of stupidity undertaken by me. What's the hurry?
7. Don't be a pleaser. Pleasers excel at self-hatred. Best to avoid this one.
8. Don't ignore the problem. Cut out the cancer right away. It will continue to grow, even when you convince yourself it won't.

9. Don't fall in love with vendors. Just because they show an interest in you doesn't mean you have to marry them. Casually date them all.
10. Don't be stupid. This is worth repeating. Repeatedly.

My phone rang. It was a Tulsa exchange. Immediately, I thought it was the Tulsa law firm, or maybe the Bristow police dispatcher calling to tie me to neighborhood loitering complaints. It rang again, and what I really wanted was for it to be Andy, calling to wave the white flag. But when I answered, it was a lawyer named Terry from Crowe & Dunlevy. He had heard some of my story, but not all of it, and asked me to start over. When I finished for the second time—this time, the clock definitely ticking—I felt I had a lawyer in my corner, a guy outraged by the Brennan brothers and all of their stunts. I liked his self-assurance and didn't mind much when he chuckled a bit to himself, having a small laugh at my expense.

"Don't you know any better?" Terry asked.

"Know what?"

"Never to do business with anyone from Creek County, Oklahoma."

Terry thought that was hilarious, repeating it aloud again, really pleased with his heightened witticism. Once he finished laughing—a little too long for my stepped-on ego—I asked him what we were going to do about it.

"What do you want to do about it?"

"I want to get my truck and all my parts. Right away."

"Okay, then let's get your truck and parts."

"How?"

"You're going to take it all, Dan. You're going to walk in and drive it right out," Terry replied.

"Just like that?"

"It's a place of business. It's yours, and you say you're paid up, right?"

"Yeah, then some, I'd say."

"Then wait for him or any of his employees to show up, and drive it away when they do."

"I can do that? I can tell them I can do that?"

"Absolutely. He didn't live up to the contract. Just don't get shot. Not worth it," Terry added in a good piece of lawyerly advice. "We'll abide by Oklahoma law, but that doesn't mean they will."

With that, he asked for a five-thousand-dollar retainer. If I were in a hurry, which went without saying—the wellhead of all my problems—I could wire it. But first, he needed to do a conflict check, especially since I had mentioned the leviathan Schlumberger. Following that would be a simple retainer agreement. In the meantime, I was to send over all the contracts and communications, and he'd start in once I was cleared.

"We'll get the son of a bitch, Dan. Andy's just hiding. That's typical. That's what people do when their businesses are failing. Eventually he'll surface."

The moment we hung up I dialed Adam at Lightspeed and asked him to watch my emails. If a retainer agreement hit, I told him to forge my signature and send it back with a $5,000 wire.

"More money, huh?" Adam responded.

"Yeah," was my weak response. I didn't bother asking about Lightspeed because we both knew Lightspeed was no longer the reason for my calls. Always generous, Adam, in his very cool and cheeky way, suggested I do my best to avoid getting shot.

Then I returned to waiting. An hour in and the feel-good buzz from the lawyer was wearing off. What were the chances Andy was going to show up now, when he was barely there before? So I called him and left a message again, just to poke him.

"Andy, pick up. It's me. Dan. Hey, I'm in Tulsa, right outside your house. Just wondering if you'd like to go out to dinner? Your choice. Isn't there an Applebee's or something out by you? They got that riblet platter you like. Anyway, I'll swing by and pick you up. Say, six? Leave your front porch light on, if you don't mind. See you then, ol' buddy."

Thursday evening. 6:00 p.m.

It was dark when Terry rang to tell me we were all good on conflicts. The retainer agreement was on the way, and I promised him the money would be, too (lawyers like to feign a disinterest in talking money, unless, of course, you fail to provide money). I asked if I should stop in and meet him, and he said absolutely, we'd get to it, which meant no need.

"What should I do now?" I asked.

"Keep waiting for him."

"Okay," I said, wondering why I'd hired a lawyer to tell me to do what I had already been doing. But when Terry told me he'd write up a demand letter and get it to Andy first thing in the morning, I smiled. Redemption no longer seemed so far out on the horizon.

We hung up and I called Andy back.

"Hey, Andy. It's me again. Sorry I'm running a little late, but a friend of mine, a lawyer, wanted to come along for dinner, too, if you don't mind. We're heading over now. See you in a few minutes."

Two hours later, under a starless, pitch-black sky, I headed back to my hotel. My thought was that I'd try to sleep after sitting all day in my Pacifica. As I stepped into my room with a bag of fast food, Mary called to tell me she had gotten the girls to sleep upstairs in their cribs. She was back in Pittsburgh and sitting on our living room couch, surrounded by jumpers and car seats, fencing, toys, scattered books, and a broken Baby Mozart. She wondered how I was doing.

"Pretty good," I lied. "I'm more worried about you up there."

"We're good. The girls are sleeping. I've got Elroy. You want to say hi?"

"Sure," I said as Mary held the receiver to our little terrier's ear. "Hey, Elroy! How's my little boy, Elroy? You being a good little boy and watching mama?"

Something about the little dog wagging his tail picked up Mary's spirits. She promised me that all the doors and windows were locked, the stove was off, and that they were all fine. She promised, too, that she'd call me as soon as everyone woke up in the morning. Her dad had started a business, too, but nothing like this. This was all way, way beyond his start-up stories.

Friday morning. 7:00 a.m.

When I woke to light filling my room, I shot out of bed.

My God, I've slept in! was all I could think as I threw on my clothes and grabbed up everything I owned, in case I got lucky and got to go home. I rushed outside without brushing my teeth. Within seconds I was in my Pacifica, racing out of the hotel parking lot toward the highway, thinking that if I didn't get my ass in gear, this could be the one time I missed Andy.

I drove into town, past the police department, and turned right at the little casino, gunning for Andy's shop, thinking today was my lucky day. I'd run right into him in the lot, drive right between him and his truck and block him from making a quick getaway. I'd snatch my keys and my truck and roll away forever.

Then, as I closed in, I saw Andy's shop was just as I had left it—empty and lifeless.

It's funny how thinly constructed expectations can be. It's silly that I should have assumed Andy would be there. It was just me breathing life into hopelessness. Dispirited and stricken by another bad outcome, I spun around and headed back into town toward the Kum & Go. I thought I'd finally try one of those breakfast sandwiches Andy had raved about a few months back.

A couple of minutes later, as I was paying for the sandwich and a cup of coffee, Douglas called. I took it as I walked out to my car.

"How you doin' up there? You find Andy yet?" he asked.

"I'm trying. Not much luck. I had to hire a lawyer," I said as I got into my Pacifica.

"Ahh, not so good, huh?

"Yeah, pretty much not so good."

"Well, you'll get it. Truth always comes out. You'll get it. Hopefully sooner than later, though." Douglas laughed.

"Yeah," I said as I turned toward Andy's.

"We're not going anywhere. We'll be right here. Gonna build you a helluva blender once we get started."

"I got no doubts, Douglas."

"Just itchin' to get started."

"Me, too, my friend. I was thinking, though. You think Zahir could talk some sense into Andy? Maybe tell him no deal on the controls. That he won't support him?" I asked.

"He already tried, Dan. Andy won't answer his calls, either."

"Big surprise—"

"I got an idea, though, Dan. Why don't you bust into Andy's building an' drive the truck right through that busted old building-a his? I'll repaint your truck free-a charge once it's down here in Texas."

I laughed. "I'd love to, but I already asked the lawyer."

"Well, what he say? Probably somethin' legal or somethin' stupid like that?"

"He said, 'Don't.'" Up ahead I could see Andy's shop coming into view.

"'Course he did."

"Not unless someone's in there. Without that, it'd be breaking and entering—"

My heart stopped.

"There you are!" I shouted, surprising myself.

"What?" Douglas asked, startled.

"Holy shit! *Holy shit!*"

"What?"

"Not you! Not you! *Andy!* Jesus! It's *Andy!*"

"Jesus!"

"There he is! He's right frigging there! His truck is…he's there…right *here*. I gotta go!"

I dropped my phone and ducked as I rolled past Andy's shop, risking running right off the road or planting myself into an oncoming car. When I popped back up, I caught sight of the big rolling steel door, open, and right there inside, my big bright blue International.

My God, my God! I was thinking to myself. By some miracle, by the grace of God and the Kum & Go, I may have otherwise missed him. If I hadn't run for the sausage-and-egg, he would have seen me out front and driven right by.

Down the road a ways, I found a lot and spun around in a cloud of dust.

I needed to get back. Before he left. Or closed the door. Or someone else showed up.

I'd call Terry. That's what I'd do. He'd tell me what to do. I dialed and started back on the road.

Please, I thought. *Please be there.*

I passed Andy's shop a second time, covering my face with my phone, though I snuck a sidelong glance anyway. Still no sign of Andy with the building dark like a cave, a metaphor for the same black hole I occupied.

A hundred yards past Andy's shop, I turned onto a dirt road and slow-rolled back alongside the building, until I could no longer see the front lot or Andy's truck.

"Is this Dan?" I heard over the phone, crazily having forgotten that it was even in my hand.

It was Terry, my lawyer! I had gotten through!

"*It is!*" I shouted breathlessly.

"How you doing today, Dan?"

"Good. Terry. Listen, I'm out at Andy's. He's in the building. His door is open. I think he's inside."

"Hey, that's good news!"

"I can see my truck in there. But I can't see him."

"Go in and find him. It's a business, and it's business hours. I can attest to that."

"You sure?" I asked as I turned in behind his building and parked out of eyesight.

"It's a place of business. You can go in," Terry reiterated.

"What about taking the truck?"

"It's your truck. Take it."

What sounded good a few minutes ago now scared the bejesus out of me. What was I going to walk into this time? Who else was in there with Andy?

"Okay. I'm going in," I said as I slipped out of my car. "You mind staying on the phone, though? I'm going to tell him I have a lawyer on the phone."

"That's good. That's fine. I'll be right here. Just don't get yourself hurt."

I skirted the building, moving quickly toward the front of it, having to hop and jump over the red-stained oil-field trash tossed about. At the front of the building, I snuck a glance around the corner. There was Andy's truck and the open garage door, but no Andy or anyone else.

"Jesus, my heart is racing," I whispered into my phone.

"Just don't get hurt," Terry repeated. "And don't hurt anyone else," he chuckled.

My thinking had me meeting an unfriendly dog or a guy with a wrench in his hand. But that wasn't Andy's way. He wasn't confrontational. He was more suited to a sneak attack than any sort of direct, blunt-force charge. But those guys that "go postal"—I had read that they weren't confrontational, either.

"When you see him—Andy—make sure to tell him I'm your lawyer. Better yet, put me on speaker and I'll tell him for you."

"Thanks, I will," I quietly said. "Let me go in and see."

I took a breath and stepped into the big black hole of a building.

"Andy? Andy? It's me, Dan Doyle," I called out.

There was no reply. Nothing in return. It was dead silent and so dark that he could have been right in front of me and I still would have missed him.

As my eyes adjusted, I looked for movement. When I didn't see any, I cautiously stepped ahead.

"Andy? It's Dan Doyle."

I got to the back of the truck, then cautiously came up the other side of it.

"Andy? You here?"

Then I saw him, at least part of him. Sticking out from underneath the side of the truck, just back from the driver's-side door, were a pair of shoes, toes up, with pant legs attached.

Good God, it was Andy! He was under the truck! Lying on his back—underneath the truck!

I hit the speaker button on my phone. "Terry, Andy's here. He's under the truck. My truck, I mean. He's under my truck. The blender."

"What do you mean? What's he doing under the truck?" Terry's voice echoed back.

"I don't know. But he's under the truck." I stepped closer to the feet and squatted down for a better look. "Is that you, Andy? I can see your feet."

A few eternities went by before Terry's voice shattered the silence.

"What the hell's going on there, Dan? You okay? Is it Andy or not?"

Finally, a weak voice came from somewhere beneath the chassis. "Yes, it's me, Andy."

Caught! He was caught!

"What are you doing, Andy?" I asked.

"What's he doing?" came Terry's voice over the phone.

"Nothing," Andy quietly added.

"Andy, I have my attorney on the phone. He's from Crowe and Dunlevy in Tulsa." I held out my phone so Andy could hear. "Terry, do I have a right to be in Andy's shop?"

"You have every right to be in STIM SOLUTIONS Manufacturing, Dan," Terry boomed over the phone, his voice filling the cold dead space around me. "It's a place of business. It's business hours, and if Andy is inside, then he is open for business."

"You hear that, Andy? I can take my truck. Correct, Terry? I can take anything here that was going on the truck that I paid for? Is that correct?"

"That's correct. You are well within your rights to take your truck and all parts attached or in the vicinity. Mr. Brennan cannot legally stop you from taking what is your property."

Terry's voice was clean, authoritative, and irrefutable. Suddenly, I loved him and all lawyers as I stared at Andy's feet sticking out from under the truck, just like the Wicked Witch of the East under Dorothy's house. I was so appreciative, no matter how incredibly weird it all was.

I told Terry I'd call back immediately if I had any problems, then hung up and stepped over Andy's feet to pull myself up into the cab. I was looking for the keys, just like I did at Bill's place six weeks back. And once again, they were right there in the ignition.

Thank you, God! Thank you for the Brennan tradition of leaving the keys in the ignition.

I grabbed them and jumped back down and immediately started gathering up everything I could find and chucking it into the cab.

Andy pulled himself out from under the truck and rose slowly to his feet. I watched him, waiting to see if he'd come after me. But he didn't and kept his distance.

"What were you doing under the truck, Andy?"

He didn't respond. He just watched as I filled the cab with parts. When I ran out of space, I started throwing things into the stainless-steel prime-up tank that my partner Wallace had insisted on. Parts and pumps, hydraulic hoses and fittings, valves, and even bolts were flying. I even threw the Mickey Mouse stainless-steel drums up onto the chassis. I was grabbing everything in a race to get out of the shop before Andy decided to do something, before it turned into a fight with no one there to stop it, in a shop full of hammers and heavy wrenches. If that was where it all went, reasonableness or a soft touch wouldn't prevail. It would come down to who could walk out at the end and who couldn't.

Andy wasn't his brother, though. His brother got all the testosterone and rage. Andy got the leftovers. I kept my eye on him anyway but didn't stop working, not for a second. When I started throwing whole boxes onto the truck, Andy protested.

"Those aren't yours."

"You're lying, Andy. I'm your only customer. I'm taking everything I paid for. By the way, where's the pod? Still no pod, huh?"

Andy met my words with a blank stare.

"Where's all your employees?" I added.

Again, nothing.

I tossed the last few things into the truck and was done. All that was left to do was drive away, but Andy remained standing at the driver's-side door, right where I needed to go. I made it look like I had no qualms about it, not a worry in the world, as I menacingly bore down on him and the cab. Maybe he'd stand pat and stake his claim, but he didn't. He passively stepped back as I brushed past him and pulled myself up into the driver's seat. I slipped the ignition key in, knowing that if a turn of the key didn't work, I wasn't getting my truck. Turning it, I held my breath, praying *God, please. Please, God,* until the engine rolled…and rolled… then started.

Thank God for new batteries!

Though I had the truck started, I couldn't move it. Just like at Bill's place a month back and a lifetime ago, I had to wait on the air pressure from the onboard compressor to build. Without enough air pressure, the brakes wouldn't disengage. Nearly two minutes I'd have to sit at idle for a "good enough" charge, two minutes in which Andy could simply shut the big rolling steel door and block me in. The condition the building was in, though, I could drive right through the door and let Douglas repaint the truck like he promised. As I considered it, I wondered about bringing the whole building down on me. Stalling Andy would be the better solution. Knowing that he liked to talk, I'd engage him in conversation.

"What were you doing under the truck, Andy?"

Andy shrugged. "I wasn't doing anything."

"It's the first time I've ever seen you dirty."

Andy shrugged. "Where you taking the truck?" he asked.

"Tribute's going to build it. Down in Granbury. Down in Texas."

Andy's head snapped up in surprise, his mind likely racing around Zahir selling the computer to Douglas rather than him—the very computer and controls he had ordered for the job.

When he started for the door, maybe to get out of the way, or maybe to close it on me—I didn't know which—I shouted, "You shut that door, I'm driving right through it!"

I revved the engine and pushed the truck into gear. The air was only halfway up, but when I eased the clutch, the brakes released, and the truck lurched ahead. Andy jumped back just as I clutched in to kill my momentum.

"Thanks for returning all my calls, Andy!" I shouted out the window. "I'm sure my lawyer Terry will want to talk to you about it!"

Whether or not he replied, I have no idea. Behind the wheel of a truck I didn't know how to drive, I was too scared shitless to pay any more attention to him. That, and sunlight was burning white-hot spots into my eyes as I cleared the shop and bumped along the front lot onto the county road. Almost to neutral territory, I went to grab a higher gear but stalled and lurched forward into a dead stop, slamming my chest into the steering wheel. Sucking air, I checked my sideview mirrors. No cars or trucks were coming. Nothing was going to hit me, even when the truck disappeared into the cloud of trailing dust I had sucked up from Andy's lot. When the cloud rolled past, I restarted the engine and caught a glimpse of Andy standing motionless inside the doorway of his shop, glaring after me—his lunch ticket—escaping with his fab shop dream.

Chapter 31

I-44 WEST

Oklahoma

An eighteen-speed transmission should have given me plenty of options, but as I tried grinding my way into gear, I couldn't find a single damn one of them until I finally punched the shifter into third or maybe fifth and feathered out the clutch. Immediately, the engine bogged down to the point of stalling until I frantically clutched in and out and got the truck rolling.

At fifteen miles per hour or so I was winding out the engine as I crawled toward downtown Bristow. I needed to get out of there and out of Creek County, and hopefully soon enough, out of all of Oklahoma. If I could make it through town and get onto the interstate, I'd lay down some miles between me and my nightmare. The only obstacles left were Andy calling the police and the likely chance of wrecking.

The first time I stalled out in town was at the first traffic light on Main, coincidentally within eyesight of the Bristow Police Department. Under the green light, I shoved it into first against a horrible grinding sound and popped the clutch, stalling out all over again. The cars behind me didn't honk. This was Oklahoma, after all. Instead, they patiently waited.

The second time I stalled, I found a gear and hoped for the best as I revved up and feathered out the clutch. Too bad for the guy behind me, because I was in reverse and damned near crushed the front end of his little Chevy. This time the cars honked, every single one of them, as they pulled around me in a confused band of traffic, heatedly looking up at me as they shot past.

This was too damn much. I called Wallace Kane but didn't reach him, so I called his son. In a panic, I asked him how to shift the big son of a bitch.

"You own trucks and you can't drive a truck?"

After a short but good-natured outburst of laughing, he tried to explain something that was as familiar to him as taking a breath. Pretending I understood, I hung up but kept repeating my mistakes—grind, stall, grind, stall—in a mental block that was killing the batteries every time I restarted the truck. Finally, when I got it moving again, I was laying down tracks at something like eight miles per hour, trying to time green lights and determined not to stop again.

I could smell it. My clutch was burning. Smoke was everywhere. Cars swarming all around me. Everything had become tenser, much worse than the terrified I started with. Horns honking and one guy flipping me off from a battered Ford Econoline van. Jesus God, if only they knew.

Just keep going; get on the highway and turn toward Granbury, Texas, and go. There I'd find a high-enough gear, and once I did, the only thing stopping me would be fuel. Not even a bathroom break would stop me. I'd pee my pants if I had to.

A mile or so and four or five traffic lights later, I hit the ramp for I-20 West. I kept the truck moving by smoking the clutch right up to the one last obstacle I had to clear—a toll booth. I clutched in and rolled up to the window, stinking of burning metal and rubber. Miraculously, I stopped right where I was able to take a ticket from the lady attendant. It was a miracle, too, that I didn't hit her and the booth, given the scarcity of clearance on either side of my chromed-out sideview mirrors.

"How you doing," I yelled out to the lady in the booth.

She was about to hand me the ticket, but stopped short, distracted by a white pickup in the next lane. I couldn't see or hear its driver, but when she turned back to me, she yelled something that I couldn't hear over my truck.

"I'm sorry. What'd you say?" I yelled back.

The woman leaned out of her booth and shouted, "The man in the truck there says you're leaking oil!" She was pointing her thumb at the pickup in the lane behind her. "You can pull over right ahead to the right there."

I followed her line of sight to a parking lot and small building with an Oklahoma state trooper car parked out front. Without a pause, I shouted back a lie. "That's water. I just washed the truck, and it's water dripping off the truck. Not oil. Thanks, though."

That was good enough for the booth attendant, even though the truck was filthy and hadn't been washed since the last rainstorm swept over Bill's yard.

I released the clutch, hurrying to get the hell out of there. Then stalled and winced as I slammed my chest into the steering wheel again.

"Ah, dang!" I shouted with a dopey grin I flashed at the attendant.

Immediately, I got it restarted and did a slow, winding crawl away from the booth.

Leaking oil? What the hell? I thought. *Leaking oil?*

Even if I was leaking oil, I wouldn't be able to see it in my rearview mirrors or with my head out the window. I had to pull off. But if I stopped too soon, I'd attract the attention of the trooper. *Wait until you're out of sight*, I thought. *Just wait.*

Two miles later, I pulled off the interstate onto a grassy, narrow berm and dropped down out of the cab after a few cars sped past. Fighting a flight impulse, I forced myself under the truck into the dark void between the steer and drive tires. Having to lie flat on my back, I slithered along the frost-covered pavement. Two or three inches above my nose was the truck's undercarriage, hotter than hell, 150, maybe 180 degrees in the sump and anywhere else oil accumulated. It felt like I was the fire under the frying pan. I could hardly breathe. It was too damned hot, and tight enough that I shut my eyes with the onset of a claustrophobic freak-out.

Inch by inch, moving ahead toward the center of the truck, I heard it before I saw it. A car was approaching, fast. From my point of view, just a set of tires and a front bumper bearing down on me at 70 mph. Right at me. My God. Not a damn doubt in the world that my time had come. Reflexively, I shut my eyes in silent horror as the car raced in, but then blew past me, seemingly over me, in a torrent of wind, dust, and stones.

I found myself panting. But I stopped that immediately because of the heat filling my lungs, causing me to cough and gasp, and then another car, right after the first, bearing down on me all over again.

This wasn't a good place for indecision, that was unambivalently clear, so I started looking around for the leak. Unexpectedly, it was my feet that were the first to find it. Hot oil was dripping from somewhere above, covering my boots and turning them what felt like red-hot. Twisting and dragging, I spun myself around to get my head where my feet had been.

The woman at the toll booth was right. Oil was leaking right out of the back of the transmission. I drew in closer and saw that wasn't it—it was the splitter box, the power take-off bolted to the back of the transmission. Oil was pouring out in a thin stream, not an enormous amount, not anymore, anyway; but driving down the highway, it must have been puking oil.

Looking around, I could see that the casing wasn't cracked. It wasn't a loose hose connection. I knew because I burned the palm of my hand wiggling a few. It was the drain plug. It was missing.

How the hell was a drain plug missing?

Lying there still as a stone and thinking, thinking, and then arriving at Andy and why he had been under the truck. He'd been lying right there, right where I was, the same exact spot. Without the drain plug, the sump at the bottom of the splitter box would bleed out. Inside were the gears that split one driveline into two: one for powering the truck, the other for the blender hydraulics. No plug in one of the lowest points on the truck and there'd be no oil. No oil and you'd junk the transmission, the $24,000 splitter box, and possibly the entire drive line, with some engine repairs to boot.

It was the first time I had ever seen Andy dirty, just like I told him. I didn't see a wrench in his hand, but that didn't mean he hadn't left it under the truck.

I was so deep in thought that I didn't even notice, or even much care, when an eighteen-wheeler thundered past, whipping me with dirt and sand and a blast of hotter-than-hell air.

Then the realization hit dumb ol' me. I now understood what Andy had been doing under the truck.

The shitty son of a bitch!

The son of a bitch had been disabling my truck. The son of a bitch was trying to hobble me. He was sabotaging me. All over again. He had to have known I was lurking, waiting for my chance to take the truck. Somebody must have seen me hanging around. Until I wasn't. And then Andy, by disabling it, had assured I wasn't going anywhere.

Lying under the truck with traffic racing past, I found an ill-fitting pebble and pushed it up against the drain hole. After a few seconds, with my fingers burning and scorching hot oil still leaking out, I began laughing at myself, my own absurdity. It was hilarious. That made the last laugh mine. I had gotten away! Andy hadn't stopped me after all! He would never want a part of this problem, an illegal and crippled truck stranded on a remote section of interstate. This was a costly problem, no longer the easy, low-hanging fruit of keeping it locked up in a building.

Right then, I was free of Andy and his brother and of everything outside of debt and oil prices. I was overcome by a barmy joy, no longer finding the radiating truck heat to be scorching. Rather, it was suddenly warming, giving me a feeling of joy and vindication and an incongruous good humor that played out against the cars and trucks rushing at me, peppering my eyeballs with entrails of dust and dirt dragging behind them.

I didn't bother thinking up some better-suited action plan. This was all I had. Oddly, purposelessly, I lay there relieved, until I drifted off and remembered Samuel Beckett's *Waiting for Godot*, a literature class assignment I'd read back in college, years and years before. I couldn't help the farcical parallel, the improbable realization that I had just found myself inside the play as the more useless character, the one who's highest order was plugging a hole that leaked oil. But at least I had my truck. The other characters, Vladimir and Estragon, they didn't have shit. Once I figured out what to do next, I'd drop the rock and drag myself out from under the truck. Those other guys, they'd still be waiting.

It seemed to me this would be a fitting time to call Douglas, to tell him we had a deal. Even if he wouldn't have a truck, not right away anyway, I was ready now to sign the agreement. That would take a phone call, but doing so under my truck was the wrong spot, so I pushed and pulled and twisted my way out to the berm, where I got my footing and climbed up a grassy bank. There I sat, near a barbwire fence holding back a few bony, disinterested cows, and reached for my phone and smeared it with the grease and oil and roadside dirt caking my hands.

I dialed and cupped the phone so I could hear over the whoosh of traffic shooting past. Lisa answered, and after a short chat, mostly me yelling to be heard and explaining where I was, Douglas got on.

"How you doin', Dan? We been worryin' 'bout you."

"I heard. Yeah. Thanks. Doing okay. Pretty good, all in all. Doing really good, actually. Under the circumstances."

"Where're you? Hard to hear you."

"Yeah. I'm on a highway. Loud out here. Listen. I wanted to tell you. We have a deal. If you're still up for building this blender, we have a deal," I shouted over the blast of a truck passing, the trucker inside hitting his horn and pumping his fist.

"You say we got a deal? I can't hear."

"Yeah. We got a deal."

"Son of a gun, that's some good news, partner. We been worried—"

"On one condition," I interrupted.

"One condition? All right, what're ya thinkin'?"

"You gotta come and get me. Me *and* my blender."

"You got the blender?"

"I got it. And I didn't even have to break any laws, either. Not that I know of, anyway."

"Well, that's good, partner."

"Yeah, but it's broke down on the side of the road. Your side of Bristow."

"Well damn, that's no good. What's the problem?"

"Andy. Andy's the problem."

A few minutes later, yelling and explaining the missing PTO plug and leaking oil, Douglas answered that he was sure he had a replacement.

"I got every kind of plug you can imagine," Douglas assured me. "Don't you worry, I'll have a guy out first thing in the morning. Any place around there you can spend the night?"

"I don't know. Probably. I'll start walking and let you know."

"Hang tight, Dan. We can look that up for you. Hang tight, and I'll get right back to you."

We hung up and I lay back in the grass and waited. If I'd had a beer, it would have been a good time to drink one. But I didn't, and instead I wondered what the hell I was going to do about my Pacifica back at Andy's. Thrifty was going to be pissed, sure to hit me with some kind of pickup charge. That, and I doubted they'd be mailing back my toothbrush and spent underwear, and the favorite T-shirt I left in the back seat of the car.

"Not too far down the road, Dan, there's a Best Western," Douglas said when he called back. "Maybe a few miles. Just walk west, away from Bristow. That should be easy enough for you, shouldn't it?"

"Real easy," I grinned, then thanked Douglas profusely. When we hung up, I wasn't in much of a hurry but started walking west along the berm. I was fine with it, even a little happy-go-lucky. In fact, it was fitting in this odyssey of trucks that I should be hoofing it like some wheelless and broke vagabond without a change of underwear. Hitchhiking or even accepting a ride never crossed my mind. I was content as it was, walking along, destitute and down-and-out, free and ecstatic, and right where I wanted to be. On the westbound lanes of I-44.

After a few easy miles, with my beloved blender just a speck behind me, I saw a bluish sign ahead. Then, a few hundred yards later, as though emerging from a mirage, I saw it was the Best Western—a big and plush

Best Western Hotel. I climbed the embankment and jumped a barbwire fence and saw that it had a restaurant with warm halogen lights filling its windows. A few people were moving about inside, which meant it was open and serving food. I needed no more, not a better car back home, a bigger house, or even a truck that worked. As I was seeing it at the moment, it was much more than just enough. It was a gift. The cloud that had been raining on me for months was drifting off without me. Gravity's hand was letting go.

Godot had arrived.

Everything was going to work out just fine.

Until it didn't.

PART II

I hate getting bit.

—Lennox Lewis

Chapter 32

GENETICS OF AN ENTREPRENEUR

Rasselas, Pennsylvania

The missteps, the abysmal timing, the pitiful, stumbling overreach, none were recent developments. All were part of an early onset failure, all wired into my DNA from the start. The symptom, that was my fledgling frack company, but the cause, the reason, that was all me. I'll make a hurried, overly zealous decision to do something, then just do it. I'll assume that if I do, I'll land on my feet. The bedrock of all my assumptions has always been *Why shouldn't I land on my feet?* Why though? Why so damned cavalier?

It is because I am an entrepreneur.

I have an entrepreneurial restlessness that overwhelms common sense and other well regarded human instincts like fear and fear of failure. Reasonable personality traits like caution and restraint are pushed out of the way. Entrepreneurism consumes all the air in the room, riding roughshod over benevolence, dignity, good and proper manners, and everything else living under the umbrella of civility. I'm not necessarily proud of it, either, this inescapable disarrangement, irrepressible and agitating against authority, seeking difficulty over ease, naivety over season. It's the same bullheadedness that marks all entrepreneurs; our cacophonous, messy catchall of a group which, by all reasonable standards, is a shit-poor group to belong to.

How, though? How?

Because I am my father's son. It is from him. He, too, would jump first without looking for bottom. The nervy sort, he was all entrepreneur. Back when his children were somewhere between diapers and bicycles, he started a steel fabrication business but wasn't first a fabricator. He drilled an oil well but wasn't first an oil man. He started a commercial fishing business but wasn't first a commercial fisherman. Again and again, he acted on his ideas, which meant he walked the walk. And because he was a role model to me—but overwhelmingly because he was my father—it is all his fault. He is to blame. Endlessly selling his seven kids on the conviction that anything was possible makes it all his fault. It is his doing—his malfeasance—my ungrounded bearing on life, my unqualified disregard for risk. My assuming I can fix bad decisions and capitalize on good ones, that I'm fast enough on my feet to keep out of trouble—that's all him, too. But because I am him, it's me, as well. All my endeavors, good and bad, successful and not, sleeping on floors and in cars and trucks, broke and not so broke…he put that all on me.

Golden Gloves boxer, outdoorsman, and dreamer with little regard for barriers, that was my father. At fourteen, during the height of World War II, he lied about his age and shipped out on steam-powered freighters. Nothing his mother did could have stopped him. He just pushed some clothes into a sack and went to work on one of the hulking, snub-nosed freighters that carried ore out of the northern Lake Superior mines.

A few years later, he was clearing a North Korean minefield when an antipersonnel mine exploded in his face. Because of his helmet, he kept his head but lost half his eyesight and most of his teeth. He suffered shrapnel wounds in his forehead, down his back, and right through the big, meaty right hand that held the knife that stabbed the mine. After a year of lying around in MASH units and army hospitals in Seoul, Tokyo, and Walter Reed in Washington, he went back home to Erie to convalesce, with three Bronze Stars and a few Purple Hearts, none of which he ever mentioned. Neither did his mother, my Grandma Doyle, who suggested her son get off the couch and get to work and save himself. From Grandma's way of seeing it, the only salvation known to her was work. It was the remittance and the payoff that came from a hardened sense of self-reliance after her young husband died of pneumonia and left her alone with two little boys.

I heard she never complained. It was just the way life turns for some. There were no handouts or casual dating or second marriages and honeymoons. It was just work and whatever fun could be cooked up on the cheap in her working-class, maritime neighborhood in Erie, Pennsylvania.

Taking his mother's advice, my father scratched together a few bucks, finished college, and bought a business. Then he married Kathleen, beautiful and refined, a surgeon's daughter whose picture he had seen in the newspaper. Daring himself, he took a shot and called her. When fatherhood came, he and "Kate" settled into the predictable chaos of pregnancy, seven times over, and sleepless nights and debt, but never any diminished dreams. When it was my turn to walk away from home, I walked into college with an undeclared major—not pre-dent, as I had promised my mother—instead drifting, until I made it home one weekend and changed my life by listening in on my father and his boyhood friend Norby Hardner at our kitchen table talking about oil and drilling oil wells. They weren't talking about drillers listed on the American Stock Exchange, or buying into the swarm of Regulation D oil- and gas-drilling programs circulating at the time.

They were talking about drilling their own oil well.

The outbreak of the 1979 Iran-Iraq war had just triggered another Middle East oil shock. A boom was on, and investors were rushing the gates. Adding fuel to the fire was a tax code allowing for nonrecourse leveraging that Wall Street could securitize—a boom all its own.

It was just too much for two dreamers, just too much temptation, the closest thing to treasure hunting left on earth. But what the hell were they thinking, this business of drilling their own oil well? My father and very intrepid mother had seven kids and a business to run. And then there was Norby, who watched over dozens of employees in his construction company. It was a crazy idea and absurd to consider something so far out of reach. But it didn't matter. They did it anyway.

Once drilling and completion began, I started coming home from college every weekend to ride along with my mother, brothers, sisters, and dogs, all of us stuffed into our family station wagon where the windows glazed over from our dogs' panting. Up front, my dad and Norby, with one of my little sisters wedged in between, drove and talked shop, always warming up on their respective construction businesses before drifting to the well, always to the well, dreaming out loud about oil.

Quietly, I listened in on these two middle-aged men. They were starting over, washing away all the drivel and disappointments of their day jobs. It was a fresh start for them, like being twenty years old all over again. This drilling, this digging for treasure, this was boyhood stuff. It was two men reborn as wildcatters, going over all the possibilities. What if it comes in big? What do we do with the money? Where do we drill next?

When the well finally came in, it made some oil, but it didn't flow in long laminar sheets or spray into the tank. The well never got wild. It dribbled in and brought along an ocean of brine water in the infancy stage where you keep pumping, quietly pleading with God or your bankers or your wife for more time and oil. Eventually, though, the well pumps off and the story is told, whether you're ready for it or not. It's the backside of the American dream that no one wants to cover. It's failure to some, but to others it's just a failed attempt. It sucked and was altogether disappointing. Cleaning up any mess without revenues always is. But to my family, that's all it was—a disappointment, not a setback.

Norby and my mother and father didn't drill another well. This one alone cost a lot of money, probably about $140,000 in today's dollars. It was a big move for a guy with seven kids. But my father was smart. His reach didn't affect anyone's lifestyle. We didn't go without. No one had to drop out of school.

But for me, it was different. I got to be around two guys who had the balls to step into uncertainty. It was pure risk and reward—hits or misses—this bit of gambling dressed up as a business, as a provocation. That was the takeaway, and these were the unmarked parameters I knew I wanted to live in. It was digging in the spot marked X, with the buzz of expectations so much more appealing than the grindingly slow crawl of any other career awaiting me after college, other careers I could have comfortably slipped into.

And it was legal.

So I redid my class schedule, transferred to the geology department, and started an academic sprint to get done in two and a half years what should have taken four.

Such it is when you're smitten.

Chapter 33

WEST BY SOUTHWEST

Oklahoma to Granbury, Texas

I had to pee. I was only an hour into driving the blender to Granbury, Texas, and I already had to go. An hour later my bladder felt stretched beyond all reason. After another hour, three hours into my drive, and coming up on the Oklahoma-Texas line, I was bent over double against the steering wheel.

Earlier in the morning, I drank a cup of coffee, enough only to stave off a caffeine withdrawal headache. But then I had another, because it wasn't bad for roadside coffee. When Douglas's guy showed up at my motel in a service truck, I poured one for him, and just for the hell of it, another one for me before we drove off for the blender.

Circling back to the interstate on the perfectly squared-off county roads, we came upon the soon-to-be blender, a lonely black-and-blue dot that my driver, Douglas's guy, had already found. He'd left Fort Worth at two in the morning and had already run a plug into the splitter box and filled it and the transmission with oil. All I had to do was start the engine, build air, and get it up to speed. If I could do that without destroying me or the truck, I'd drive the four hours to Granbury without stopping.

"So, you think you'll miss those guys?" Douglas's guy joked over the low roar of the engine after I started it.

"Yeah, I was hoping they'd stay in touch," I laughed from the berm as a car shot past. "You can have my room if you want, catch some sleep. I never checked out."

"No, man, I want to get out of here, too."

I nodded and shook his hand for the third or fourth time, terrified of what lay ahead. Then I climbed into the truck and wound down the window to say goodbye one last time.

"I'll follow you for a little, make sure you're doin' all right," he said in a way that suggested he wasn't so sure I'd be all right.

I thanked him again, pushed the shifter into a gear, and popped the clutch. The truck lurched forward five feet and stalled.

In the sideview mirror, I could see Douglas's guy was laughing wildly, stomping his foot, until a semi blew by and nearly knocked him on his ass with its trailing gust of wind. When he finally straightened up, he threw me a thumbs-up and I threw one back and got the truck restarted. This time, I smoked the clutch and strained forward in third or maybe fifth gear—whichever it was, I wasn't sure. But I was able to keep moving by grinding the edges right off each successive gear as I upshifted and gained some momentum. At 50 mph, I backed off the accelerator and settled in there. *Good enough*, I thought, but my God, the damage I had just done to the truck.

A few minutes later, Douglas's guy shot past me, blaring his horn and waving out the window. I pulled the air horn tether and pumped my fist with a fading gusto as I second-guessed myself for not having asked him to stick with me. *What a hapless move*, I thought, as the kid disappeared ahead of me into the endless, flat horizon.

Three hours later and I couldn't keep going. Twisting around in the seat and holding onto my crotch to keep from peeing myself, I somehow made it through Oklahoma City and its 70 mph bumper-to-bumper traffic. As I crossed over the Red River into Texas, I saw an exit for a Texas Welcome Center and—screw it—took my chances and pulled off. I had to. No way I could keep going.

Stupidly, I pulled the truck out of gear as I turned into the exit lane. I shouldn't have. That was my first unforced error, leaving me without a gear to drag and slow me down. I was rolling too fast for the exit, and as much as I tried to shove the shifter back in, I couldn't find a lower gear, the vibration on the stick so violent that it was vibrating my right arm right out of its socket.

With no way to swing back into traffic, I could only brake hard as I committed to the exit, smoking the brakes and plunging the dash-mounted air-pressure needle deep into the red. Immediately, the engine stalled and with it the chance to build any more air pressure. That locked up the rear end, which responded with a violent bouncing sway. It was too much, too quick, the ass end of the truck skidding around, slamming me into the door panel as I came upon the cars stopped ahead. A buzzer sounded and a dashboard dial flashed that I had dropped through the critical low-air point, leaving no recoil, no pressure, nothing left of the brake pedal but the feel of stepping on a wet sponge. Unless I could find a low enough gear to stop me, nothing was left to do but run off the road and risk a rollover.

Discarding all concerns about the blender's well-being, I shoved with all my might against the shifter, pushing it into a horrible, stinking grind. Whether by miracle or pure force, the shifter finally sank into an unseen slot, redlining the engine in an awful cry as a gear caught, and *thump-thump-thump*—the truck bounced along the pavement, abruptly stopping and throwing me into the steering wheel, folding me right in half as my chin hit the horn.

I was too shocked to feel anything other than relief, even when the truck stalled out in a cloud of smoke and steam, the engine popping and crackling, with a hiss coming from somewhere, maybe the brakes bleeding off the last bit of their stored energy. Only gradually did I become aware of the smell of burnt rubber and clutch, every bit the smell of burnt money.

With traffic stacking up behind me, I thought I should try and restart the engine. When I wiped my sweaty palms on my pants, my hands stopped moving, caught in a wet friction. That's when I felt a warm and damp clamminess. Jesus, my crotch! I'd leaked right through! It wasn't much, but it was enough. A few hundred miles of self-flagellating masochism, then a toilet two hundred yards ahead, and I had pissed my pants!

The hell with it. Let it all go and get it over with, I thought.

I let go of whatever muscle was holding my bladder back...and waited. And waited. Nothing happened other than everything hurt. For Christ's sake, now I couldn't pee! Contorting myself ten different ways, looking for some relief as the pain of a balloon-tight bladder came back, I restarted the truck and waited on air to recharge and unlock the brakes.

When I released the clutch, I wound out the rpms and crept up to the front of the Welcome Center. Carefully, wincing in pain, I slid down out of the truck and hit the ground with a small jolt. A rush of urine came on so quickly and forcefully that I was afraid to stop it. There wasn't any point anyway. My legs had already turned a sloppy, hot wet, so I kept going and going, feeling a warm, creeping sensation that coursed right into my boots.

I finished in a dumb sort of relief, waiting on the last dribble, aware that nothing hurt any longer as I emptied out both urine and pain. In a slow realization, it struck me that I was standing wide open in a parking lot, in front of a bank of Welcome Center windows, with my legs spread and urine pooling and running across the dried-out pavement. I started to consider just how many people might be gawking at me, at the grotesque stooge—the guy whose faded blue jeans had just turned purple and whose expression belied some sort of weird ecstasy.

Then I saw it—*please no!*—a Texas state trooper car. And me urinating in public. Was that legal, or not so legal, or one of those things law enforcement left in the gray spread of indecipherable human comportment? But if my privates were in, and not out, what could be the charge? Littering? Organ failure?

With my legs turning from warm to wicked cold in the Texas winter wind, I needed another sort of relief. I needed to get out of my pants. There was no way I was getting back in my truck, not with me still dripping urine all over the pavement. Besides, I had no spare pants, socks, shoes, or underwear to change into. So I charged off toward the glass-wrapped Welcome Center, hoping that if I looked to be in a hurry no one would stop me.

"Howdy-do!" I heard when I entered the building.

An older woman inside a central kiosk, a state employee, was smiling and waving.

"Hiya," I responded as I passed by, trying to shrink away, each of my steps leaving a wettened imprint of urine.

"How can Texas help you today?"

"I was just looking for a bathroom—"

"Just a bathroom? That's all you came to Texas for?"

"Well," I said, searching for words, soaking wet from the belt down. "That would be for starters."

"Okay, then. Maybe afterwards you'll have a look at all-a our wonderful attractions here in the Lone Star State," she said, indicating the standing displays of colorful flyers selling all the local attractions. "Y'all'd never run out of things to do in Texas."

"Beautiful state," I offered, one squishy step after another on my way to the men's room door.

Once inside—and alone—I immediately stripped down to bare-assed naked, knowing that the faster I got done, the less chance anyone, including the trooper out in the lot, had of walking in on the naked dude in the men's room.

I rinsed and wrung out my clothes, then hurriedly tugged them back on. Giving in to guilt, I sopped up the water I'd left on the floor with a wad of brown paper towels from a dispenser. Then, dropping my haste, I casually, purposefully walked out the door—right into the Texas trooper, who was leaning against the kiosk with the chatty woman, staring straight my way.

I froze, waiting for the inquisition, trying to come up with something reasonable, some line of blither, from where I stood, dripping wet. When the trooper kept staring, gawking really, I saw it as a pass and stepped ahead, out of my puddle, shuffling my feet because I wasn't able to shove them back into my shrunken boots.

"You enjoy your time in Texas," the chatty and oblivious woman called out as I passed by.

"Thanks, I will. Thank you, ma'am."

At the door I made a break for it and stiffly crossed the lot for my truck. Pulling myself up into the cab, I got it started, then waited. Air had to build, a forever proposition, but when it did, I slid the shifter into some unknown gear and slowly released the clutch. The transmission grabbed, the engine didn't stall, and off I went at four or five miles an hour. As soon as I cleared the parking lot and was far enough down the ramp, I pulled onto the berm, set the brakes, and stripped out of my sopping-wet boots, socks, and jeans. My wet underwear, though, I left on in case I died in an accident.

An hour later, I pulled into Tribute, killed the engine, and took in a long, slow breath. *Good God*, I thought, *I made it!*

Douglas and his guys began streaming out of his office and shop.

"You may not want to look," I called out as I opened my door. "Sorry to do this to you," I said as I slid out of the cab and dropped to the pavement in my underwear, holding onto my pants, socks, and shoes. "I know, I know," I laughed. "Not a good look, I know."

"Whatcha got goin' on there, Dan?" Douglas asked, quizzically.

"I pissed myself."

Instantly Douglas's guys lit up, laughing.

"Damn, son," Douglas grinned. "Y'all didn't have to be so honest about it."

"Afraid if I stopped, I'd never get the truck moving again," I admitted as I leaned in against the fender to pull on my cold and wet pants.

"Y'all 'bout naked!" one of his guys shouted, triggering another uproar from the rest of them.

"Well, we appreciate you bringin' it down," Douglas said. "Now which one of you fellas wants to drive Dan's truck 'round back?"

"Screw you!" someone shouted. "I ain't sittin' in that truck."

A minute later, with everyone still laughing, Clayton walked in with a sheet of cardboard. "No offense," he smirked as he laid it on the driver's seat and climbed in.

A few hours later, one of Douglas's guys dropped me at DFW, and I found a few connecting flights and a way home to Mary and the girls. While I was flying, my Christian friends back in Oklahoma returned my Pacifica to the Tulsa airport with a warning that if I tried to pay them for it, they'd put a dent in the car. A day later, Douglas had the spare blender parts inventoried and found a few things he might be able to use. He'd even given me a small break on the price.

All the news was good. There was just too much of it….

Chapter 34

WINTER—SPRING 2009

Pittsburgh, Pennsylvania

Winter had arrived, and with it came a cold, dull-witted lethargy that covered Pennsylvania's oil fields. Sapped by the weather and low oil prices, there was little movement or inclination to move.

The Kanes were up on the hilltop, grinding it out in a start-stop-start approach to drilling our wells. Whenever a whiff of outside work blew in, down they'd come. Two or three weeks later, they'd be back, but not to work, more to talk about it, about having to drag the rig and pipe boats and all their equipment back up the hill again. Each of their moves was on my payroll, all the fuel and labor, but not one was my decision. As much as I privately cursed and moaned over the cost, the waste, the frustration, I should've been smart enough to have anticipated it. I should have been able to look deeper into my own deal before I made it.

On one of my trips to the hilltop, I met with Eli so he could show me what had been done, and what hadn't.

"Quit worryin' so much. We'll get it done," he told me.

"Eli, it's like three times up and down the mountain so far, and we've got like one well drilled so far. Why don't you just drill all the wells and then come back down and stay down? Wouldn't that be easier?"

"It'll get done. Just takes time."

"Yeah, but three times as long. You don't think these guys calling for work could wait until you're done up there?"

"They'd just call someone else."

"They're in that big a hurry? Oil at fifty dollars a barrel? They can't wait an extra week or two to lose their ass on an oil well?"

"Then why you in such a hurry? So we can just lose our ass, too?"

Eli's passivity was easy to handle, but it didn't abate Wallace's fatalistic, in-due-time approach to life and our oil company, Arcade. Still, Eli had become my sounding board on the direction the Kanes were pointing at any given time, the one person I could appeal to.

"Well, how about if I started coming up every day? I can start helping get this done."

"Oh yeah? What're you gonna do?" Eli grinned, taunting me.

"Show me how to run your 'dozer," I said, pointing at the bulldozer sitting nearby, dead still under a coat of snow. "I'll start building the roads."

"Nah. I can't do that."

"Why not?"

Eli kicked at the frozen ground. "We need it to build a road for a guy in Tippery."

"You gotta be kidding me."

Down in Texas, things were different. It was all feel-good with Douglas and the pictures he was taking and emailing to me. He was on time and on budget and didn't look to be going out of business anytime soon. Costs were as expected, and all was refreshingly boring. The promised April 2009 delivery looked to be holding, and I was doing what I could to prepare for its arrival. The missing piece of the puzzle, though, was cash. Douglas's fire sale helped, but not enough to offset what I had lost with STIM. No way around it, I was going to be short come the April delivery date.

Over in central Pennsylvania, fabrication on our first sand dump was underway by a guy named Tork. When I first met him, his lot was stuffed full of recently finished Universal Well Service sand dumps, looking like showpieces with their polished-aluminum bodies gleaming on top of brand-new International Paystar chassis. A few months later, when I dropped off the chassis for our second dump—the one I bought with stolen money—Tork's exuberance had taken a precipitous fall, and so had his now-empty parking lot. There was no more making hay while the sun shines. Low oil prices, and a shift to bigger transports needed for the onset of shale, had wiped him out, causing him to vow to quit as soon as he could push my two dump bodies out the door. No surprise to me, he kept his word.

Back in Pittsburgh, a few body-shop guys from the neighborhood converted a 4x4 Ford Econoline into a data van with a laminated U-shaped desk, a bench seat for customers, and rows of windows we cut into both sides to watch the unstable wellheads we would be tying into.

Other things ancillary to the trucks, like crushingly expensive $1,300-per-set walkie-talkies and push-to-talk sound-attenuated headsets, were put off as long as possible for no good reason other than that I was nearly broke. The same went for over $100,000 in parts like swages, Chiksans, tees, check valves, a pinch valve, pup joints, suction and discharge hoses, remote pressure gauges, high-pressure grease guns, data-van computers, monitors, and three or four dozen other parts and pieces. All of it had to be bought with cash. But whatever cash I had, I was throwing at the Kanes' hillside. That meant I had to look for credit, but credit is hard to come by in the oil business, and for good reason. Vendors are well-conditioned and hardened to our "down on my luck, gimme a break" implorations. The well-intentioned dreamers among us—guys like me—generally receive a skeptic's first glance from the staid foundrymen who cast our parts.

Without credit, I had to time my purchases, a juggling act all its own. Shale was sucking suppliers dry with enormous, previously unheard-of orders. Their easy money was being tossed around in a torrent of "We don't care what it costs! We need it now!" Enormous frack companies, seemingly born overnight, were buying up future supplies of essential parts and locking conventional guys like me out. Frack iron was absolutely unavailable to me, until I found a guy who made a few calls on my behalf and found a little iron company in Houston with a big heart and a small supply.

Cheaper items, like eight-pound sledgehammers, thirty-six-inch aluminum pipe wrenches, gloves, and general hardware-store stock were bought and stacked up in my office—a meager sign of progress, but something, anyway. Other things normal to a start-up, like logos and stationery, stickers and company-embossed pens, and PPE equipment like hardhats and flame-retardant coveralls, were being accumulated. A payroll account with a processor was opened—better than me screwing up withholdings—and then began the insurance discussions, always the insurance discussions. A website was also needed, which shouldn't have been a farce but was. My web developer, whose day job was handling equipment for the Pittsburgh Steelers, asked for pictures, but since I didn't have any, he wondered if it was okay if he borrowed an image from another company. "Sure, why not?" So, of all places, he grabbed a picture of a Universal Wellhead Services truck off their website, photoshopped it black and blue, and uploaded it to our website. Typical of the rushed confusion at the time, the website went live—and I got a call.

"Clearly, this is one of our trucks," Universal's lawyer started in on me over the phone. "It looks like it's been paint-shopped or something, but this is clearly our truck on your website," said the lawyer from Universal, our soon-to-be-biggest competitor.

"You should be flattered," I told him. "It's your fault. You didn't have such nice-looking equipment, we wouldn't have done it."

After an awkward moment, the lawyer finally spoke up. "You're going to take it down, right?"

"Yep. Right away."

Chapter 35

SPRING 2009

Reno, Pennsylvania, and the Globe

Something had to be done.

Waiting on the trucks, I was starting to have frack nightmares: my subconscious mind untethered and punching up scenarios of more failures, of more shortcomings, of wholly new and unforeseen sets of dread and fear. And I hadn't even started fracking yet. Though frack nightmares were new to me at the time, I didn't know they would last for years.

I needed more money to shovel into the Kanes' furnace. Their third-party work had run out, but the malaise hadn't. We just couldn't get anything done other than run up costs. I had given up on raising money. I'd stopped calling around and chasing down leads, people I knew or sort of knew, who knew someone who knew someone.

I began another round of humiliation, of calling well-heeled people who might have an interest in investing. It didn't go well, given that my pitch sounded too much like a plea. All through it, I'd consult with my older brother Pete, an engineer who had once worked in the oil business, too. Like me, he had ridden along in the same station wagon and listened in on our father and Norby. Thank God for the sympathetic ear of family. Even when there's nothing, sometimes that's enough.

Pointless and embarrassing, all I had left was what Lightspeed was bringing in, which had become less and less as rentals fell off when a housing recession took hold. My sole source of income was collapsing, sucking me inside an imploding global economy that someone somewhere named the Great Recession.

A bank run was on, and big capitulations were coming. Bear Sterns and its outsized share of subprime mortgage loans had already fallen.

Lehman Brothers was next, about to be gored by its $600 billion in debt and a shaky mortgage portfolio four times its shareholder equity. Massive public assistance—bailouts—were being pushed by the Fed, ultimately to be underwritten by the usual suspects, the go-to beasts of burden: us unwitting rubes, the US middle class, the standard-bearer of all bad public policy.

That sentiment was soon enough reinforced by the International Monetary Fund's call that all standards marking a recession had been met in early 2009, not just in the United States but around the entire globe.

Stupidly, all of us in the middle and lower classes had gotten sucked into Wall Street's NINJA loans. Those Wall Street dodgers, though, they just couldn't help their shitty maelstrom of greed.

It was all just so bleak. All of it. Including me. Arcade's and Reliance's burn rates were too much. The mounting costs, the up and down the hill, the clawing and fighting, the leveraging and monetizing of idle assets into low-cost oil production, were crumbling right out from under me.

Unable to stop the conflagration of good capital after bad, unable to disentangle myself from my own edacity, I set out for a reset. I called for a meeting with the Kanes—a real meeting, with a budget and assigned responsibilities—and an end to their "money bags" regard for me. I needed to herd all the cats, set timelines and deadlines, and establish assurances that we'd be ready for the frack trucks, so that in the absence of outside work, we could at least get oil moving as soon as we got them. So I pushed and got my meeting. It would be at our shop, the place I rented that was filled with the Kanes' trucks and gear.

When the morning came, I was prepared with a calendar of hard deadlines, budgets, checklists, points for discussion, training ideas, safety ideas, duty assignments, and the often discussed but never committed-to roles of Wallace and Eli—as in, what exactly would they be doing on frack jobs? They would be selling and supervising, right? But would they also be running trucks?

We gathered in a dark corner of the shop, each of us standing around or leaning on whatever was nearby, because no one in the oil field ever sits.

"I made us up a schedule here," I said as I pulled pieces of paper out of a folder I was carrying. "I laid it out like a calendar."

I passed one to Eli, who took it. And another to Wallace, who didn't. I felt stupid holding it out, so I gave up and laid it on a backhoe bucket, alongside one of Wallace's propped-up and muddy Wellington boots. It was a telling position he had taken, noticeably turned away from me and Eli.

"Here's what I'm thinking," I said. "I'll just read it.... We really need to have all five wells drilled by mid-March. That's in two weeks. Just two weeks away. The cementer will have to follow the rig, so that's going to shave off like three days; so we really have to get those last wells drilled now. Like, right away. Let's see.... Casing. I know you guys have a string or so up there, but we should get the rest of it up there while we're drilling. And we should get all the tubing and rods up there, too, while we're drilling, before we get too far into the thaw, you know?" I asked, glancing up to see if Wallace was paying any attention. He wasn't. His gaze remained straight down, staring a hole into the concrete floor.

"Plus, we gotta get electric in and finish the roads and get all the jacks up there, too, and take some time to learn the trucks once we get them. Jesus, that's a lot to do yet," I said, suddenly sickened by the thought of it all. Saying it aloud just made it all the more overwhelming as I dragged on.

"I'm thinking once we get our trucks, we can set up a test tank with a pinch valve and practice some, maybe a week or so or, you know, whatever you guys think works, maybe right here," I said, indicating the cleared lot outside the shop. "We get some practice on whatever everyone's doing. We need to know what everyone's doing, too, you know? Whatever you think everyone's gonna be doing, who's doing what. And then I'm thinking we head up the hill. But *just once*, you guys. I mean, no one's fault, but all the up-and-down we've been doing, all the damn time it takes? So just once up the hill with the trucks. Just frack one after another and get them all producing. You guys think we could do that?"

No one said anything, leaving my pitifully eager plea exposed.

"So what do you think?" I repeated.

"I think you just said a mouthful," Eli said.

"I know, but we gotta get going, don't you think?"

"Easy for you to say," Eli said, belying some indecipherable unwillingness to get back on the mountaintop.

An outburst of rowdy laughter erupted from the Kanes' crew at the other end of the shop. Someone had just painted someone else green with a paintbrush.

"Cut it the fuck out!" Wallace roared, startling everyone as he abruptly came to life, and just as abruptly slid back into his cantankerous gloom.

The laughter and taunts immediately stopped as our bootless crew returned to work, painting an oil-water separator tank, two of them with brushes and four of them watching.

"We're building the separator," Eli added defensively, partly a mild protest, partly an embarrassed omission, as he pointed at his crew. "That's something, isn't it?"

"It's something. I know. It's just that we got to get things going, don't you think? What about just driving the trucks around, getting them to the location? How many of your guys have CDLs?"

"Some do," Eli replied.

"We gonna have enough drivers? How we going to move them around?"

"Well, I'm not driving them," Eli flatly stated.

"Yeah, you said that. But you mean it?"

"You gonna drive one, then?" Eli asked me.

"I got a CDL. I can."

"No, you better not," he laughed.

I acknowledged him with a shrug and half-hearted smile. "If I got to, I will." I glanced back at my calendar, ridiculously spot-on and entirely disregarded. "Plus, a big thing—we gotta figure out who's doing what. Like who's running what?"

Eli shrugged, like he was used to it. "We'll have to see," he said.

"Yeah. Okay," I said, checking a budding annoyance, a resentment. "And now we got this big data-acquisition system we weren't gonna have. And I don't know a damn thing about it. Any of your guys any good on computers?" I asked.

"Them?" Eli joked. "Maybe video games, but I doubt any-a them're computer geniuses."

"How about one of you two? One of you runs the van. You've got all the experience."

Eli snorted. "I don't know nothin' about computers. I wouldn't even know how to turn one-a them on."

I looked at Wallace, actually at his back, but thought better of asking him.

"Then we have to hire someone for that. I've got nothing in the budget for it. We don't have anything for—I don't know—nothing," I said, altogether disaffected. "You guys got any idea who we could get?"

"Nope," Wallace stated unequivocally, surprising me. Then offered nothing more.

"How about you, Eli? You know anyone?"

"How about you?" Eli asked, challenging me with a stare.

"Me? I don't know what I'm doing, either."

"Don't worry. We'll teach you. Most-a the other operators don't know what they're doing, either."

I let it go. We had gotten too close to the edge of a fight. Another push or two and my partners could turn and walk. I'd bring it up again later, after a reset in everyone's state of mind.

I took a last, defeated look at my calendar. "Last on this, we have enough drivers for bringing the trucks up from Texas?"

"Yep," Eli said. "We got you covered there. They all wanna go."

Chapter 36

TRIBUTE OILFIELD SOLUTIONS

Granbury, Texas

"Come on down, buddy. Let's fire these trucks up," Douglas said when he called to tell me the trucks were done.

"You tested them already?"

"Passed with flying colors."

"You had *them* on your test stand?"

"More'n once, buddy."

Douglas was going for gold, for the shock factor of being the one to end my crusade in one good phone call.

"Bring your crew on down, and we'll fire 'em up. Get you out in the field makin' some money!"

A celebration was in order. Drinks and dinner and "hear, hear" toasts to success should have been first up. I should have called Mary and my partners. We should have been shouting with joy, slapping each other on the back, making big, big plans for a night out. But we didn't. I didn't. That sort of self-congratulatory zeal seemed a bit much, a departure from reality, a bit of poor taste given the FUBAR I had just fumbled my way through. Toasting each other, for what?

What a birdbrained embarrassment, was the real truth.

So, there was no party or after-party, not even a cold beer on the way home. I just started calling people. Wallace first, then Eli, and decided who would go and who wouldn't.

When the day came, four of us packed into a plane in Pittsburgh bound for Dallas–Fort Worth. Flying with me were Ford, Bo—a big, good-hearted kid—and Ken Carson, the mechanic known as Griz.

Of the four of us, only two had ever flown before, and I was the only one who fit in my seat, all three of the others being too big for theirs. Wallace didn't want to fly, so he and his wife Cassie had already started to drive. Eli stayed back, as he said he would, promising to take over if we all crashed and died.

We made it to Fort Worth and warm springtime Texas weather and met up with Wallace and Cassie at the Stockyards. The big longhorn steer out front was corny as hell, but it turned it all around for us. Everyone was happy, a real departure from the last six months. The following morning it only got better when we rolled into Douglas's shop. His place had the look of good manners and fresh, private equity money. I didn't have to apologize to Wallace or the rest of them for any missing walls, trip hazards, or piles of dulled steel rusting away.

The second we arrived, Douglas's office door swung open and out he stepped with Clayton, Lisa, and Zahir, smiling and welcoming us. Everyone got a handshake or a hug, and after twenty years, Douglas and Wallace reconnected.

"Wallace, that you, you ol' son of a gun?"

"How you doin', Douglas?" Wallace grinned under his walrus moustache and ever-present ball cap, genuinely touched to see the man that had built his first frack truck a lifetime ago.

"Couldn't be better, young man. You haven't changed a bit. Lookit you!"

"Ha!" Wallace chortled.

"Been a few years, huh?"

"Does it look it?" Cassie chimed in with a laugh.

"Hasn't changed a lick!" Douglas grinned, as he moved on to introducing his team. I followed by introducing mine, and in no time, everyone was grinning and feeling good as Douglas walked us into his office and guided us to seats around the conference table. A minute later, Lisa and Clayton returned with coffee and bottles of water.

"Whatever happened to that little combo unit I built you, Wallace? That little truck was so tight you couldn't push a stick into it. You 'member that?"

"Oh, yeah. I remember that part pretty well. Caught a lotta jobs with it," Wallace said, obligingly.

"I was awful proud of that truck. Couldn't see a damn bit-a daylight through that thing. You still runnin' that, or you wear it out?"

Wallace kind of shrugged, avoiding Douglas's grin.

"That one got caught in a flood," Cassie finally said, stepping in for her husband.

"A flood? You mean water, like a flood?"

"Yeah, river come up next to our shop," Wallace said.

"Well, that's too bad," Douglas said, as baffled by it as Wallace was abashed.

"Yeah."

"Good truck when it was running, though?"

"Yeah, helluva truck. Never had any problems with that truck."

Jesus, I thought. *So much for our feel-good meeting.* Everyone walked into Douglas's with high spirts, and somehow it had turned into a cautionary tale about neglect and poor truck maintenance. I was about to change the subject when Douglas beat me to it.

"Well, you got some brand-new trucks to replace it, now," he said, striking a chipper tone, then moving on to oil-field gossip as Clayton passed out hard hats and safety glasses.

After letting our collective anxiety build—everyone wanted to see the damn trucks—Douglas finally stood and suggested the obvious. "You all ready to see those trucks?" Our group let out a "hell, yeah!" and immediately was on its feet following Douglas down the hallway and out the shop door.

While waiting my turn, Cassie quietly grabbed my arm and held me back.

"This is really good for all of us, Dan. It's all just, you know, right and, well, I wanted to thank you," Cassie whispered in her warm way. "This is really good for Wallace."

"Yeah, sure, Cassie. Probably good for all of us." I smiled. "Hopefully Wallace likes the trucks."

"Oh, he will. Trust me. It's just what he needs…after everything else."

We caught up to the others on the raised platform, standing above a mostly empty shop absent of all the earlier activity. I didn't call attention to it, instead following the crowd along the broom-clean floor toward the open overhead doors in back.

Framed like a picture was a clear view of our pump and blender—like a calendar shot—the two trucks majestically poised out back on the glaring white caliche ground cover.

"Son of a bitch," Wallace said aloud as I stepped up alongside him. "Those're some good-lookin' trucks."

Fully assembled, massive, and extraordinarily beautiful, the blue, black, and silver metal-flaked paint gave the trucks the look of huge, rolling bruises. They were stout and heavy-shouldered and done. Four-inch rubber hoses ran like tendrils in and out of the blender, and a high-pressure, three-inch, lipstick-red pipe joined the back of the pump to a 20,000-gallon wheelie tank in the distance.

The younger guys couldn't contain themselves and broke away for a quicker and closer look, "oohing" and "ahhing" and shooting questions back at Douglas and Clayton as they ran ahead of our group.

"How many horsepower?"

"What kinda rate you think we can get?"

"I get to go first!"

I stopped alongside Wallace, who had stopped to stare. "It's not a vortex blender," I said. "But it's going to work."

"Don't matter. Long as it pushes water," Wallace said, then walked off without me, leaving me behind with Cassie as he did a slow circle around the trucks.

"Don't think anything about it. It's just his way."

"No problem, Cassie. I don't blame him. I want to take a good look, too."

Ken, our mechanic, was already on top of the blender, poking around and giving it a critical eye. I wanted to see what he thought of it, so I climbed up its side-mounted ladder onto the "party deck." About five feet off the ground, the deck covered the entire truck chassis. On the backside were the mixing tub and pipe-wrapped auger running down into the sand hopper below. The centerpiece of the deck was an air-conditioned operator's cabin, and up front were valve stacks for diverting water, stainless-steel chemical totes, and up by Ken, an oil cooler hanging like a painting from a guardrail.

"What do you think?" I asked him, barely able to contain my pride.

"Too small," Ken harrumphed.

"What's too small?"

"Oil cooler."

"The oil cooler's too small?"

"Hydraulic oil's gonna get too hot."

"Huh? You think I should tell Douglas?"

Ken shrugged. I had no idea whether he was right or wrong, so I let it go.

Then I heard it.

The big Cummins deck engine on the back of the nearby pump truck rolled and caught in a slow-motion firing sequence. Even Ken looked over as the engine idled up into a steady and deep-throated rumble, broken by the tinny clatter of hinged muffler guards popping on top of the exhaust stacks.

Douglas's operator was running the pump at an impromptu test stand. Cheap but good enough, it was nothing but a folding table with two folding chairs and an overhead umbrella. On top of it was our remote box, a stainless-steel suitcase of sorts, controlling the computer that controlled the deck engine and pump. It was set up about a hundred feet off to the side of the pump, far enough away to allow you to get a running start.

"Let's get this show on the road!" Douglas shouted good-naturedly to a man running in.

"Comin', boss. Comin'," shouted the man, joking and passing out earmuffs to everyone at the pump stand. Everyone put them on except

Wallace, who was already half deaf from all his years around oil-field equipment.

"Boss says you gotta wear these," the man shouted as he pulled himself up onto the deck beside me and Ken, handing each of us a set of earmuffs as he stepped into the control cabin. "You all gonna join me?" he smiled through tobacco-stained teeth as he sized up Ken. "I don't know that you'll fit in here, but you're welcome to try."

The man slipped on a radio headset and called out, "Ready here," and immediately began throwing switches and bypass levers on a stainless-steel console that looked like it belonged in an airplane. When he dialed up a rheostat that fed hydraulic horsepower to the suction-side pump, I felt an abrupt and jarring lurch as the impellor inside began spinning and filling the oversized mixing tub in back with a blast of frothing water.

As loud as it was, even with ear protection, I heard the pump truck coming up in the distance and stepped out of the control cabin to watch.

A deep-throated *woof-woof-woof* sounded as its three big chrome plungers began stroking back and forth, punching at the pressure side of the pump like a heavyweight boxer's fist. Their push and pull rocked the pump truck into a back-and-forth sway, becoming more pronounced as the gear-driven torque of the enormous eight-inch-thick driveline picked up speed. In a burst of kinetic energy, it spun into a blur between the transmission and pump, converting 1,500 horsepower into enough pressure to crush a submarine.

Out across the caliche, Ford was sitting in the chair next to the operator. Behind him, Bo leaned in, and back another tier were Wallace, Douglas, and Clayton. Further back were Cassie and Lisa, turned away and trying to talk over the noise.

I grinned at Ken and he grinned back as the blender took off. Kidding around, I made a show of holding on. The operator had engaged the big suction-side centrifugal pump and was throttling up the 400-horsepower, 15-liter road motor. Underneath us, at an intersection of hydraulic hoses, tangles of wiring, piping, and manifolds, a pressurized rush of water pressed through the blender and out to the frack pump through the four-inch hoses that snapped like angry, twisting snakes.

I heard a gear change, then another as the pump operator next to Ford grabbed second, then third on the remote box. With each successive gear and boost in rpms, the decibels reached higher into an ascendance that made me question just how loud it could all get. How soon until the whole damn truck unraveled? What piece of steel, I wondered, would turn into shrapnel and take my head off? Looking for some assurance, I turned to Douglas, watching him for any telltale fear, but he was beaming at Wallace and prodding him with an elbow, as in—how'd ya like that?—getting even Wallace to grin along.

I was thinking we weren't going to blow up until I changed my mind again, as fourth gear came next, and the yawing turned into 72,000 pounds of truck bouncing, which only got worse when Douglas tapped the pump operator on his shoulder and jiggered his thumb upward for even more.

"You gotta be kidding me," I said out loud as the operator obliged him and grabbed the fifth and final gear. A thunderous and stupefying burst of horsepower responded as the engine wound out and the pump took off. Douglas turned to me and Ken and held up two fingers, then three. We had just hit a rate count of 23 barrels—1,000 gallons—per minute against a pinch valve pressure of 3,000 psi. This was him bragging as we passed 95 percent of throttle, then 96, 97, 98 percent. Douglas raised his arm again, this time holding up two fingers, then five. Twenty-five barrels a minute! There we paused, hopefully topped out, with the truck engine screaming a kind of *run-away, you're-gonna-die* scream, like this was all about to turn horribly bad.

Boom!

A sharp metal clang echoed, and a forty-foot geyser of water shot out of the top of the wheelie tank. The pressure had blown the heavy steel tank lid open—as it did on my first trip to Douglas's—causing water to spray up and out and rain back down around us like confetti.

The operator hit instant neutral on the control box, knocking the truck out of gear and letting the geyser fall back to earth. Douglas reached in and hit a red "kill" switch—a doomsday device—strangling all the horsepower and pressure.

What followed was a sudden, though short and vacuous, silence.

And then—

"Whatdya think-a that!" Douglas shouted in a rallying cry. After a few seconds of collecting ourselves, our group finally broke out and matched him in a wildly boisterous howl.

"Whatdya think-a that, Wallace!? Whatdya think-a that?"

"It works!," Wallace laughed. "Really works!"

"Son of a gun pumps, don't it?"

Wallace was nodding in disbelief, while Cassie and Lisa were walking briskly toward the shop, as in *the hell with this.*

"Go ahead, Wallace," Douglas called out, grabbing Wallace's elbow and coaxing him toward the pump stand. "You'll love how smooth it shifts. Not like that son-of-a-bitch lever I put on your old one, remember that? About three feet long!"

"Yeah, I remember that!"

"This one, you just push a little button. Go ahead'n try it out."

Wallace resisted and right away, Ford chimed in. "Yeah. Come on, Dad. You take it," he said as he cleared the seat next to the operator.

"Go ahead," Douglas pleaded. "Have some fun with it, Wallace. Just like a ride at the 'musement park. One big thrill!"

"Nah, let the boys run it," Wallace said, holding up a hand and digging in. "Let 'em have some fun. I'm too old."

"Ha! I bet you could run this in your sleep." Douglas turned from Wallace and looked for another volunteer. His glance landed on me across the way, and he called out, as a kind of afterthought, "How about you, Dan?"

I nodded toward Ford and Bo. "They got it. I need to see how to run this blender."

Douglas didn't protest. He wanted to keep the show going. "Okay, boys, you're up," he said to Ford and Bo. "You two ready to take a shot at this big son of a gun!"

"Hell yeah!" Ford shouted and retook his seat.

Chapter 37

TRIBUTE OILFIELD SOLUTIONS

Granbury, Texas

I'd been up on the blender controls for about an hour when I noticed Zahir and a small entourage coming our way. They converged with Douglas and Wallace in a mix of handshakes and back slaps. It was beginning to look like a party around the test stand, like one I should attend, so I climbed down off the blender and walked over with Ken.

"There you are, Dan," Zahir called out as I approached.

"You all meet Zahir? The genius who built the controls," I announced to my group.

"You're too kind, Dan. Too, too kind, my friend," Zahir beamed. He shook my hand and grabbed my shoulder. "This is Dan," Zahir announced to his group. "Everyone meet Dan. Dan, I'd like you to meet my partners. They came all the way from Oklahoma to meet you."

"They did?" I asked, as I was pushed into the zeal of their outstretched hands and delighted congratulations.

"Gotta feel good about this, Dan," one of them said.

"Those trucks'll be worth their weight in gold," another said.

"Ordering more in no time," the third partner interjected.

"Is now a good time?" Zahir asked, pulling me in. "My partners would like to have that word with you I promised."

Zahir had been promoting his three partners and had promised me a long and mutually rewarding relationship with them. "This will be very good for all of us, Dan," he vowed as the five of us began a stagger-step back toward the shop where a laptop had been set up for us. "My partners and I do more than just computers. We've been talking about your area up in Pennsylvania, and we think we can really help you there."

"What're you running up there? Chemicals, I mean," came one of them.

"Friction reducers and clay control, right?" came another.

"Some iron sequestrant? Little biocide?"

"You running cats or anionics?"

"Cats," I said, short for cationics.

"Good choice. More expensive, but the right choice."

"Dan?" one of Zahir's partners asked.

"Huh?"

"Who you buying your chemicals from?"

"Ah, well, I was thinking Weatherford."

"Weatherford? Well, that sounds expensive. But let me ask: Weatherford ever take you out to dinner?"

"We will," another of them quickly offered.

Off in the distance, the pump wound up again. I turned to watch as a geyser shot up in the air, followed by a spirited outburst at the test stand.

We stopped just inside one of the bays, under the open rolling steel door, where a table was set up with two chairs and a laptop. An ethernet cable had been strung all the way across the lot to the blender, terminating in a CAN dongle, a signal-altering gadget that Zahir plugged into the computer.

"You're going to love this, Dan. I already did some run-throughs, so no surprises here, I can promise you." Zahir said as leaned in and opened a Quantum icon on the screen. "Seriously, this is just the cat's ass. Sooo, sooo smooth."

I took a seat beside Zahir as he navigated through his program. Then, with a bit of flourish, he punched one last key, and we watched as data began importing in second-by-second rolling columns of numbers.

"Jesus," I said out loud, astonished, watching in quiet awe as data loaded and poured down the computer screen in cascading sets of numbers. Sensors onboard the trucks were reconfiguring blunt force into pulses and hertz and transmitting them to the laptop, where they were digitized and sorted into amorphous ribbons of numbers, representing a dozen different functions.

It was all so damned impressive. But more so, it was so damned *confusing*. Our $1.7 million in trucks that had become $2.5 million in trucks, hanging in the balance on the other end of a cheap Radio Shack cable. It didn't even seem plausible until I sat there, agog, watching and so thoroughly relieved.

"You try, Dan," Zahir said, startling me, as he closed his Quantum program. "Try from the beginning."

"I don't know, Zahir, I don't want to screw it up."

"How can you screw up a one-way stream of numbers? Even an idiot can't screw that up."

"Right. Okay. Yeah. An idiot," I laughed. "You gotta show me, though."

Zahir walked me through a few keystrokes and windows—and *voila!*—data started piling up in my page view, numbers clipping by at an update rate of sixty times per minute across twelve different columns. That was over five thousand data points in a typical frack stage for us, tens of thousands per job. It was a mind-boggling mountain of numbers, precipitating into one big lump of confusion.

"How in the hell am I supposed to make sense of all-a this? How do you graph all-a this?" I asked over an escalating rumble of the trucks in the background.

"What's that?" Zahir asked back.

"How do I pull up the graphing function? Is there a tab or something, somewhere?"

"What do you mean?"

"How do we graph this?"

"We are."

"Isn't this a chart?"

"Yes, it's a chart."

"Well, I thought we were going to graph all of this. You know, a squiggly line, like this," I said, drawing an imaginary line in the air.

"You don't want to chart it?"

"We can chart it, fine, but how do you graph it? There another tab or something?"

Zahir didn't answer. He just looked at me, blinking. Was he pulling my chain? Yet nothing in his look suggested that he was.

"We've been talking about a graph all along, haven't we?" I continued. "We've been talking about graphing, right?"

"No, Dan. Charting."

"No, no. Graphing. Every discussion we've had, Zahir—like on an X-Y axis. A graph, like on an X-Y axis. Just like Universal's computer, like we talked about, condensed in like three or four squiggly lines, going like this," I said, chopping at the air, tracing the same imaginary graph line as before, and over-modulating, talking way above the noise of the trucks. "What am I gonna do? Print this out?" I shouted, jabbing my finger at the laptop screen. "It'd be a box full-a—that's a big box full-a—"

"You saying you want a graph? You mean a *graph* graph?"

"Yeah, yeah. We have to graph. A *graph* graph."

"Dan, graphing is very, very complicated," Zahir stated flatly. "A graphing function is much more…ah…tricky. You're talking something very tricky."

"We were talking about graphing all along! You quoted me a graphing—"

"No, we were talking about charting."

"Listen, I know I don't know shit from Shinola, but I can't give this to a customer! How are they going to decode this? It's bewildering, Zahir! They wouldn't know where to start! That's like hundreds of pages. I'm gonna get laughed at!"

"You put it on a thumb drive, Dan! You give it to them on a thumb drive!"

"A fucking *thumb drive*, Zahir?"

"Exactly!" Zahir exclaimed, as though he had just solved it all.

"So, they open a thumb drive, then what? It's still a pile of numbers."

Jesus, Jesus. This bullshitter. This fraud! I thought as I pushed back, knowing I needed to cool off, that arguing with Zahir wasn't going to solve anything. So I sucked in a breath of air and hung onto what self-control I still had, noticing for the first time Cassie and Lisa in the bay next to us, staring blankly back at me on one side and Zahir's entourage smiling like jackals on the other.

"Zahir, tell me. Can you just fix this? Not fix it, I mean add it. A graphing function. Can you add that? Isn't there some software out there that could convert all this to a graph?"

Zahir shrugged. "Well, Dan, you know, anything is...ahh...possible."

"All right. Great. Then let's do that. You think you can do that?"

"I will have to think about this. I would have to see what platform. I'd have to work up a quote."

"What do you mean, a 'quote'?"

"It could be expensive."

"What do you mean, 'expensive'?"

"It can be done, you understand. I'm not saying—the trick is not rewriting everything. Not to start over from scratch."

"Uh-huh," I said, biting my tongue.

"I'd have to talk to my partners. We will work something out that is very fair to you. But, in all honesty, Dan, this is a very unexpected development," Zahir said, in a manner suggesting he was the reasonable one. "Maybe we can work this out. But let me get an answer for you. Just be calm, Dan, and I will be right back."

Zahir rejoined his pack, and the four of them moved off toward an exit in the fence. I kept watching as they huddled around a banged- and beat-up Lexus sedan, glancing back at me over their shoulders, furtively looking for weakness, a wobble, blood—an advantage.

As I waited for their verdict, I turned to Douglas and Bo climbing up onto the blender. Ford was still on the pump, throttling up for another run, seemingly thrilled by it. But Wallace hung back, his big frame distorted by the wiggly optical effect of heat radiating up from the white ground cover. He stood watching, by himself, keeping his distance, interested but lacking interest. Diffident, it appeared.

Oddly, he must have sensed my stare and glanced back, right at me, the two of us locking eyes for just a flashing moment. But it was enough, because right then I knew. That's when I realized Wallace wasn't going to run our equipment. Maybe he'd pick it up later, back home, where he could slip scrutiny and judgment. But I didn't think so.

No doubt Ford would be running the pump. But the blender—as I saw it—was complicated, and now was the time to learn it, but Wallace wasn't learning it. As encouraging as it was to see Bo climbing up on it with Douglas, it was also pointless. Bo had a job elsewhere and wouldn't be sticking around with us. He was there because he could drive and because the Kanes liked him. That was it.

It struck me that there was no mystery as to why I had been left alone with Zahir and his data-acquisition system. No one wanted to get stuck inside the van with the customers and their questions and observations, directions and dictates. So what simpler disqualifier was there than to plead blind ignorance? That's why no one was coming my way. It wasn't due to a lack of interest; it was for self-preservation.

It was a theoretical fallacy, a stumble between a hoped-for outcome and real-world reality. Staying home while the Kanes sold jobs and fracked wells looked now to have been a poorly conceived delirium. I'd be on every job, in the van, on the computer, far from home in a position that normally took years of experience.

And no one bothered telling me. They let me figure it out on my own, in an aha moment in Texas, trapped and without a choice, reserving all my self-inflicted anger for my gullible, dim-witted self and not my crew, who were out on the caliche without a care in the world.

And there wasn't a damn thing I could do about it. I didn't have the money to hire a full-time treater, which right then meant I didn't have a choice. What I thought my life would become had just changed. I'd forever be on the road, suddenly fulfilling Wallace's dream far more than my own. I thought of walking over to Cassie in the next bay. Maybe she'd have some insight into her husband and his plans, but as I stood there looking over, neither she nor Lisa noticed me.

Something was off in the way they were engaged, something about the intensity with which they were holding onto each other's gaze, deep down in a conversation that shut everyone else out. It struck me that I knew what they were talking about, that I knew something about each of them that they were just discovering about each other. Lisa must have been sharing with Cassie her daughter's story, about something so random and unthinkably cruel as HIV having found its way inside her home. And having to accept it because there was nothing less than acceptance. And, surely, Cassie had to have let on about the inconceivably painful shift in life she herself had felt. Something so beautiful as a child—nothing more beautiful—lost in a tragedy too staggeringly disruptive to the whole premise of life. Just too much. Too, too hard. A child in the front yard running to answer a phone call from her friend and getting struck by her brother's motorcycle, being pushed instantly off this earth and living on in shattered memories.

Years later, I met up with a friend, a reservoir engineer who brought along his soon-to-be wife. She told me of growing up in Venango County and going to school with a childhood friend, Wallace and Cassie Kane's "sweet" little daughter. And how it was she who had made that call that day....

The afflicted, Cassie and Lisa, talked and persevered and hid their incomprehensible grief behind benign, everyday smiles. Twenty feet, a world away, I turned back to the computer and simmered about the insignificant and slanted deal I had made.

"Dan!" I heard and turned. It was Zahir, a walking reminder of my new life, approaching with his gang. "Dan, Dan, we have a compromise for you," Zahir said as he closed in. "We talked it over, and since you've been a very good customer, we all think you're going to grow your company and keep us fed for a long, long time."

"We really like what you're doing, Dan," one of Zahir's partners let out.

"I think there's a way to do this," Zahir announced. "There will be a lot of programming work, but it is possible."

"You can fix it?" I asked.

"I can build off the same platform. I think that is very possible."

"Great."

"Of course, now, Dan, this is tricky business and will be very time-consuming," Zahir warned. "Lots of effort, but the best news is we have a one-time deal for you!" Zahir beamed. "To help you out."

"Right," I nodded, bracing myself.

"Just for today. If you can decide today—because we are all here—but if you act today, we can make a better price for you. I had to bend my partners' arms for this price break."

"Come on," one of them laughed. "Not that much."

"Just for our costs though, Dan. No profits. Absolutely not," came another.

"Then how much?" I insisted.

"Normally to get a graphing functioning in the software, we would charge fifty thousand dollars. But if you act today, right now, Dan, we will give it to you for twenty-five thousand."

"Twenty-five thousand dollars," I said so loudly that even Cassie and Lisa looked over.

"The scope of work, Dan! This is a special one-time offer!"

"Twenty-five thousand?"

"Yes. Yes. And that's cheap! For you, cheap! For you, it's a favor!"

"Are you seriously kidding me, Zahir?"

"No. I am making you the deal of a lifetime!"

"Plus, you have to buy your chemicals from us," interjected one of them.

Off in the distance a cheer erupted as another geyser shot up and rained back down on the equipment and crew. When I turned back, there was Zahir and his posse wantonly staring, athirst and starving for cash every bit as much as I was.

Chapter 38
LITTLE RENO LEASE

Venango County, Pennsylvania

The day had come.

My alarm rang at 1:00 in the morning, but I didn't need it. I'd been awake since midnight, though I didn't dare turn the alarm off, my mortal fear being that I'd fall back to sleep after only getting an hour or two of it.

Trying not to wake Mary, I slipped out of bed and peeked outside our bedroom window. Rain on the glass turned the cars parked out front opaque, with uncertain, orangish outlines. Like an Edward Hopper painting, the halogen streetlamps punched holes into the Pittsburgh night, with the shadows left fuzzy from the chilling, distorting rain.

I wasn't moving, because I knew that when I did move, I'd be just as cold and wet as the view out my window. So I stood there in my underwear, hanging onto the security of my bedroom, wondering about the next twenty-four hours and how my first frack job would play out.

"You going to be all right?" Mary asked, startling me. She was still in bed but just as awake as I was and had had as little sleep.

"I'll be fine. I didn't mean to wake you."

"I was up anyway. Don't get hurt, okay?" she said, leaving not much left to discuss.

Thirty minutes later, I was weaving my truck through my dim Shadyside neighborhood. Force of habit had me stopping for traffic lights on the otherwise empty streets. In little time, though, I had my truck straightened out and pointed north on I-79.

All the arrangements had been made, the equipment and materials had already been dragged up the hill. Everything and everyone we needed would be there, except for any real working knowledge of how to run the trucks, given that we didn't have the time to run them once we got back from Texas.

Other than Wallace and Eli, we all sort of knew what to do, but that didn't mean we knew what we were doing. The idea was to take it slow, keep out of trouble, and try to keep anyone from getting hurt. That was as far as we got with the whole abstruse matter of safety. That was what I was wondering about as I made my way north by northeast, driving through the joyless ether of a darkened and indecipherable landscape into Pennsylvania's ancient oil fields.

Eventually, the thruways pinched down to highways and then to a dirt road that ended at our shop. The doors were all wide open and the lights were on, though no one was around, which instantly roused me. All that was inside was our van. We wouldn't be running it on the first job. Too much too soon.

I drove up the hillside behind our shop in a hurry, feeling like I was late even though I was on time. That's the way it is in the oil field, though. Being on time means being an hour early.

Alongside me was the plunging ravine where the road turned steeper. I hit it as fast as my truck and the rain-slickened, mud- and rock-topped road allowed, feeling a few times like I'd gone airborne but needing every bit of momentum I could get. On top of the ridge, I parked on ground that looked hard enough to keep my truck from sinking to the frame, then jumped out into predawn air that felt like a cold, wet slap to the face. As much as I wanted to duck back inside the truck, I didn't. Instead, I pulled on a filthy old sweater, then a hooded sweater, then my rain gear, and finally a pair of steel-toed Muck boots, and started walking into the noise along our freshly laid shale road.

Ahead, the glow from our truck headlights and markers and a light plant burned a white hole in the nighttime sky. It was blinding, walking into that radiating bloom, and then into a wall of sound created by the idling engines and the sharp strikes of steel against steel—sledgehammers smacking hammer unions.

Like a curtain being drawn back, I came through the last stand of trees to the well site. The frack crew was moving slowly through the soup-like mud, their heads down in humorless expressions, dragging their feet like zombies to keep from tripping and falling into some unseen void. They were wearing the same dark green raincoats and pants as I was, though theirs were smeared with mud, which made me feel all the more like I was late.

Across the hollow of mud and steel, I saw Wallace standing inside a tree line next to the pump controls. As I made my way over to him, trying to step over the mud because it was nearly impossible to wade through it, one of the crew ahead collapsed under the weight of his end of an eight-foot-long stick of iron. The rest of the crew cried out in cackles and jeers as the kid folded over into the mud, trying to right himself.

Undeterred, he squatted and pushed up under the unimaginably heavy load, wearing a humiliated grin and starting off again with his partner, lead-footed, toward the wellhead. Once there, their piece of pipe was added to the end of a pipeline that the rest of the crew beat together with sledgehammers. When there was no give left, the pipeline was unceremoniously dropped into the mud and immediately swallowed whole. Then it was on to the next joint, and then the next, as the pipeline of frack iron grew its way from the back of the pump truck to the wellhead, leaving me feeling, for the first time, that our crew wasn't making nearly enough money.

Sucking air from my push through the slop, I got to the pump stand and Wallace. He grunted, his only response to my cheerful greeting, and continued watching over the crew. It had been decided that Ford would share the blender with me for our inaugural job. In his place on the pump would be another kid, a friend of the Kanes who had some past pump experience.

"Couldn't-a picked a better day," Eli said, smiling, when he stopped by. As a punchline, he dipped his head and let rainwater spill off the bill of his ever-present ball cap.

"If the trucks leak, we're never gonna know it," I shot back, thankful for Eli's comradery.

"Maybe five minutes more on water," he said to me, but meant it for Wallace.

"Okay," I said, playing along.

Wallace seemed to nod. I wasn't sure. Whatever it was, though, was good enough for Eli.

"We're pumping all the way up the hill. Couldn't get any head pressure. But we got it now," Eli went on.

"Should be good, right?" I asked.

Eli shrugged. "We'll see."

Eli whistled loudly toward a kid on top of one of the two skid-mounted tanks. Eight feet up in the air, he was filling one of them with a three-inch lay-flat hose. In their unspoken language, the kid held his hand like a knife blade to his chest, three-quarters of the way up his body. Eli was satisfied with the translation, that the tanks had a quarter of the way more to go. He tipped his hat one more time to me, spilling some more rainwater, then disappeared somewhere back into the black mist.

Once he was gone, Wallace's booming voice hit me like a thunderclap.

"Listen," he bellowed. "I don't want to fuck this well up 'cause we got greedy."

"Wha— Huh?" I stammered.

"I don't wanna have to trip pipe 'cause we got greedy on sand. You don't need all-a that sand anyways. Fuck all-a that sand. No more'n fifty sacks a stage. That's it!"

Then I understood. Wallace was referring to one of our previous points of contention. I wanted a bigger frack job, with more sand, "proppant" as it's referred to. More of it correlates to better reservoir drainage. But it comes with risk. Too much, and the formation may sand-off and close up during stimulation. Wallace didn't want that risk. Hog in too much sand, and he'd be stuck flushing the well with his rig. He wanted to play it safe, get in and get out.

"Fifty sacks a stage. That's it," Wallace added, angry over the discussion he'd started.

"You want to see how it goes?" I asked. "We can watch the treating pressure—"

"Fifty sacks. No more'n a pound and a half, maximum. That's it," Wallace declared, then stormed off, effortlessly bulldozing his way through the mud to the rig and his other son, Rusty.

Up on the rig deck, a couple feet above the ground, Rusty and his crew of three were running frack pipe into the well off an enormous traveling block. It was a winch-and-cable system working off a huge drum that Rusty controlled from a console. Together, they were adding one thirty-foot stick at a time to the string hanging down into the eight-hundred-foot hole.

Left alone and feeling stupid for it, I made my way across the sucking mud for the blender. Just as I got there, reaching for the ladder to the raised deck, I tripped and went down, soaking myself in more mud than any of the crew who had actually been working in it. Struggling to right myself, trying to keep my hands out of the mud, trying to go unseen, I missed the rung and went down again. This time my hands caught me and sank out of sight into what had tripped me: the snaking coils of black water hoses pressed down into the mud underneath me.

I pulled myself up the ladder and looked back to see if I had been seen. Maybe not, until I heard Ford above me, glowing under the light in the blender's cabin, laughing and pointing at me and desperately looking for an audience. He was shouting something into his radio, something like "Man down! Dan Down," but dropped it when I stepped inside the cabin alongside him.

"Everything okay?" he asked, still laughing.

"Yeah," I said, meeting him with a smile. "Just trying to fit in."

Ford freed up a little room for me at the one-man console. Before joining him, I purposely made a point of knocking the mud off my boots, a pointless exercise given that it was already everywhere. Worse, Ford paid no attention to me. Anything new about the truck was already gone.

The two of us were to split the functions. Running all of it was too far beyond our individual ability. Ford would take water on both the suction and discharge side, and I'd take chemicals and sand. That put us shoulder to shoulder, sharing the five-foot-wide console full of gauges and dials, rheostats, digital screens with counters, levers, actuators, and a liquid crystal screen resembling something you'd see up front in an airplane.

It was just so damned overwhelming.

From outside came the sharp pierce of a whistle, audible over the baseline roar of the rig and truck engines. It was Rusty up on the rig deck, whirling an index finger around in tight circles over his head. It was time to go. Right away, Ford toggled a lever next to me, engaging the $30,000 splitter box underfoot. The truck shook and water began filling the big tub just outside our rear window. Chemicals and sand came later, so I didn't have anything to do just yet, but I was aware of a fear in me, the same fear I'd known as a kid before my wrestling matches, when my opponent and I would eye each other as the ref's whistle blew, when it was far too late to back out.

Ford keyed his push-to-talk radio. "Got a charge. Pick it up."

I slipped on my headset and right away it was broadcasting. Ford or someone else had already keyed in the channel we were using, a relief because I didn't know how.

"Shove that water right in your ass—" I heard over the radio, then a crackling laugh.

"Get ready. Here it comes. Right up yours. Nice'n cold," Ford shot back as he dialed up the discharge pump and pushed the engine rpms up, shoving water to the pump.

They were all so damn easy about it all, every one of them. I couldn't even remember what exactly I should be doing. I knew the process, but I couldn't remember the procedure. I was shutting down. Where there had been receptors, there was now just vapid air. Nothing was there for my neurotransmitters to run along. I had disconnected. Nothing was getting through.

Surreptitiously, I watched Ford for some sort of clue, for something to jar me, but was only further intimidated, further afield, as I watched him spinning dials like some kind of DJ under the otherworldly, sickly green light in our cabin.

A psychoanalyst might have called it sensory overload. My mom would have told me I just needed a good night's sleep. But my high school wrestling coach, Mr. Pikiewicz, would have cut right to the chase. "Pay attention, meathead! Come on, Doyle. Let's go! Let's go!"

Calm down! I thought. *Calm down…calm down.*

Concealing my panic, I watched the digital counters for rate and volume rise, accompanied by the dull, throaty growl of our engines. Then I watched Ford watching them, like he understood, or was just good at pretending like he understood.

"We gonna treat this water?" he asked loudly, outside his microphone so as not to broadcast it. A moment passed before I realized he was talking to me.

"Treat it?"

"Yeah. You want to run chemicals on the flush?" he asked again.

"Yeah, yeah—no. No. We don't need to on the flush," I answered like a deer in the headlights, but one that managed to jump off the road.

Where'd that come from? I wasn't sure, but it was the right answer. Ford nodded his approval, then turned back to the console. The way he was looking at me, though. It wasn't like he was challenging me. It was him protecting me.

Like a shot, water erupted from the frack pipe thirty feet up in the derrick. Water was suddenly everywhere—raining down on the rig crew and onto the 20-mil plastic liner covering the location.

With a grim delusion, they all found it to be funny, getting soaked with cold well water, a bit of gallows humor for the boys. Something about forty-degree water on a forty-degree day had them revived and grinning and boyishly pushing each other into the cascading water.

We'd been pumping water down the backside annulus of the well. Now, it was returning through the downhole frack pipe all the way to surface, where it was jettisoning out of the "el" on top. What had started as clear water suddenly turned gray, and then black, as gobs of gravel plug-back were swept up off the bottom of the well and then up and out the flush el overhead.

All around, gravel was hitting everything, bouncing off the steel rig deck and pipe boat and off the hard hats of the retreating crew. When the blitz of falling gravel stopped and the water cleared up, Rusty set the brakes on the two-thousand-pound traveling block. Ford and the pump operator shut down their onboard pumps, and the water dropping out of the hanging pipe dribbled to nothing. The crew returned, achromic in their lifeless, mud-drenched green raincoats. In a scrum of backs, shoulders, and arms, the wellhead was replumbed, redirecting our lipstick-red, 15,000-psi-rated frack iron into the pipe leading downhole.

Frack pipe is milled with thick square threads, and each piece connects to the others with heavy, winged collars. Wrenches aren't used to tighten the collars. Extreme and violent percussion is. So, when the hammer man stepped in, everyone else stepped back. Lining up his target like a pool player lining up a shot, he took a huge swing with his sledgehammer, arcing right into the collar. Then another, and another—one blow landing with such reverberating force that it snapped his brand-new Reliance-blue hard hat off his head.

Whack! Whack! Whack! he went, pounding the guts out of the connection, until there was no give left in the threads. As quickly as he came on, he left, dropping his hammer without regard for where it landed and drifting off for a cigarette in the rig's steel-plated doghouse.

Rusty and another crew member jammed a forty-eight-inch pipe wrench onto the hanging frack pipe and gave it a hard twist to set an expanding packer 800 feet below. In the same manner, they dropped the wrench without fanfare or recognition of our moment in time—the completion of the first stage of our very first well.

Through the wash of rain, through the blender windows, I watched the blurry hulks of men moving away from the rig, their forms as foggy as my thinking. The last I saw of them was Rusty spinning his index finger around in the "let's go!" signal as they scattered under a wetted sky that had grown less dark, though not at all bright.

It was time...time to frack.

Chapter 39

LITTLE RENO LEASE—FIRST JOB

Venango County, Pennsylvania

"Bringing it up," Ford called into his walkie, dialing up the motor to a raucous scream, the blender yawing and swaying under us as water rushed through it and into the hoses connecting us to the pump.

Following was a bellowing of horsepower, an absolute roar, as the pump came up and the three big plungers on the back side of it came on. Flashes of chrome punctuated the gloom as they whipped back and forth with enough thrust to rock the 70,000-pound truck. Pressure built and water became supercharged as it was pushed downhole at a climbing rate of speed.

Edgy and spooked, I nervously gazed about, looking for the next bit of trouble. My eyes landed on Wallace, but nothing about him conveyed any sort of misgivings like my own. He was a fixture, standing rock-solid behind the pump operator, unflinching and every bit like Lieutenant Colonel Kilgore on the beach in *Apocalypse Now* as mortar rounds exploded in the sand beside him. Nothing about the thunderous 1,500-horsepower pump in front of him seemed to bother him in the least. He just watched, not missing a thing.

In front of me, the body on our polished-aluminum sand dump began to rise, climbing ten, fifteen, twenty feet into the air as sand hogged out of it into the blender hopper. Nothing about it was any longer theoretical. It was actual and unmistakably happening, all of it bawling at me to ready myself over my half of the blender console, my looped rejoinder, my mind's eye screaming, *Don't screw this up—don't screw this up!*

I nudged the sand rheostat and saw the auger above the tub budge, then spin, and immediately I backed it off. Good. It worked—and that was good enough. Next to me, Ford was working on his side of the console, seemingly unflappable and altogether at home. But he had grown up around this. He was five years old when I saw him running around his dad's frack jobs. This could have been his family living room, for all the calm he showed.

Abruptly, water stopped flowing and the big deck engine caught and bogged down. The well was resisting. The formation was shouldering back, blocking the onslaught of water from above. Our pressure gauges looked to have been shocked, the way they jump-started and pegged into red as the rate crashed from eight barrels a minute to zero. The battle was on between what would break first, our equipment on the surface or the rock formation below.

Something had to explode. Surely something would snap and turn all this energy from potential to kinetic. A fleeting thought I had—*Am I safe?*—passed, and I thought…*maybe.* But the control cabin's aluminum skin wrapped around me was measured in millimeters. It was good at keeping out the rain and dust, but that was it. I'd get it as bad as anyone else. "Pink mist," we called it, back when we talked about this day. "Take your head off!" "Hahaha." "Why would you want to start a frack company? You have a death wish or something?" "Hahaha!"

I caught Wallace coolly keying a thumbs-up at the pump operator. More throttle was added, and then more and more, more than I ever thought we had—over 1,500 hydraulic horsepower shoving itself into the hole. The rate counter laid flat but flashed some indecipherable number, a trickle of water, a ray of hope, then went flat again. If nothing came apart, the expectation was that we'd see a "breakdown," meaning the formation would break and take water. We'd hit the point when pump pressure exceeded rock pressure, when water and frack sand split the formation rock and squeezed out along its bedding planes into the oil and gas waiting there.

2,800 psi. 2,900, 3,000, 3,050 psi…

Wallace motioned for more, and the rate counter ticked up to one barrel per minute (BPM), then settled back to nothing. I kept watching, thinking Wallace would keep pushing, but he slashed his palm instead, signaling "that's enough," and there we held—a foothold—rocking back and forth at 3,300 psi.

A handful of seconds later, like a rubber band snapping, the pressure dropped 500 psi or so, and the rate shot up. It broke! The rock broke! We had a breakdown right at 3,300 psi. Wallace jiggered his thumb up, and the operator came into it with a rush of hydraulic horsepower as the $200,000 pump threw haymakers—*foom-foom-foom*—into the rock face below.

Eight barrels per minute, then 10 BPM, 13 BPM, 16 BPM, with the operator catching one gear after another as he kept pushing with brute, unyielding, kick-the-door-down force. Pressure settled into something around 2,400 psi as the pump and its chromed plungers, three streaks of liquid silver, pushed water downhole at our target rate of 18 BPM—the equivalent of about 800 gallons per minute, expanding out across a horizontal plane in rock a quarter mile down.

My thinking was mush. I was all over the place. Water was flowing, and it needed to be covered with chemicals, but I couldn't get it right. I fumbled with four different chemical knobs, frantically trying to find the right pump rate for each one of them. But I couldn't hit my marks. I was wildly dialing up, then down, in a crazy sine curve of too much and too little as I stumbled along the peripheral edge of incompetence, hardly aware of Ford's elbow poking me in a rapid "let's go" rush of jabs. He was saying something, something in a quick, staccato fashion, repeating it over and over. I was staring blankly back at him, trying to decipher, hearing but not understanding.

"Sand! Sand! Sand!" Ford was shouting.

Yes, of course. Sand. I should start sand.

"We got fifteen barrels in! We went past it ten barrels ago. You gotta get the sand!"

The sand! Damn! Dammit! I hit the rheostat that controlled the auger, the part that carried sand from the hopper below to the mixing tub above, but got nothing. It was stuck. Nothing! For God's sake, how?

I turned it up all the way, into the red, pegging it at wide-open, but still got nothing. In a wild panic, and for no good reason, I spun the rheostat all the other way to zero, then turned it all the way back up. Something about that woke up the auger and made it turn. But even with it turning, there was still no sand. I rushed out the cabin's side door and looked down into the hopper. It was full of sand from the big sand dump, but there was still no sand making its way to the mixing tub above. The two crew guys running sand below peered up and threw me a thumbs-up, but even with their assurances, there was still no sand.

Suddenly, without warning, it was everywhere. Sand was belching out of the spinning auger and into the water-filled tub, to the point of locking up the mixing paddles inside. *How the hell!* I jumped back into the blender and spun the dial back to zero and the sand stopped. I looked up at Ford. He'd caught it all, me and my foolery, watching me out of his left-side eye, his calm manner poles apart from my artless, flailing rush of madness.

But my biggest worry right then wasn't sand. It was Wallace. What if it all got back to him?

Calm down. Calm down, I thought. *Screw Wallace. Get ahold of yourself.*

I got the auger turning again and found something close enough to my target of a half pound of sand to every gallon of water. Earlier, fortuitously, I had made up a cheat sheet. I read through it and saw that I had another twenty barrels of water to go before sand hit bottom. When it did, I'd dial up another half pound of sand to the mix, and twenty barrels after that, another half pound. Incrementally, you add more sand per gallon as the fracture develops. But for the moment, for about a minute, I'd have a break. I'd clear my head and regroup.

I never got the chance, not with Ford elbowing me again.

"Where's your chemicals? You didn't start none-a your chemicals!" he shouted.

Chemicals! My God. My God. I forgot!

I raced through the four chemical pump rheostats. Instantly they all took off at different speeds, right past where they should have been. I adjusted each back by half, but all my rates and ratios and volumes were wrong. I was all over the place, trying to find my marks, and in no time missed my twenty-barrel sand mark again.

Shit!

I jumped to sand and dialed it up, then down and up again, until I hit a pound and a half—right where it would stay for the rest of the job. Then I shot back to sorting out my chemical runs, embarrassed and sneaking a sidelong glance at Ford. He didn't say anything, so neither did I. But how was it that on his side of the blender everything was so damned spot-on? How? Was he screwing up and I was missing it? Or had he known what he was doing all along? How?

Five minutes later, with five thousand pounds of sand in, and a mish-mash of chemicals pumped, Ford called out over the radio, "Sand's in."

I cut sand, not daring to run more of it, as I had wanted, and as Wallace had warned against. Not after my performance. No way.

A minute after that, after twenty barrels of clean water were pushed in behind the sand-laden water, I dialed out all the chemicals and called the job.

"Shut it down! Shut it down! Stage's in. First one down!" Ford called into his mic.

He killed the suction-side water and pulled back on the throttle, bringing the roar of the blender motor down with it. The pump's big diesel dropped off, too, leaving behind a sudden and sedative quiet, something stunningly peaceful even with the engines at a loud idle.

It was over.

We had fracked our first stage.

No one was dead or hurt, and our equipment was still standing. But it was ugly, and Ford was already out of the cabin, down the ladder, and heading off somewhere, maybe to his father to rat out me and my dismal performance.

No rest for the weary, a sideways geyser erupted in a *whoosh*, shaking me from my momentary calm. It was Rusty, Ford's brother, out by the wellhead, releasing an in-line valve with a long steel rod and jumping back. Pressurized frack water was shooting out into a backstopped pit and exploding into the graying sky. It was astounding, unleashing the force of pressure, but when I looked around, it seemed to mean nothing to the rest of crew. Gathered in the wings, they waited in boredom for the eruption to trickle away into a static, atmospheric balance. With the pipe and wellhead deenergized, they swarmed back to the rig, and assholes to elbows, replumbed the frack iron with sledgehammers and grit. When they finished, Rusty whistled and spun his finger for water. A moment later, his older brother Ford boomed up into the doghouse alongside me and engaged the suction and discharge pumps.

"Got a charge," he called into his walkie as the blender shook and began pushing water to the pump truck.

There had been no time, no spare time at all, to think through what had just happened. I was still transferring numbers from the digital gauges onto an old waterproof field notebook I had from my college geology days, a cheap substitute for not bringing the data van and its computer. But then, hardly a breath later, we were flushing down to the next frack stage. Water and gravel plug-back were spouting out of the flush el thirty feet up in the derrick and raining down in a torrent onto Rusty and the crew. Lowering the traveling block and frack pipe six feet deeper into the hole to the next stage had them all sopping wet and freezing cold. Their horsing around, I noticed, looked to have come to an end.

"Gonna run outta water next time, we don't get sand started sooner," came Wallace's voice as he barged into the cab right behind me.

He was looking at Ford, but it was meant for me.

"Yeah, I gotta get the hang of it," I admitted, stumbling. "I'll get the auger set this time, so there's sand, you know, as soon as I turn it up..." I shamefully trailed off.

I was thinking he was about to critique my chemical delivery, too, until Eli appeared atop the blender ladder and called out from the rain.

"Whatdya think-a that? Truck's got some power," he grinned.

"Yeah. Worked pretty good," I said, pretending to wipe sweat from my brow.

Eli dropped out of sight, and after an intentional pause, Wallace left as well, silently leaving me and Ford behind.

Not wanting to hold us up again, I finished transferring the stage totals to my notebook. The digital numbers would be wiped away on a reset for the next stage, so I had to rush. But something was wrong. I was checking and rechecking, working through simple subtraction. But still, my totals were wrong. Wildly wrong. It had to be me, though. With the muddy condition of all my thoughts, it had to be me. Yet every time, the numbers came out the same. We should have run about 125 barrels of water on the stage, but our gauges showed nearly four times as much.

"You zero out the suction side before we started?" I asked Ford, pointing to the suction-side totalizer, speaking up over the engine noise. "This right?"

"What's that?"

"It's what the computer said we pumped last stage. It's kinda high, though, isn't it?"

Ford looked. "Huh." He shrugged. "Shouldn't be that high."

"No. You reset it?" I asked. "Before we fracked the last stage?"

"Probably. I don't know. Maybe I didn't."

"No big deal. I gotta turn it in to the state, for the completion report. But it's showing like four times more water than we pumped, than I think we pumped. Maybe from all that flush. I can fix it."

Ford shrugged. "I'll reset it this time."

"Yeah. We don't even have that much water in the tanks."

I keyed my walkie and asked the tank man to check the levels of the two tanks. He held a hand to his throat, signaling that the first tank was full, then made an ill-conceived leap to the adjacent tank. Nearly skidding off its long cylindrical top in his muddy boots, he caught himself just in time. Regaining his balance, he gauged the tank with a look and cut a hand across his chest, marking it as three-quarters of the way full. That made for 400 barrels on hand, a solid starting point.

I heard a sharp whistle and looked up to see Rusty twirling a finger and clearing the wellhead with his crew. It was time to go. Already. Again.

"You ready this time?" Ford asked as a put-down, but he said it with a smile so maybe it was only partly a put-down.

"God willing," I smiled back, in a self-depreciating way.

"Zeroing it out," he added, making a point as he reset the suction- and discharge-side volume totalizers. I nodded, and we were off as he dialed up the big suction- and discharge-side centrifugal pumps, packing their volutes with pressurized water.

"Got a charge," he called into his walkie.

And up roared the already deafening pump truck as it came online, making it impossible to hear anything else but the pump. A half minute in and the pressure gauges bounced up as the hole loaded with water and fought back. Resistance was met with more horsepower in a battle of wills—1,000 psi, 2,000 psi, 2,800 psi—until the formation broke and the pressure dropped, and the engine revved a multitude higher, with the pump operator throttling up through each successive gear. In just a dozen seconds or so, fluid was racing downhole at our targeted rate of 800 gallons per minute through the three-inch frack iron.

This time I'd be ready. I had preloaded the auger with sand so that it was poised and ready to drop. I was doing a little better with chemicals this time, too. Each of the control knobs had its own learning curve, all of them so damn touchy and calibrated so wildly different from the others. But I was getting there.

At fifteen barrels in, right on cue, I started dribbling in sand at a half a pound per gallon. Twenty more barrels and it would hit the formation face below. When the rock face took it, I increased the sand to one pound per gallon and started another countdown to my next density change. That came and went, and I was at a pound and a half per gallon and growing more confident. Wallace wanted me to leave it there, but a higher density of sand required less water and had a better effect on a well's performance. So did more sand, more than Wallace's five-thousand-pound limit.

I shouldn't have, but I did. I worked my rheostat up toward two pounds and kind of grinned when I caught Ford's glance. Half a minute later, when the higher density hit the formation face, nothing happened. The well took it.

It was bullshit of me, though. I should have made a bigger stand against Wallace up front instead of sneaking it in. But he was right about one thing: A spike in instantaneous pressure, caused by stuffing the formation face with too much sand, could create a bomb. Pressure had to go somewhere, and that would be straight up. Pipe would be pushed right out of the well and over the rig like a rocket launching. That's the way it was when fracking open-hole wells like ours. In a few years, I'd be on a few wells like that, where heavy-walled pipe backed up out of the hole, hit the surface, and twisted like licorice sticks.

Then I felt something behind me. I looked back, fearing it was Wallace, and it was indeed Wallace, standing right there with his considerable bad-ass kind of presence, glaring at my gauges.

Aww, no, is all that registered. I wondered if Ford had signaled him over, or if it was just plain bad luck. He'd see my sand concentration and would come unhinged. Or maybe he'd just stepped into the cabin to say hi. Hah! Doubtful. But then, with some good luck and bad, there was a sudden noise—*clang!*—followed by a rasping, a shearing of steel. Everyone's attention shifted to the pump truck as its rear end jarred upward off its axle springs like some sort of mechanical hiccup, then settled back down and continued pumping.

"Might-a picked up somethin' in the water," Wallace said dismissively over all the engine noise.

Yet Wallace kept staring, maybe knowing something that we didn't. Without another word, he stepped out of the cabin and disappeared somewhere into the frack job.

I turned back to the controls. The digital sand counter was already up to 5,200 pounds in. I had overshot my 5,000-pound limit, as I had intended. I let it run—5,300, 5,400—then at 5,500 pounds in, I felt Ford elbowing me. A few sacks later I shut it down.

"Sand's in," I called into my walkie.

Nothing more was said. Maybe Ford agreed with me. I don't know. He didn't say. But the well took it just fine, and we continued with water only until the flush was in.

"Shut down. That's two down, five to go!" Ford called into his walkie. The blender and frack pump dropped out, and both Ford and I pulled off our headsets and set them on the console.

"I'll check on water," I told him.

"You do that," Ford said and dropped away out of sight, surely on the way to his father.

I slid down the blender ladder after him and landed in mud halfway up to my knees. Each step felt like rubber bands were attached to my boots as I cut off on my own and made my way to the water tanks across the location. Wanting to see the levels for myself, I pulled myself up the steel-runged ladder to the top of one of them. It was half full, so I jumped to the top of the second tank and went down—hard. All that saved me from an eight-foot fall was my knee driving into the open tank lid and stopping me. Christ, it hurt, but no one seemed to notice, which would have been far worse than hitting the ground. Shaking it off, I looked inside the second tank. It was also little more than half full.

Back at the blender, I called up an old equation, one that converted spherical volumes into gallons—$\pi r^2 d \times 7.48$ gallons $\div$ 4—and came up with 150 barrels of water pumped during the stage, right about where I should be. But Zahir's digital controls read 525.

How the hell? How were we so far off? What about everything else? The chemicals? The sand? Were they out of calibration, too? But the sand, the sand holds the fractures open. How much sand were we even throwing?

Recklessly, I slid down the blender ladder and made my way to the dump's hydraulic controls. I dropped the bed and crawled up along it to the hatches. Lifting one of them, I looked inside and did a quick estimate.

We had used about 20 percent of the bed's capacity on the first stage. That made the sand count right, maybe the chemicals, too, but not the water.

I slid off the dump, smearing the wet mirror-glaze finish with mud and hating myself for it. But I kept going, thinking I needed to get to Wallace, to explain why I did what I did and try to get his blessing to continue. I thought he might be on the rig and found him there with Rusty. Something about his demeanor, though, his turned-away posture, made me hesitate and hang back. I waited off to the side for a few awkward minutes until he started back in my direction.

"You think we picked up something in the water back there? The way the pump jumped?" I asked Wallace, a benign beginning to explaining my overbaking the sand run and the possibility of the sand count being wrong.

He never stopped to answer. He just pushed past me like a force of nature, effortlessly plowing through the soupy ground in boots big enough to waterski on.

So there it was. The silent treatment.

Five minutes later, the rig crew dropped their hammers and headed for their cigarettes and Cokes. I was already up in the blender at the control console when Ford swung in alongside me. Like his father, he had nothing to say.

"Charging water," he said into his walkie.

The relative quiet was shoved away as the blender and pump came on. Stage three was underway, and my earlier panic was moderating with familiarity. Sand and chemicals were running, and I was all over the knobs, still messy, but I was tightening up the sine curve of too much or too little—and of what I was starting to think wasn't just me. It was in the hydraulic controls, too. Or something in their design.

After twenty barrels in, I took sand to a pound. After another twenty, to a pound and a half. In another minute, after another twenty barrels in, I kept it right there, doing as I was told, rethinking my aggressiveness. I'd get back in good stead with Wallace and Ford instead of running off in my own direction. I'd behave.

Then all hell broke loose.

Sounding like a cement mixer spinning out of control, breaking out above the engines in a metal-striking-metal grind—*tat-tat-tat-tat-bang!*—all six tons of the big triplex pump began bucking up and down in a harsh obliteration, a screeching cacophony, a ruinously expensive, horrid noise.

"Shut it down! Shut it down!" the pump operator screamed over the walkie as he throttled down the pump.

As soon as he did, the tub on the blender began backing up before Ford killed it, instead shouting at me to dial out the sand and chemicals. I did, and we both ran out of the cabin onto the deck for a better look.

Eli and Ken Carson were rushing in, too, Ken in his fluorescent hunter's cap, with all hell breaking loose around them.

"*Goddammit! Keep pumpin'! Keep pumpin'!*" Wallace shouted as he marched across the site toward me and Ford.

"I shut it down!" Ford shouted back.

"Bullshit! Keep pumpin'! Who said to stop pumpin'?"

Rusty rushed onto the location for the in-line release valve, ready to relieve the pressure with the steel rod he'd picked up along the way. Just as he was about to release the pressure—

"What the fuck'r you doin'?" his dad shouted.

"I was gonna blow it off!"

"The fuck you are! Keep pumpin'! Clear the sand outta that well. Fuckin' snakebit, broke-down, piece-a shit. Keep pumpin' the job!"

Ford, Rusty, and I stood motionless. Slack-jawed still.

"Let's go or I'm gonna pump this motherfucker myself!" Wallace rushed the pump operator, who immediately started throttling up as everyone else ran about in a goat rodeo of confusion, all built on a filial fear of Wallace.

Ford grabbed my arm. "We better go," he stated flatly as he started back to the cabin with me.

"You think that's smart?" I asked, so far outside of understanding anything about any of it.

"You wanna tell him?" Ford shot back.

"Just clear the sand outta the pipe. First gear only!" Wallace bellowed over the trucks. Then he caught my eye from across the location and pointed right at me. *"No more fuckin' sand!"*

I held up a hand in acknowledgment. No sand. Promise.

Ford engaged the blender pumps, pushing water out to the frack truck. The operator grabbed a gear, then another, then ran into a wall—a sharp *clang-clang-clang.*

Down below, Eli had stopped near the tanks, hanging back, knowing better than to get anywhere near them. The rest of the crew was filling in behind him, all of them on cautious footing, staring as though gazing into fire.

Then I saw Wallace coming my way, his presence worse than the pump truck disintegrating. He'd put it on me, the extra sand, the higher ratio. But that was before, on the second stage. This time I wasn't. He didn't know that yet, that this time I was running it his way. For Christ's sake, though, there he was, coming right up the tiny ladder and into the cabin with enough force to knock both me and Ford over.

"What's your rate?" he demanded from Ford.

"Like seven barrels, Dad," Ford answered defensively, shifting into me, away from his father.

"Radio that asshole and tell him to take it to ten," shot Wallace, referring to the hapless kid on the pump controls.

"*Take it up to ten barrels!*" Ford shouted into his walkie.

The pump truck responded on the rate gauges, but I couldn't hear its engine, not over the obliteration taking place inside it, the *incurable grinding* that had overtaken the job site.

"What's the pressure?" Wallace demanded from Ford.

"Twelve hundred pounds. Ten barrels a minute."

"Keep it goin'. Jesus Christ, this is bad. This is fuckin' bad!"

Then, unfortunately, he turned to me.

"No sand!"

"Nope, no sand. Just chemicals. Just treating the water."

"Why the fuck would you do that? It'll never hit the goddamn formation."

"I'll kill it. You're right," I admitted and dialed out all the chemicals.

"How much until clean water hits bottom?" Wallace asked Ford.

"About fifteen barrels."

"How much you got in?"

Ford looked at me, hoping I knew. I drew a blank. Not with the computer problem.

"I don't know," I answered for him. "It's hard to—I think the rate is right, but the totals are screwed up."

"You don't know how much you got in?" Wallace bellowed.

"Maybe five barrels, based on how long—"

"Jesus Christ!" Wallace spit in disgust, then turned to Ford. "Run it for a minute. It'll clean up by then."

Then we waited. Whatever damage we had done during the job was only getting worse as Wallace continued directing the flush. *Clang-clang-clang.* It had me shuddering, but I went along with it, too bewilderingly stupefied to do anything but keep feeding more water to the pump, like drugs into a dying junkie.

In a small moment of clarity, during the minute we spent destroying whatever was left of the pump, I did wonder what the hell we were doing. Why? I knew that the settling frack sand could stick the packer, and to free up a stuck packer you might have to run a narrow flush pipe down inside the frack pipe. But that was maybe a half day's work. Maybe $1,000, $2,000 tops on a third-party job.

Instead, we were risking a $200,000 pump?

"Shut it down!" Wallace bellowed, and instantly Ford called it, and the blender and pump went dead quiet.

Down on the location, Rusty ran in and threw open the backflow valve. The well burped then trickled off to nothing. It didn't blast out across the location. It just fell flat.

Wallace turned to me, and I waited for it. But when nothing came out of him, nothing but a glowering silence, I hesitantly, stupidly asked, "What do you think?"

Instead of answering, he bounded out onto the blender deck, up over the crew that was approaching the pump as though in a procession.

"Rack up that iron and hoses," he barked, "then get these snakebit hunks-a junk off my goddamn mountain. *Right fuckin' now!*"

Wallace slid down the blender ladder and started on a crash course for the gathering of drab olive-green raincoats. They jumped the hell out of his way, clearing a path as he blew right through the middle of them and kept going, to where I didn't know.

In a hurry, I slid down off the blender and rushed for the back of the pump.

Eli and Ken were already there with a handful of wrenches and sockets, Ken tentatively feeling it with his fingertips when I ran in.

"What do you think?" I asked when I got there.

"Hot," he said as he fitted a socket to one of the five-eighths-inch bolts circling a small inspection plate that he began ratcheting out.

"You think we trashed it?"

He grunted something indecipherable. I didn't understand, but I stopped myself from asking again. I'd sound desperate if I pushed it, more desperate than I was, so I waited, just like Eli was waiting, quietly watching as Ken ran the bolt out.

"Really, really hot," he said when it was clear, bouncing it in his palm like a hot potato before tossing it to me. "Here. Careful," he warned as it landed in my palm.

Instantly, I was tossing it up and down to keep from burning myself. "Jesus, that's hot!"

Eli grimaced. He didn't need to say anything.

"I mean, it's kinda hot, but it's not *too* hot," I offered, trying to sell the idea that the pump was just fine. "Maybe it's not so torn up?"

Ken let out a kind of guffaw. That was it. A foot taller than me, he stared down at my hopefulness through a beard that covered most of his face and all of his expression. It didn't matter. His perpetual poker face didn't hide anything. I knew from his and Eli's silence that it was bad, especially after Ken unbolted it and billows of blue-tinted black smoke rolled out of the opening.

"Smell that?" Ken said.

It was hard not to. Everything suddenly stank of burnt oil.

Eli and I stepped in a little closer, haltingly staring at what I was beginning to see as tens upon tens of thousands of dollars burning up inside.

"Jesus Christ Almighty! That's got a lotta heat!" boomed a voice behind us.

I spun around to Wallace and the whole crew bravely filling in behind him, rubbernecking for a better look into the dark hole exhausting black smoke and all hope.

"What happened?" someone in back imprudently asked.

"It broke," another of them jeered.

"Yeah, ya dumbass."

"Maybe it's just taking a break."

"Hahaha!"

"Yeah, 'a break'! A break!"

"It's just havin' a smoke."

"A smoke! Hahaha!"

"Will you all shut the fuck up?" Wallace shouted, having lost some of his earlier vigor, as curious now as the rest of us.

Ken dipped a box wrench into the inspection port and held it up for a look.

"Brass," he said, examining the small specks of bright gold immersed in the blackened oil.

Eli smeared a finger across the smoking wrench. "Bearing."

"All of 'em, I'd say," Ken responded.

"Well, that's that. We're done," Wallace said.

"Can we fix it? I mean us? Right here?" I earnestly asked Ken.

"Humph! It's more than bearings. Probably lost your bull gears, too."

“How bad’s that?”

Ken shrugged. “Probably the pinion, too, if the bull gears went. That kinda heat, the pinion would go.”

He pulled a small flashlight out of his pocket and rose to peer inside through the smoke.

“What do you see?” I asked.

“I can see broken off teeth on your one bull gear. That gear’s shot.”

“What else?”

Ken took a while to answer. “The whole damn pump,” he said resignedly, as though he didn’t want to say it aloud.

The crew stopped their horsing around, mostly watching me, curious to see what I’d do and how far a meltdown might take me. I could see it in their expectant stares, but I knew better.

“Let’s go,” Wallace quietly said to the crew. “We all seen it. Let’s just get outta here.”

Wallace turned back to the pump and me. “Maybe you should call Douglas,” he suggested, the empathy in his voice surprising me.

“Yeah. I’ll call Douglas. Yeah.”

Chapter 40

THE TRIPLEX PUMP

Venango County, Pennsylvania

"Looky! Oil!"

I looked up from the blender deck. Out by the rig one of the crew was excitedly pointing at a skim of crude on the flush pit.

"Oil!" he shouted again, dipping his fingers into the pit and rubbing them together for me to see.

I didn't bother going down to have a look. I just smiled back at his hopeful grin, feeling too gut-punched to move. No one else bothered to join him. No one wanted to take a slog through the mud to see what they'd seen before. No one cared, not in the tireless rain and the ground fog wrapping around and smothering us.

With just a single bar of reception showing on my phone, I stepped into the quiet of the blender cabin and called Tribute. Right away, Lisa was on the phone, excitedly asking about the trucks and whether we'd given them a whirl just yet.

"Yeah, Lisa. That's what we're up to right now."

"Are you lovin' 'em, Dan?"

"Yeah, love them, Lisa. Beautiful trucks. Really beautiful. Listen, sorry, but I'm a little worried about losing signal up here. Any chance Douglas is there?"

Always gracious, letting my slight pass, Lisa patched me through to Douglas. Immediately, I told him of our troubles, explaining things as best as I could.

"What it sound like?" he asked.

"Like banging. Bang, bang, clang, you know? Loud. Really loud. Like something was breaking up inside. The whole back of the truck was snapping around."

"Was it smoking?

"Yeah, when we opened it up it was—through the inspection port. It was hot, like *hot* hot. The one bull gear was missing a tooth, maybe teeth. I could only see the one."

"What was your rate when it come apart?"

"About twenty barrels—at the end, when it was really getting bad."

"You shut it down right away, soon as you heard it?"

I paused. "Not really..."

"Not really?"

"Wallace didn't want to have to flush the hole...to clean up the sand in the well."

"He didn't?"

"Uh-uh," I said, leaving it at that.

Douglas went tip-lipped too, uncharacteristically so. After a long and thoughtful pause, he finally spoke. "Well, Dan, I hate to tell you, but it sounds like you got yourself a catastrophic failure."

"A what?"

"Catastrophic failure. In your pump. Missing teeth, bearings, all that smoke."

"How's that happen?"

"Usually, it means somethin' got screwed up. Sometimes it's operator error. Sometimes it's the pump. Your case, I'd say...well, Dan, I'd say it sounds like both."

"You mean, like, as in it's ruined—it might be *ruined*?"

"Doesn't sound good. Bring it down an' we'll get right into it. Maybe we'll get lucky."

"You think you can fix it?"

"I don't know about that, but I can tell you what's wrong with it. Gardner Denver's not too far up the road. We'll call 'em down if we got to an' see what they think, see if they'll cover it."

"You think they will?"

"Gardner Denver? You never know."

"Well, what do you think?" I kept on, clinging to hope.

"What do I think? I think you kept pumpin' it when it was comin' apart. So, I think probably not."

Our conversation ran redundant, with me looking for hope and Douglas offering little of it. When it ran dry, I promised I'd call him back with our plans. Then I hung up.

Two-hundred-thousand-dollar pump…

Catastrophic failure…

First well… Lost revenues… And another trip down the hillside hooked to 'dozers and a clock.

I stepped out onto the blender deck and quietly watched as the crew sucked the iron and hoses up out of the mud. There was no more engine noise, just a few sharp hammer strikes, and a few distant spring crows.

I'd go down and help rack up, but not just yet. Because when I dropped to the ground, I'd have to come across with composure. I'd have to be reasonable and measured. I'd have to act like a boss and feign a stern resolve. If I didn't, whatever thin and irretrievable line of respect I had would break.

A few hours later, after picking up and moving off location, Wallace, Eli, Ken, and I gathered on the ridge above the descending shale road, watching a bulldozer winch the pump truck down the steep lease road.

"There's a pretty goddamn good chance Douglas didn't set it right. Maybe he screwed up the plumbin' on it or some other pissin' thing," Wallace said in a slow burn. "You think you can call 'em, those guys at Gardner Denver that sold you the pump? We should call 'em an' see what they say before we send it down there, jus' so Douglas can't cover up somethin' or another."

"Yeah, I'll call them."

"Maybe we see if they'll look at it. They're right in the same town, so why wouldn't they? An' see what they say 'bout his 'operator error' number. That really what that son of a bitch said, he really say 'operator error'?"

"Yeah—"

"Bullshit!"

"Yeah."

"You gonna call Gardner Denver?"

"Yeah, I'll call them."

Chapter 41

RENO SHOP

Venango County, Pennsylvania

I called Gardner Denver and found an engineer there by the name of Paul. He said the same thing Douglas had.

"Bring it down."

I said I might, and we left it at that.

I had called from our shop, where I'd been waiting for the last hour. Wallace and Eli had promised they'd be right back but hadn't returned, and that left me alone without any tools to tear into the pump myself.

When I heard a truck approaching, I ran out of the building to meet it. It wasn't them, though. It was Ken.

"Should we open it up or wait on Wallace and Eli?" I asked as he walked into the shop.

Ken harrumphed, an uninterpretable grunt, and kept going. I followed along, the lap dog looking for a friend.

"You need a hand? I can give you a hand."

He ignored me, looking instead over the pump's cover. About two feet wide by three feet tall, it was big enough to crawl into.

"Whatdya think?" I asked.

"Seein' what tools I need."

"Yeah. Nothing much laying around here."

Ken said nothing in return as he started for the door, with me following along on his heels.

"You going to get tools?"

"Gotta let the dog out."

I thought he was kidding. But he wasn't.

"You want me to go let the dog out for you? You could get started, if, you know, you wanna—"

"Dog won't like you."

"Dog won't like me?" I laughed. "Why not?"

"Dog don't like nobody but me." Ken started for his truck. "I'll be back."

"I'll wait for you."

"I'm all right. You want, I can call you."

"You sure?"

"I'll be fine," Ken said in a way that made me think he wanted to be left alone.

"'Cause I don't mind."

"Gonna be awhile. Dog likes to take a walk, too."

I bit my lip, but I understood. The pecking order was dog first. Got it.

As much as I wanted to open the pump, I needed to get back to my office, too. This was going to be expensive, whatever way it went. Maybe ruinously so. It was either give up and surrender, or find more money to stuff into the insatiable maw of Reliance Well Services—the boundless furnace, the conflagration of overreach and dreams.

Ken and I exchanged phone numbers for the first time, and I left with the promise that he'd call me once he backed out the two dozen heavy bolts holding the pump cover in place, right after he fed the dog. He also wanted the engineer's number at Gardner Denver, a call I wanted to be on, but thought I'd better not push it.

It was dark by the time I made it to my Pittsburgh office. With all the prostitutes, pimps, and petty thieves in the nighttime neighborhood, I was relieved to see my next-door neighbor James's lights on. Having come across the southern border all the way from Nigeria, he knew about trouble and would watch out for me.

I got inside without any problems and slipped into my office behind my computer. First up was looking for whiffs of money in Lightspeed's receivables. There wasn't much, nothing to overcome the estimated oil sales I had anticipated from our first oil well. There would be none of those sales, maybe forever, depending on what Ken had to say.

Last ditch was looking for money in my mail. Looking for checks, I opened the accumulated stack of envelopes, and of course found none. There was a letter from my lawyers at Crowe & Dunleavy in Tulsa, though, maybe good news on our recovery efforts from STIM and Andy. "Only a matter of time," went the puffed-up pitch when I paid their retainer. But when I opened it, standing up to read it in anticipation of something possibly good, it was only a bill with a legal document tucked inside.

Ten seconds of reading and I understood. It was a notice. Andy and his wholly owned STIM SOLUTIONS had just filed for bankruptcy protection.

No recovery there.

I sat in self-pity until my phone rang. It was Ken. In earlier days, hope would have had me wishing for a blessing. Nowadays, I sat and readied myself for the next kick in the nuts.

"Rod bearings are burned up," he reported. "Teeth on your bull gears are burnt black. That's the ones that're left."

"Pretty bad, huh?" I asked.

"You can replace that."

"So, not so bad? Some new parts?" I said, tricking myself into finding hope.

"It's what happened after."

"What do you mean? What happened after?"

"Took the crank out."

"The crank?"

"Yep."

"All shit, huh?"

"You can feel the gouges in it. Engineer down there had me feel it for any damage."

"You talked to Paul?"

"Yeah."

"What he say?"

"Said to turn the crank."

"You try? Turn it from the shaft?"

"Yep. Don't turn."

"Don't turn," I repeated, beginning to capitulate, feeling myself falling. "So, what's that mean?"

"Means your pump's shot."

I didn't have a response. I hadn't prepared. I hadn't gone so far as to submit myself to the possibility that the $200,000 pump was shot.

Likely sensing it, Ken went on for me. "Paul said he wants to see it."

"All the way in Texas?"

"You want, I can drive it down for you."

"To Fort Worth?"

"Yeah."

"When?"

"Tomorrow."

"Really, you would?"

"Yeah, I gotta do a few things first."

"Your dog?"

"No. Wife."

"Oh. Okay."

"Figure I can leave about four."

"Tomorrow afternoon?"

"No, in the mornin.'"

"Four in the morning? That's like only seven, eight hours—"

"Yeah. Wife don't take as much time as the dog."

When I finally made it home, Mary was asleep, so I turned off the baby alarm on her bedside table and slipped into the nursery. Elena looked to be sleeping, too, but that didn't keep me from nudging her and listening for a breath. Satisfied, I did the same with Maria, nudging her and watching her recoil then settle back to sleep like Elena. Double-checking their blankets and every other perceived hazard, I finally lay down on the nursery floor between them, my way of spending time with the girls, and of taking over for Mary.

Immediately, my thinking went to Wallace. Why would he do that? Why would he call for us to keep pumping when our pump was being destroyed? Just to save himself the hassle of tripping in flush pipe?

I couldn't get past it. I couldn't get past *Why?*

Knowing, too, that in the morning I'd have to tell Mary I was heading back to Texas, on another unplanned trip. I'd tell her, too, that Ken was driving the truck down, and not Wallace or Eli, and that eventually Ken needed to be paid something, even if he wasn't asking. I'd tell her that we might need another lawyer, someone down in Fort Worth, some other miracle worker who might get someone other than me to pay for the newest mess. I'd think about how to tell her in the morning when she was rested, when it wouldn't keep her up all night worrying alongside me.

Then I sensed a change in the room and saw Mary hovering over me, just a featureless hole in the night, but at that moment as waking as a midnight apparition. I'd called her a few times during the day but had been short on details. Now she'd want to know, and there was no escaping it or my insuppressible failings.

Chapter 42

GARDNER DENVER CORPORATION SHOP

Bentwood, Texas

My flight descended into DFW with its crisscross of concrete runways and geometric patches of grass. Watching out the window, my first impression was that I was seeing a phantom, but as we soared past, it turned out to be a billowing American flag stuck into the crow's nest of a towering top-drive drilling rig. Right there in the infield of the fourth-busiest airport in America. Right there in Texas.

All during my flight, I'd been rethinking the promise I had made to Douglas, to call him the minute I touched down. Cojoined to that was his promise to meet me at Gardner Denver's facility in Fort Worth. He'd meet me at the drop of a hat, he promised. By the time I landed, though, I rescinded my part of it. Inviting him to join me would imply that Douglas was blameless in the whole mess, that it was me and him against the Goliath, Gardner Denver. Knowing, too, that in short order it could be just me, I did what I'd become accustomed to doing. I called a lawyer.

I had found my newest lawyer in Dallas the day before. He took my call, heard me out, then asked for time to check on conflicts. He'd never heard of Douglas's company, but Gardner Denver, with their size and global scope, they were different. "Trophy client," he said—not about me but about them. The following day I heard back.

"All clear," my newest lawyer told me triumphantly.

I was immediately relieved, but he wasn't, not when I told him I was only *maybe* considering an engagement.

"So, you're saying there's no dispute?"

"Not yet…but one might develop."

"Okay, so what am I doing?"

"I'm thinking like a deal where, you know, where I can call you when...when it looks like I might need you... You know," I continued, trying to keep his interest up, "see how it goes after I talk to them."

"Aren't you sort of done talking to them?"

"Well, not all the way. Tribute's blaming Gardner Denver. But Gardner Denver, they haven't said much yet. I'm only thinking they might try and screw me. But neither one has actually screwed me yet. But I'm thinking that's what's coming next. One or both of them screwing me..."

"Huh... Might be a dispute. Might not be a dispute. Okay. Then what is it you want me to do?"

"Just be ready, is what I was thinking."

"You mean, like, be on standby? You're envisioning I remain on standby?"

"Right. Exactly. That's it. Exactly. There...ahh...a charge for that?"

"Waiting on standby? I doubt it. I never did it, not right at the initial—"

"Is that okay? I mean, you okay with that?

"Yeah, sure, screw it, why not? I'll just hang out. Hey, it's worth the laugh, right?" he said, summing it all up.

Two hours later, I rolled into Gardner Denver in a rental and ran right into Ken in the parking lot. He had beat me by a few hours in the pump truck and had news.

"I found the problem," he announced, the second I opened my door. "Weld splatter. It's all over the inside of the pump casing. Down in the sump, too, gears, everywhere. There's splatter everywhere," Ken said, excitedly.

"Weld splatter?"

"Right through all-a the pump. Chewed right into the teeth in the gears. An' that's not all. Bearings walked right out from under the pinion. Pump's out of timing. Maybe from the slag, or maybe just built wrong. But it's lucky the whole thing didn't come apart an' kill everyone on that hill!" Ken exclaimed, nearly giggling.

"So, you saying that rules out operator error?" I said, grinning, feeling the beginnings of enormous relief.

Ken curled an index finger, as in "follow me," and started away.

"Where we going?"

"Goin' to meet Paul. He'll tell you all about it."

Obediently, I followed Ken into one of the several buildings on-site. It made no mark on him, none at all, that we were inside a multinational with security and passcodes and protocols. He just blew down a hallway, filling every bit of it in his humongous steel-toed Frankenstein boots, his long gray-and-blond hair streaming behind him.

At an office well known to him, he turned in without a knock or a pause and loudly introduced me to Paul the engineer.

"Nice to meet you, Dan," Paul said, standing. "I see Ken helped you find your way. He's getting pretty familiar with the place," Paul said, ribbing Ken a little, but not too much.

Ken harrumphed and I stood still, grinning stupidly.

"I'm guessing you want to have a look at your pump?" Paul reluctantly offered. "You came a long way to, anyways."

"I sure do, Paul. That'd be great."

A moment later I was following Ken and Paul back down the hallway and outside into a lot where I saw my dismembered pump truck, missing the pump and fluid end, looking like its back half had been cleaved away.

We continued into one of the buildings, past a smattering of technicians. All of them seemed to know Ken, giving him the room he required as he barreled on with a point to prove. In the back of the shop, we arrived at my pump, sitting there unceremoniously on the floor, still seven feet wide and five feet long, but diminished without the truck chassis underneath it.

Right away, Ken was grabbing my hand and guiding it toward an open inspection plate in the pump's sheeted steel housing.

"Feel right up here," he told me.

I reached inside the cavernous six-ton pump, my arm disappearing into what looked like the ass end of a mechanical elephant.

"Deeper in. All the way in, so's you can feel up above."

I did as I was told, apprehensively pushing my arm in deeper and waiting for a trap to spring and cut off my fingers. I kept going, past one of the darkly skeletal bull gears, thirty inches in diameter and big enough to suck me inside whole, until my fingers touched the back side of the steel sheeting. I felt it—what Ken was talking about—an oily, knobby texture. What should have been a flat sheet of steel was instead covered with tiny metallic beads.

"You feel it?" Ken joyously asked, thrilled to have found a problem not of our own making.

"Yeah, I feel it," I said.

"Smooth?" Ken asked, his eyebrows raised expectantly.

"No. Not at all. Like pebbles."

"That's right. Smell it."

I pulled my arm out and smelled the blackened oil smearing my hand and shirt sleeve.

"Yeah. Burnt."

"Weld splatter. That's what happened to your pump. It got in your gears and tore 'em up. Plus this," Ken said, pointing at an eight-inch-thick shaft circled in bright rings of polished brass. "Bearings walked right out from under the pinion. Pump's out of timing. Probably from all that splatter. That's what was shakin' the truck."

I turned to Paul, who had been quietly hanging back. "What do you think? You guys think that's what got into the gears and bearings…that splatter?"

"Maybe. We're looking, I promise you," Paul said. "But we're concerned about how your fabricator built your truck, too."

"How's that?"

"Well, they didn't install any protection. We publish installation guidelines, and they didn't follow them. OEMs generally follow them, even when they don't like them. Avoids the liability."

"What do you mean?" I asked, sensing a deflection, a shifting of blame.

"There wasn't any filtration between the sump and the lube pump. Then there wasn't anything between the lube pump and your power end on the return. You had no protection. Your builder didn't plumb in any protection."

Ken and I shared a glance. *Here it comes.*

"Well, what do you think?" I asked Paul directly. "You think it was the weld splatter, or you think it was the no filtration? I mean you, personally."

"Dan," he said, smiling, "I'm not paid to think. We gotta wait till Gaylord gets here. He's the one that gets paid to think."

"Who's Gaylord?"

"He's my boss. Gaylord runs the place. He's seen everything there is to see with these pumps. He'll know right away."

"So, when's Gaylord gonna get here?"

"He'll be back tomorrow. Plan is we're gonna have a nine o'clock meeting, right after he looks over the pump."

I nodded along. "You mind if I meet you all, too, back here? You know, to make our case?"

"You don't need to make your case, Dan. No one here's gonna try and pull the wool over your eyes."

My phone rang. "It's Douglas," I said aloud, then directly to Paul, "the guy who built the truck." Paul shrugged and my phone rang again, then a third time before I sent it to voicemail. "I'll call him back later," I said and pocketed my phone.

"Just plan on meeting us at nine o'clock tomorrow," Paul continued. "We usually meet in the conference room over in the offices." He looked at Ken with a smile. "Ken should be able to find it. He's probably been in it."

We started back out of the shop, weaving around pallets and parts, Ken and Paul nodding to a few of the Gardner Denver employees along the way.

Then, just as we were emerging, Ken and I stopped dead in our tracks. We had just run headlong into Douglas, standing right there in front of us, talking on his phone. Suddenly, mine was ringing again. I didn't need to look at who it was.

"There you are," he called out, waving his phone. "Hope you don't mind, but I thought I'd come down for a look for myself."

"Oh, hey, Douglas," I said, awkwardly stepping forward with Ken and shaking his hand. I introduced him to Paul. The two of them shook hands, too, both keeping a wary, tentative space between themselves.

"Good to meet you," he said to Paul, then turned to me. "Let me see that pump-a yours."

"We're still assessing it, sir," Paul interrupted. "Once we've made some determination, maybe Dan and Ken here can—"

"Oh, come on. I'm just gonna have a quick look. You all got nothin' to hide, right?" Douglas asked pointedly.

Paul didn't want this any more than Ken and I did, but he stepped into it anyway and hesitantly took the lead back into the shop. "Just for a minute, all right?"

Douglas shrugged. "That's fine. Won't take me any longer'n that."

No one was talking as we retraced our steps. Missing too, I noticed, was Douglas's genial, get-'er-done Texas swagger.

Looking at the pump in silence, Douglas reached inside and smeared a finger with oil. "Smells-a burnt oil, doesn't it?" He held it up in the light for all of us to see. "Lookit that. Got some brass in here, too, I see. Looks like your bearings come undone." He turned to Ken. "What'd you think, Ken?"

"Bearings are shot," Ken replied, offering no more.

"Crank, too. Crank's shot," Douglas continued, staring down into the inspection port.

He pulled up a sleeve and reached inside, all of us watching, though no one saying a word.

"What's this? They're all over… Feels like BBs… That weld splatter?" he asked Paul, holding up his oil-soaked fingers, pinching something between them.

Paul finally spoke up. "There was an issue that we acknowledge—"

"What was the issue?"

"There is some weld splatter that should have been caught by an inspector."

"Got in the gears, didn't it? That's what knocked that pinion off its bearings?" Douglas casually asked, without expecting an answer. "I bet there's plenty-a those BBs down in your sump, too. Probably got into everything."

"You're right about that, but there wasn't any protection on the pump to stop it," Paul said flatly.

That got Douglas. "What do you mean, 'protection'?" he asked.

"I'm not sure if you're aware of our build specifications, but we require a filter between—"

"Twelve-thousand-pound pump blowing up, and a filter's gonna stop it? Uh-uh. I gotta call you out on that one, sir."

"Hey, Douglas," I jumped in. "No one's saying—"

"That splatter tore the pump apart before oil even circulated outta it. A filter in between woulda tore open like a bitty sheet-a toilet paper!"

"Listen, Douglas," I said, feeling duty bound to break up a fight. "We're going through it all at a meeting first thing tomorrow." I turned to Paul. "Maybe Douglas should be there, too?"

"Yeah…I don't think so," Douglas said with an emphatic firmness that caught even me by surprise. "Their pump blew up, an' I'm supposed to make another damned trip out here? I don't think so. Tell you what, fellas. You think this is *my* problem, then it's gonna be *your* problem. You all can talk to my lawyer, you think this is my problem."

That was it. Douglas was finished. He turned around and walked straight off, yelling back as he went, "Next time you buy an SPM pump, you want to avoid Gardner Denver's chickenshit!"

And just like that, he was gone, leaving us behind in stunned silence.

"What the hell was that?" Paul finally asked, searching for words as much as I was.

"My guess is he don't think it's his fault," Ken giggled, and right away we were all right there with him, laughing out loud as if nothing else could possibly have been on our minds.

Chapter 43

GARDNER DENVER CORPORATION CONFERENCE ROOM

Bentwood, Texas

After a night at a cheap hotel, Ken and I were back inside Gardner Denver by 8:00 a.m. This time, there was no free rein. We were immediately intercepted by Paul at the gates and led into a small, unused office outside a conference room. We'd be called on when the time came, he told us as he backed out and joined the gathering of Gardner Denver engineers and executives next door. When I heard the conference room door close, and their indecipherably muffled voices, I knew they were discussing me and my start-up.

Absent much hope for redress, I did as I was told and sat still under the suffocating weight of judgment, in a dim and horrible brown-on-brown room last decorated in the 1970s. At least I was sitting beside a man who had stuck by me like a brother. When he finally spoke, I didn't hear him, not until he raised his voice and repeated himself.

"I wrestled a bear," Ken said.

"Huh?" I asked, thinking I hadn't heard right.

"I wrestled a bear."

"What do you mean?"

"Man came though Oil City, a carny with a bear you could wrestle, so I wrestled it."

"No way."

"I'm not sayin' I wasn't drinkin' when I wrestled it, but I wrestled it."

"Come on."

"Why they call me Griz."

"Like what, a friendly bear?"

"I don't know. Never talked to it. Just wrestled it," Ken guffawed. "I had to pay, but if you didn't quit or get kilt, you got your money back."

I set my phone down. I'd been thinking of calling my newest lawyer, the Dallas guy, but this was better.

"And you, like, got in the ring and shook its paw and started wrasslin'?"

"I got it down. Right on its back."

"How big a bear?"

"Six-hundred-pound bear. Big ol' fat bear. Had a muzzle that covered up all its teeth, an' it didn't have claws, but it was still all bear… Went a whole minute an' wanted to keep goin', but the man said no more, so I got my money back."

"That's it? You got your money back, was all?"

"Better'n losin' it," he said, getting me to laugh right along with him. "You know what, though?"

"Huh?"

"I really stunk after wrestlin' that bear. I had to throw my shirt out… *an' I really liked that shirt!!"* he roared with laughter.

Ken was howling and I was right there with him, the two of us loud enough to be heard through the conference room walls. That's what I thought when Paul stepped into the room. I thought he was there to tell us to shut the hell up.

"Excuse me, but you want to join us, Dan and Ken?"

That knocked the laughter right out of us. Suddenly nothing was very funny.

Ken and I stood and took a few apprehensive steps forward, me toward a lifetime about to be marked by success or failure. It was nothing less than a gallows walk as we entered the room next door, into the maw of six or seven Gardner Denver engineers, admins, and an older guy at the head of the conference room table who I rightly guessed was Gaylord. He was the first to stand. Everyone else followed, shaking our hands and displacing most of my apprehension with a budding sense that at least they'd be polite about screwing me.

"Gardner Denver wants to apologize to you, Dan. We're plain sorry about what happened here, an' we're gonna make good on it," Gaylord said to nods and agreement around the room. "We called this meeting here, Dan, but it wasn't jus' 'bout you. It's about a problem in our Odessa plant, where your pump was built. We just design and repair 'em here. Hell, occasionally we even sell one or two of 'em," Gaylord said to grins and a few chuckles around the room. "But Odessa's problems, Dan, they appear to have landed right in your lap."

I didn't say a word because I didn't want Gaylord to stop.

"We had to let a fellow go there for some shoddy welding, and it looks like you and your pump were ground zero for that fella. But that doesn't mean your pump shoulda ever made it through an inspection. We're lookin' at that, too," he said, his voice betraying a lifetime in Texas with its deep twang. "But, Dan an' Ken, it's important to me, to all of us in this room, that you an' Ken understand that this does not represent what we do here at Gardner Denver."

"That's really…that's…" I stumbled, slowly coming to it, that this wasn't a brush-off or a repudiation—it was an *apology*.

"Tell you the truth, though, Dan, it's not jus' as simple as that. There's also the matter of your truck packager. Paul here tells me he paid us a visit yesterday evenin', an' he wasn't at all tickled. That what you said, Paul?"

"Amusing, he wasn't very amusing, Gaylord."

"Oh, amusing. Well, that, too. That an' an asshole, from the sound of it."

The room broke out in laughter, with me and Ken snickering along, just less so.

"That fella missed some very rudimentary parts, like filtration. Pretty damn rudimentary stuff. But the simple truth is our pump, condition it was in, may have thrown more shrapnel at a filter than it coulda handled. You just don't know. Bottom line, though, it's not our way to duck our part in this. So, with your permission, we're gonna rebuild your pump so's it's just like brand-new. Then we're gonna bolt it back on your truck so you all can get back to work. We're gonna do all-a that, an' you are not gonna pay us for that, Dan…but on one condition."

Here it is, I thought. The punch line, where it all retracted into one big insider joke. "What's that?" I asked, trying to cover my apprehension.

"You're gonna keep buyin' Gardner Denver pumps as you grow that company-a yours. You're gonna be a Gardner Denver man, through and through. Would that be a deal you could accept?"

"Seriously?"

"Yes, sir."

"Are you fucking kidding me?" I blurted out. "I'd never own anything but a goddamned Gardner Denver pump for that deal!"

"Hahaha!" went the room as the tension tore open and gape-mouthed laughter poured out of everyone, mostly me, as I kept ridiculously professing a lifelong loyalty to the Gardner Denver fraternity.

Five minutes later, Ken and I walked out into a cloudy April Texas day and stood there, trying to gain our footing, though still upright and shaking our heads and grinning, looking for some irretrievable logic to it all.

"What the hell just happened in there? I thought I was a dead man," I said in a whisper.

"I don't know. But I got a really good idea."

"What's that?"

"Let's get the hell outta here 'fore they change their minds!"

"Hahaha," we laughed all over again, beelining for my car.

People are good, I kept thinking. *Bless all of us, Jesus Christ, people are good.*

PART III

Ain't nothin' wrong with goin' down. It's stayin' down that's wrong.

—Muhammad Ali

Chapter 44

RELIANCE SHOP

Reno, Pennsylvania

It was a little over a week after Ken and I got back from Fort Worth when Paul from Gardner Denver called.

The pump was done and painted and refastened to the chassis, but he wanted to share some "polite advice" before we came back down to drive it away.

"We got the pump right, Dan," Paul said. "But it's on your team there to rebuild that lube circulating system. You don't, you're gonna be back. And, Dan, the next time it won't be so cheap."

"We'll get it right, Paul," I promised, thanking him endlessly.

My next call was to Ken, whose response was "Harrumph," which translated into "good idea."

I called Eli and told him the same. "We can't go through this again," I started in, consciously fearful. "We gotta build out the circulating system right, Eli. Right to spec. We don't, next time it'll break us."

Eli agreed and said he'd help. Next up was Wallace. But I couldn't reach him. Later, I heard back from Ford, instead.

"Dad says you need to get the pump back up here soon as possible."

"Right. We need a driver."

"Okay, let us know when you get one."

"How about one of your guys?" I asked and waited, hearing only muffled sounds as Ford covered the receiver.

"Dad says we're too busy."

That ended the call and all prospects of getting my truck back home, until five minutes later, when I got my old friend Woodstock on the phone.

"You stealing back another one-a your trucks?"

"Believe it or not, they're gonna actually hand us the keys this time."

"We don't even have to do a B and E to get it? What fun is that, man?" Woodstock laughed.

After a few minutes, Woodstock was in, and this time it was easy. No parrot worries or last-minute rush. No issues with the plate in his head dinging airport body scanners. He simply flew down to Fort Worth and turned around with the truck. No fires on the way home, no breakdowns, no crime spree, like our first trip back from Texas, when state troopers closed the highway for prairie fires and a nearby murder-suicide. Woodstock didn't even have to offer donuts to the angry lady at the scale house. Nothing out of the ordinary, at all. It was unusually uneventful, almost legal, even.

After that, it was a two-week rush of working day and night, weekends, and nonstop. I spent most of it under the truck and up between its frame rails, trying to get back on the hill and back to fracking and some whiff of money.

First up was undoing what had taken us down—heat. We needed to remove the heat generated by a starved lube oil circulating system. That's what Douglas didn't get right. He installed a cheap, in-line, super-fine 100-mesh screen as filtration. Thick lube oil couldn't pass through it fast enough, generating heat on the squeeze and blowing up our pump.

That was the first thing to be ripped out, and the first to be replaced with a new circulating system of hoses and thoughtfully sized filters. One two-foot-tall specialty filter we couldn't find anywhere but in an Ontario border town. Shipping it and clearing customs would take too long, so I made a deal with their salesman to drive it across the Peace Bridge. Meet me in a Buffalo parking lot, and I'd give him a hundred bucks. In a hurry—always in a hurry—we made the exchange, and I took off before the nearby customs and drug enforcement encampments caught on and thought the box held something other than a filter.

We added the new lube oil pump that I bought on a rushed drive to West Virginia, then added a filter with a vacuum gauge, an analog pressure gauge with a huge and visible dial, and a first-warning flashing red light, like the cherry-on-top light of an old police car. Should oil pressure fall, it would trigger a cherry-red strobe.

It was a race against a clock measuring both time and insolvency. The longer it took, the closer I ticked to failure. So the rush continued, right into one Saturday night at our shop. All the Kanes were there, Wallace and Cassie and their sons and a grandson, a funny little kid that everyone was chasing around a shop where there were a hundred different ways to get hurt. Ken and Eli were there, too. Everyone was in a good mood, all of us one big family. Even Wallace was talking, a rarity anymore, especially because he was talking to me.

When we found ourselves separated from the others, he began to open up, stepping out of himself in a trickling confessional of sorts.

"Snakebit trucks… Lotta struggle… More'n I ever coulda thought," he went on, the progeny of a polished, erudite past, of privilege that had so thoroughly slipped away. That was all so far away now, Wallace on the other side of a break in heritage—a backslide, as a social scientist might call it.

I wasn't sure of what Wallace was getting at, but something was being said. His hesitation, his being onto something—a struggle—made me want to help him, but when I started in, he cut me off.

"It's almost as bad as back then," he went on reflectively.

Then he let it rest, but I understood. He was saying it was too close to everything, from before.

When he lost everything.

And me meeting him with silence, unsure and waiting for more from him about the day when he gathered his little girl in his arms and watched her slip away.

The horror, my God, the horror…

I could see it, all our efforts dragging him back into that dim labyrinth, into a pernicious retelling of that break in his life. It was now too close to the broken dream right in front of us: the trucks, a mission to me and a burden to him, a reminder of everything that had gone so wildly wrong before, something he couldn't patch back together. He couldn't breathe life back into his broken little girl. But with this, we were all trying and trying and trying, and there was hope for this—but not for that, that faultless chaos that had no repair.

My God, my God… I understood…

I slipped under the truck to hide behind my work. It was easier there, underneath and out of sight and listening in on good-natured Cassie up above, with her infectious joy. To her, everyone was together, Heaven on Earth, even if we were stuck in a dark and filthy shop and gathered around a truck and a dream that had failed us all. And me, hiding under it, having given up on my dream of it all coming together, because I didn't dream anymore unless it was tormented waking dreams of fracking.

That was the last of it, that moment, the beginning and the end. It was the last of Wallace and me ever really talking, and the beginning of a preoccupation with him, an obsessive one—and a near-unworkable endeavor to get him to see things my way.

Chapter 45

SECOND WELL—LITTLE RENO LEASE

Reno, Pennsylvania

This time, the second time, it was easier.

After the world coming to an end on our first job, everything more or less fell into place on our second. The oil lube system we installed worked. It kept the pump cool, right at about a 180 degrees cool, with Ken monitoring it from the sidelines with a heat gun that looked something like a pistol. Ford kept us going, too, pushing us along as we stumbled through the stages, one after another, deeper and deeper into the well, like this was something we sort of knew how to do. I was making plenty of mistakes, but nothing like the first time, and none of them all that embarrassing. More important, I was keeping to Wallace's frack design. I wasn't sneaking in any extra sand or goosing sand concentrations. I was sticking to the playbook. No more taunting Wallace. That had been a cravenly bad play.

I needed this job to work as much for the oil income as for the urgency to win him over. Wallace knew everyone in the basin, and only Wallace could bring in work. Start by finding a way to apologize for my overzealousness on the first well. Tell him he was right and I was wrong. Desperation will do that to you—get you to say anything. So what? Just tell him we were ready for outside work, whether we were or not. Tell him we could bluff our way through anything as long as he was there.

Just sell us, Wallace. Just please sell us.

This time, though, Wallace never saw my acquiescence. He never made it over to me in the blender to meet my apology. When the sun came up, I could see him over by the pump operator, at his stand on the edge of a tree line. A few times, I saw him at the rig, talking with Rusty, or with Ford between stages, but I never was able to get close to him.

By the time we were pumping our last stage, I was keeping an eye on Wallace as much as I was the controls. When the last stage came to an end, I caught sight of him walking off the location. Jesus Christ, I wanted to run for him. But I was stuck to the controls, counting down the last seconds of the flush.

"Ten, nine, eight..." I counted aloud into my mic, watching Wallace disappear behind a water tank, back where I thought he might have parked his truck.

"Three, two, one, that's it!" I called out as I yanked off my headset and leapt off the blender into the mud.

Trying not to look like I was rushing, but nearly running, I caught up with him.

"Went pretty well, huh?" I called out, smiling.

"You say so," Wallace said, never looking up.

"What do you think?" I asked hopefully. "From what you saw? You think we're ready?" I stuck right to him, tagging along like a little dog, taking two strides for each one of his.

"Ready for what?"

"You know, to get out there. Start working for other people."

"No," Wallace said flatly, as he pulled open his pickup truck door and dropped inside.

In a moment he was gone, disappearing down the lease road, along with any thought of him selling us anytime soon.

Chapter 46

THIRD WELL—LITTLE RENO LEASE

Reno, Pennsylvania

Maybe a clear telling of my story would generate some sympathy.

That dawned on me the next morning. I was lying under the blender in the shop redoing a chemical pump and thinking about money. Mostly about how to get more of it.

I doubted my bank even understood what had happened since closing my loan. For sure they wouldn't be pleased, but maybe they'd be sympathetic enough to grant me another interest-only period on the $1.5 million loan I'd closed six months before—the loan that had since fallen woefully short of my real capital needs. I had to have more time for the simple reason that I didn't have anywhere near enough to pay the coming principal payments. Not even close.

Miss my first principal payment and I'd risk having my loan reclassified and downgraded. Miss another and it could be called, with a notice coming by registered mail, the equivalent of a bullet to the head.

Right there, with my laptop balanced atop a nearly four-foot-high truck tire, I pounded out a confessional to my loan officer, Emaline. It quickly turned into an exposé so phenomenally ugly that it was sure to capture her interest and, my hope of hopes, an empathetic response. Something on the order of another, a second, three-month deferral on principal payments.

Or so I thought.

I waited and waited after I sent my bleeding-heart email. Discouragingly, though, it met with an oppressive silence. After nearly a week, every day of which I kept myself from resending it, I finally heard from Emaline. Her email asked if we could talk. I called her immediately.

"The loan committee's curious, Dan. Actually, they're wondering what happened. You know, how it could have all gone so…badly."

"Didn't I cover that? I thought, you know, in my email?"

"You did, Dan. Really well. But usually, they were just saying, usually it takes these things a while to go so badly—not before, before you even get started. There's no fire alarms yet or anything…they're just, ahhh, super curious. Right out of the gate, not even out of the gate, really."

"Yeah, I know, but—" I started in, defending myself, making a case for an interest-only extension, calling out the cost overruns, the lost money, the stolen money, the oil crash. But all the while spare on details about the Kanes and their need for a vortex blender, or their exasperating, halting, stop-start path to oil revenues.

When I finished, a cold, hanging silence followed as I waited on Emaline to take her turn. What followed was something different than what I hoped for, something along the lines of a parent cajoling a child who just flunked an algebra test.

"Dan, I don't know about an extension. I don't think the committee wants to do that. I promise I'll work on it for you, but what they really want is for you to make this work. They think Wallace and Eli should be able to sell this for you, especially with oil prices looking like they could rebound. Honestly, Dan, your key man is Wallace, just like you said when you two were here. Get Wallace out selling your idea. You make it work, and I know they'll be one hundred and ten percent on your side."

And there we sat, on nothing.

The next time I had any chance of seeing Wallace again would be on the next frack job, our third, and a full week away. "Whenever we get there, we'll get there," I was told, as the Kanes were too busy on other work to get back any sooner.

My wait for their return curdled from frustration to an unbearable, inhumane siege. Placed on hold, I was beset by a remorseless indifference, left with nothing but my demons as I awaited their return and my own path to revenues. Left behind and alone with Ken—more a matter of being ignored than trusted—the two of us started back in, night and day, remaking the trucks and proving to everyone, myself included, that we weren't going away. It was a way to keep my sanity, too, a diversion to keep me from obsessing over Wallace and his lack of faith, his obstinate unwillingness to engage his reputation and sell us.

When the Kanes finally returned, we went back up the hill to frack our third well. We ground through it and were still rough, but our learning curve was flattening. I got ahold of my side of the blender and was beginning to catch on to everyone else's jobs, too. That should have been good enough. But instead, I remained wholly preoccupied with Wallace. I needed to explain to him all of our improvements, how we were ready to move beyond our own wells, how we were ready to make money. He had to see it, too. It was so damned obvious.

But like the last well, he never visited the blender. As had become his way, he stayed tucked into the brush on the edge of the pad, an unapproachable specter, a shadow behind the pump stand and operator.

Watching him, waiting for my chance, I finally found it when we had a long flush between stages. I dropped off the blender, pretending to be without motive or hurry, casually approached him, smiling brightly. I thought I had him when he started coming my way, too. For the briefest of moments, I felt like we'd be okay, that our union had been made whole again with working trucks. Then he blew right past me, without a word, on his way to Rusty up on the rig deck. Left jilted and with little to do but search for a recovery, I dragged myself back to the blender, as alone and beaten as I'd ever been.

Inside the cabin, I joined one of the Kanes' crew who was taking over Ford's side the blender. Ford wanted to be on the pump and left behind a guy who smiled at me as I entered—mostly, I knew, because I signed his checks. But a smile is a smile, so I took it and smiled back.

"You gonna miss us?" he asked.

"Miss us? What?" I asked as I set my controls for the next stage.

"We're gonna catch one for EnerVest after this."

Feeling like I'd just got kicked in the chest, I stopped the man. "What do you mean? You guys are going to EnerVest?"

"Guess so. We gotta get everythin' off this stupid mountain 'gain."

"When?"

"Today. After this, I guess."

"When'd you hear this?"

"I dunno. A while ago, I guess. Why, you didn't hear?"

Right then the incessant hammering stopped and Rusty whistled and spun his finger in a whirl that matched my growing panic, my sudden inability to think as I blundered with the controls, unaware of everything around me—everything but Wallace.

I couldn't see him out of the blender windows, but if I had, I would have shut the job down. I would have run to him screaming, *"No-no-no!* You can't go! Fourth well, fifth well yet to go! You can't pull off and jump in bed with another frack company! *Not again! Not without me!"*

"Got a charge," the blender man next to me radioed, and we were off. There was nowhere I could go, trapped and throwing fits inside my own equipment.

Pulling off. Pulling off. Pulling off! *No fucking way!*

"We gonna treat this? We treatin' this with clay control?" the blender man asked. "Dan, we runnin' clay? Dan!" the man shouted, finally catching my attention.

"Huh? Treat it? No. No, not the flush. On the frack. Just the frack," I said, playing with my radio, pretending that was the problem.

It was a miserable rest of the job, just one stage after another, executing every one of them better and better. Surely, if this was an audition, we would have passed it. We'd have been picked out of the crowd to move on.

But my God. This insanity. This Wallace. I needed to get to him. To stop him. Right away. He couldn't go. Or if he had to, Reliance and I had to come along with him, like a wife and kids, the whole damn package.

The moment we flushed in the last stage, I was off the blender and crossing the location. I caught sight of Ford, but he was without Wallace. I kept going, and up ahead I saw Rusty duck into the rig's doghouse. I found him tabulating his final numbers on a battered, welded-in shelf.

"Rusty, you see your dad around?"

He looked behind him, "I thought he was in here. Must be out there."

I jumped out for another look but didn't see Wallace. Thinking he might be out by the tanks, getting them ready to haul off-location, I hurried over. When I got there, it was Eli who I ran into, disassembling a water manifold with a thirty-six-inch pipe wrench.

"Wallace not here?"

"I wouldn't know."

"You guys really pulling off for EnerVest?"

"That's what I'm told."

"When you pulling off?"

"Right now."

"Ahh, come on, Eli, really? Again?"

"You're gonna have to talk to Wallace about that."

I threw my hands up. "No way, Eli!"

Eli smiled. "Just take it easy. They'll be back."

"When?"

"It's just one well."

"That's like a week, Eli. We're going to sit for another week? Then something else comes up?"

"Might."

"Well, that's a big relief! Or we could just keep fracking. We could catch four and five. Why don't we do that? For Christ's sake, we're up here."

"Couldn't answer that."

I was dumbfounded, thunderstruck. "Eli, we're never gonna be ready if we don't get a start. We just got through that well, no problem. Not one problem! Wallace never said anything about us not working. We work right alongside your rig, like we all said. You guys watching out for us, you know?"

"Might be you just got to prove it to him."

"Prove it to *him!* Prove it to *me!* He's my partner! How about he proves it to *me*? He shoulda sold us on that job!"

"He got his reasons. Maybe he just don't want to get anyone embarrassed."

"No, it won't be embarrassing when I file for bankruptcy!" I shouted, pacing. "He say anything about taking us with him? He say anything about that, about doing his job!?" I was screaming, frothing, spitting anger, unable to hide it in any longer—though aware in my rage that I might be sparking something that could catch fire and burn it all down.

"I didn't hear that," I thought I heard Eli say. I wasn't sure as he had turned his back on me and was already walking away to the next tank.

He was done…and maybe I was, too.

I had gone too far. Too damn far.

Chapter 47

FOURTH WELL—FIRST CUSTOMER WELL

Reno, Pennsylvania

To pinpoint it, this was where I developed a schism in my personality.

It was a tic, a parasomnia, as a psychologist might put it. When I did sleep, sleep meant nightmares—coming on in the early-morning REM hours, singularly about fracking, the frustration of not fracking, fear of fracking failure, the choice of fracking. I'd wake as each nightmare was peaking, with sweat around my neck and shoulders, like a phantom noose tethering me to all my bad choices. Propping myself up on an elbow, I'd hold on for a few minutes, waiting for clarity and an outcome other than terror. Once I realized it wasn't death, I'd deflect and search my thoughts for something other than hopeless dread, for a pathway to a ledge above the abyss that I could push back into and disappear.

The frustration, the worry, the lack of sleep, and then all my other problems—a failed transition to third-party work, seven other pressure pumpers competing for the same lack of work, and Wallace continuing to work alongside any of them, always without apology. I just hadn't foreseen it, the torment and jealous rush of my partners conspiring with the enemy. I thought it would always be Reliance pumping under one of the Kane rigs, following them from well to well on a pathway of profit, where their work was ours. Instead, it was anguished fits and night sweats over not participating in jobs that could have been ours with better timing or a more charitable, less barbarous partner, one that had me coming and going in the confounding state of trying to understand his bewildering intentions.

The only relief I had was work. I worked on the trucks, on Zahir's half-baked computer, and up on the hill, where I would jump in with

Eli and help push our two and a half wells along to completion, where I would hold back, bite my tongue, and restrain myself from begging and pleading for more.

Until one day, unmarked by celebration or even relief, Eli casually walked from well to well and powered up each of the three pumpjacks over our wells with an unceremonious flip of a switch. Right away—anti-climactically—each of the pumpjacks dipped like a horse lowering its head for a drink of water, then rose again, trapping and pulling an eight-hundred-foot column of fluid to the surface.

It was unnerving. It shouldn't have been, but it was. It was my first stop in the morning and last at night, and in between, anytime anybody wasn't looking, I'd race up on top of the lease and lift the hinged separator tank top and stare inside. Just like my father had done two and a half decades before, I was looking for that opaque sheen of oil, just the start of a skim, something a little heavier than you'd see in a New York pothole after a summer rain. Quietly, just like my father did, I was praying for oil to come on, making all sorts of deals with the oil gods, just like he did. I'd dip a finger into the water and taste it for the brine that comes along with oil. Instead, I'd taste frack water, which tastes like water out of a barrel. Old-timers swore that the slower oil comes on, the better the well will be. Yeah, maybe. But old-timers say all sorts of reasonless things.

Once again, I was stuck in the frustration of abeyance, waiting on oil, on the Kanes, on Emaline at the bank, on any sort of relief at all. And all the while watching the ticking clock of insolvency. Until one day I caught some news. I was in the shop with Ken, resetting the blender's auger shaft, when one of the Kanes' crew came in and casually mentioned a job we had coming up.

"With who?" I shot out.

"EnerVest."

"EnerVest? You kidding me?"

"No, man, EnerVest. Wallace says so. You didn't know? How could you not know that?"

Something had to have happened. Universal had to have pulled out. Our biggest competitor dropping what could be our biggest customer, EnerVest, likely because they were moving on to the promised land of shale where jobs were fifty times the size of ours. If it was true, it was deliverance, or at least the source of deliverance. The Kanes had a friend there, too, a field supervisor who became something of a preoccupation.

"You think you can talk to him about getting us some work?" I had implored when my partners were still listening to me.

"Those wells are way, way beyond you, Dan," Wallace or Eli or anyone I asked would scold.

"Yeah, maybe. But how do we know unless we try?" I'd insist.

Maybe there was some truth to it. Maybe. But to find Wallace and ask him, that was damn near as elusive as booking a first job. I'd heard that he'd been working on his family-owned lease, a place I'd never visited as it had always seemed off-limits to me, but this time I drove up and followed fresh tire tracks until I found him.

"Is it true about EnerVest?" I asked Wallace as I cautiously stepped out of my truck and up to a pumpjack where he was adjusting the stuffing box.

"Yup."

"Wallace, that's really good news. You know?"

"Yup."

"What do you think? One well, or you think Randy's thinking about a program?" I asked, referencing Randy, the guy who ran the field for EnerVest, the old Kane acquaintance.

"One well," he flatly stated, never making eye contact with me.

"One well?"

"An' you better not fuck it up."

Chapter 48
ENERVEST

Westline, Pennsylvania

Desperation had a hand in it. It turned what should have been fear into excitement. The EnerVest well was far too big for us, an embarkation of the Peter principle, making me run headlong into an area where I didn't belong, propelled along enthusiastically by the rumor that EnerVest paid their bills on fifteen-day terms.

My first call about getting our first well was to Mary. The second should have been to my banker but was instead to my sounding board, my brother Pete.

"We got our first big well. For that big company I was talking about."

"Hey, that's great, Dan. Maybe you're gonna be all right, huh?"

"Nah, I doubt it. Just one well. Half of one. But what the hell, it's a job."

"Yeah, man! It's a job!"

Then, having worked up some enthusiasm, I called Emaline.

"We got our first job, Em! For EnerVest. They're the biggest operator in the basin!"

"That's great, Dan. How'd it go?"

"No, we haven't— We just got it. We pump it tomorrow."

"Oh," she said, deflated.

"In case you want to tell the loan committee or anything," I suggested, keeping ahold of my hope.

"Let's see how it goes first, Dan. See if, you know, it goes well before I say anything.

Prove yourself is what I heard. We had to prove that we could perform—to the bank, to Wallace, to our customers, to vendors, to the competition, and to the one or two more employees that I really needed to hire. Because I had latched onto a known quantity, the Kanes, I thought we were past proving ourselves. That was a mistake. You can never stop proving yourself. Prove ourselves on one, and we'd have our second. Then a third, as long as we proved ourselves on the second, too. And so on.

It wasn't even a whole well. It was just the bottom eleven stages left over from a competitor's frack job that had gone off the rails, where the well came on too strong and forced the frack crew into retreat. That was our good luck—never mind that the remaining stages we'd be fracking would have the same insuppressible pressure as the lower ones. This was one of the "big wells" in the storied Allegheny National Forest that Wallace had spoken about. This was the place with the reputation of murderous frack jobs, especially with the ungodly nature of open-hole fracking, where crews stood directly on top of charged wellheads. The only thing securing the hanging column of frack pipe were thin metal slips pushed into the rock 1,400 feet below. That was it, the basis for all the stories of pipe launching out of a hole and killing whoever couldn't get the hell out of the way fast enough.

The evening before the job, Ken and I drove the pump and data van up to the location. It was an eighty-mile drive, along roads that got thinner, then slower, then ran out of berms and asphalt altogether as we pushed deeper into the Allegheny National Forest. Geologic time and plate tectonics had turned the area into a trough, where operators with leaseholds were still allowed to drill and frack alongside loggers, hunters, and fisherman on the banks of a world-class trout stream. Everyone shared the same roads, coexisting, waving as we passed each other, not as the agenda-driven news media would otherwise have you believe.

When we reached the end of civilization, at a turn marked by an orange ribbon tied to a roadside bush, we started a first-gear, single-file climb up a hill into a thick stand of trees. A canopy of oaks, black cherries, and hemlocks sprouting from a freshet closed in around us, shutting out the sky and any thought that I might know where I was going. As soon as I was certain we were lost, I came upon 'dozer tracks in a roadside clearing. I knew we were on the right track when we passed coils of extruded plastic conduit and spools of three-strand electric cable. Up ahead, where the hillside flattened, we drove right into the Kanes' service rig sitting over our well, right at the bitter end of a crushed shale path.

The moment Ken and I shut down the trucks, summer instantly filled in around us, with the chirping and bickering of birds up in the canopy pecking holes in the early summer air.

"This good?" Ken asked, referring to where he had parked the truck.

"It's fine. They'll end up moving it no matter where you leave it."

Ken harrumphed and joined me at the rig, where the two of us studied the capped wellhead rising into the rig's working deck.

"Ready?" he asked.

"Not even close," I grinned, belying a fear that had overcome my enthusiasm and was turning my gut, thinking how good we had to be the next day, how quickly news would travel if we weren't.

That night, we stayed at a nearby inn specializing in steaks and nightly bear visits to the dumpsters out back. After dinner and a bear sighting, Ken and I made our way upstairs to a few rooms where overserved hunters would normally stay. Half an hour into four hours of sleep, there was a banging on my door. When I answered it in my underwear, there stood Ken, wordless and scowling and curling his finger, as in "follow me." I did, down a narrow hallway to his room.

"Don't fit. Feet stick out," Ken said, pointing at his little bed.

We swapped rooms because my first bed had no footboard, and an hour later I fell back to sleep, reduced now to two and a half hours, at best.

At 2:30 a.m., we were out the door and into the dark. The bears were gone, but we weren't all that sure, so we stuck close together and made a beeline for the van. We were to meet the Kanes on location and were headed that way when I saw a small convoy of trucks approaching in the distance. Oddly, I was relieved, the thought having occurred to me that maybe the Kanes had changed their minds. But there they were, with the blender's headlights making a slow, labored turn up into the woods. Right behind it were our two sand dumps, and closing ranks was

Wallace's pickup. Ken and I fell in behind him, thankful he was ahead because I had forgotten my own count of lefts and rights.

Up on the location, I parked the van where I was told and immediately started setting it up. Today had to be different. I had been helping on the setups, hammering iron and hoses together, and laughing along with the crew's running commentary about my not being able to hit the broad side of a barn. "Watch out, Dan's got a hammer!" But this time, for the first time, we'd be running our data-acquisition system out of the van, and I had to get ready.

An hour later, the hammering stopped and Ford called over the walkie, "Gimme water."

I hit the standby button and started logging suction-side rate and pressure. In a push-pull, I was immediately relieved, but was just as quickly sneering at the numbers.

"What's our rate?" Ford called, just like I knew he would.

I couldn't say 20 BPM, that would be broadcasting incompetence; but that's what the computer was logging, 3.7 times more than the actual. Quickly, I ran a finger down my conversion chart to 20, then took a hard right to the converted number.

"Rate's five and a half. Five point five."

"Got it," Ford shot back, seemingly unaware of my cover-up.

Suddenly, the van side doors behind me flung open. Filling the opening was an unfamiliar, unsmiling face.

"You Dan?"

"Yeah. Hey, you must be Randy," I said, enthusiastically, too much so, too much gusto. "How you doing?" I asked, grabbing the company man's hand and shaking it.

"Just checkin' in," he replied, glancing around the van but really just taking me in.

"All set here. I even made us a pot of coffee."

"I'm good," he said, holding his stare a moment longer. "You gonna be okay in here?"

"Yeah," I replied, withering under judgment, until he pushed the doors shut and stepped back into the frack job. Flatfooted and found out, I sat staring at the door, thinking with self-disgust of what I should have said instead of offering him a cup of coffee and good company.

"Everyone ready?" Ford called out over the radio, normally something the frack operator, me, would do if not lost in self-doubt.

"Hell yeah!" came the blender operator, the same guy I had split the blender with on the previous job.

"Then gimme charge and let's go!" Ford shouted as he throttled up the pump.

The rate jumped as the pipe column filled with water. A half minute later, I heard a hitch in the engine as its unrestrained horsepower suddenly bogged down against a wall of resistance. Pressure started climbing: 2,000 psi, 3,000, 3,500, 3,600 as the pump shouldered into it with more and more horsepower…3,700, 3,800, 3,900, 4,000, 4,100 psi, higher than we had ever gone. At 4,200 psi, I caught myself ducking, wondering what I was thinking when Ken and I had hung a ten-inch-wide Martin Decker pressure gauge right inside the van, directing all that pressure only two feet away from my face.

Teetering in a standoff between horsepower and rock a quarter mile down, water began slipping into the fracturing rock like a thief, taking more and more until it became a raceway outward as the formation broke and the pump took off with a sudden drop in pressure. First, second, third, then fourth gears drove ever more water at a faster rate until we hit our target of 20 BPM, and a water-sand slurry the consistency of warm molasses.

When the stage ended, we immediately shut down. Everything was still and holding until I caught sight of Rusty rushing in from the periphery and stabbing the release valve with the long iron bar. He threw himself into it, over and over, all 250 pounds of him, but the valve wouldn't give. Another one of the rig crew rushed in like a tackle and hit the bar right alongside Rusty. The valve gave and an enormous boom sounded as water exploded into the backstopped pit. It didn't stop, either, like our little wells back home. It was screaming, wild enough for me and everyone else to hold back. Everyone but Rusty, who stood there like a sentinel, seemingly unconcerned that he was surely about to die.

A few minutes later, the pressure had ebbed enough for the crew to move in. Without a single wasted movement, they began hammering our pipeline off the wellhead, until the frack iron dropped and a wild rush of pressurized water knocked one guy right onto his ass.

As gassy as the well got, as much as it pushed against us, Rusty pushed back harder. Wallace's tall, red-headed kid with his youthful, silly demeanor was every bit as tough as I had heard. When the well started coming on and floating the 1,400-foot string of pipe in the hole—levitating it—Rusty stopped shouting over the roar and started using hand signals to push the crew deeper down into more pressure, bull-heading his way in, with his father Wallace right there alongside him.

And this was only the first stage.

The second stage was the same as the first: all the pressure returning to surface in a rushing onslaught, water spitting out of the release valve and crashing into an earthen backstop, followed by a charge of gas casting a halo under the rig's greasy yellow lights.

Then the third stage, and by the time the crew finished their connections, they were dragging themselves across the location, their green rain gear useless and hanging from them like wet garbage bags.

The fourth stage went well enough, and by the time we were into the fifth of eleven, we were into full daylight. It was all going well, and just as I was settling in, as my weary edge was wearing off, Randy threw open the van's side door again, scaring the wits out of me for the second time that day. Just like before, Randy stood there, watching, even when I waved him in.

"You're not graphing this?" he asked, staring at my monitor and the columns of numbers spilling down it.

"It's a chart," I shouted over the frack job.

"What do you mean, a 'chart'?"

"We chart it."

"Can't you graph it?"

"We set it up to chart. You kinda get used to it."

"How you get used to this?"

"Ha! Practice, I guess," I shouted, ready to deflect to our job cost, how I'd make it up on price. That and a pot of coffee.

"I don't even know what I'm seeing."

"Sorry, yeah, but charting…it's really accurate. You know, once you get used to it," I said, hearing the lying unease in my own voice. "I was thinking after the job I could make up graphs for each stage, you know, plot pressure and rate on a graph," I added, drawing a graph in the dead air between us.

"What for?" Randy asked, boring a hole right through me. "Wouldn't it be better if I had it during the job?"

"Yeah. Would help, I guess."

By the eighth stage, the pressure was coming on stronger, and the crew was pushing in harder, but all that was on my mind was my half-witted and hapless exchange with Randy.

Yeah. Would help. I guess. Would help. I guess. I repeated, paraphrasing myself, punishing myself for it, paranoid and certain the job was a one-and-done. Wondering, too, if Wallace had tipped Randy off, telling him and everyone that would listen about our software problems, and maybe something about my general incompetence. When Wallace stayed away, never once checking in with me in the van, I was certain of it.

Then we were done. It was midafternoon and quiet outside the van—just a few hammer strikes and more of the crew's youthful laughter—until the van doors flew open again, throwing my heart into another arrhythmic mess.

It was Randy again. Jesus God! How could I not have been expecting him? Groping to recover, knowing what was coming—*nice try, but*—I hung a sickened smile on my face and waited. But then he confused me with a smile and an outstretched hand.

"Good job today, Dan. I was impressed."

"You were?"

"Yeah, not sure when the next one is, probably not for a while, but I'll get with Wallace about it."

I sat dead still, stupidly blinking, incapable of responding. I should have graciously thanked him, hugged him, even; those would have been good choices, but neither came to mind.

"I still got to print your job out."

"Okay," Randy said, remaining right there in the open van doors, like he was going to wait.

"I mean, like it might take a while. There's a lot here."

"Okay. So how long's it gonna take?"

"Ahh…I don't know, maybe an hour or so to print it all, probably a few hundred pages."

"A few hundred pages? Seriously? A few hundred pages? You can't just print me a summary?"

"It doesn't print summaries," I confessed.

"You serious?"

I tried laughing, but that fell flat. "I'm, you know, working on that, too."

"Well, umm, fine, then just drop it at my office. You know where it is, right?"

"Yeah. The old Quaker State place. No problem. Right as soon as I pull out of here."

With that, Randy walked off.

I called out thanks after him, but he didn't hear or didn't care to, leaving me to wonder in another paranoid moment if I had just blown it all over again, turning a win into a self-inflicted gunshot wound.

But all my misgivings aside, we were done and had performed without any breakdowns or injuries, like we had fracked a hundred wells before—aside from my own pathetic part in it.

Needing to consolidate our win, I left my printer to print and stepped out of the van and looked around for Wallace. I wanted to tell him about the $17,000 I was printing back in the van, about how we had finally arrived, making it through the job without a hitch, how he had made it all happen, how we were ready, how even the EnerVest company man had said so. Then I'd give Wallace his turn. Maybe he'd tell me that he agreed, that the hazing was over, that our time had finally come.

When I finally caught up to him, I was too late. He was already in his truck and disappearing down the lease road, too far away for me to even shout.

Chapter 49

SECOND CUSTOMER

Warren, Pennsylvania

The day after our first paying customer, after a night when Mary and I thought there just might be a short stay from liquidation, Ken and I were back to work on the blender. An oil cooler failed during the EnerVest job, which we were furtively able to keep quiet. We'd replace it when we got home with something bigger and heavier, and while we were at it, we'd scrap all four of the onboard chemical pumps that were little more than rubble. There was no consistency, just streams of too much or too little, leaving some of an oil formation unprotected (the chemicals used were designed to stick to the formation) and other parts of it overdone in trace amounts rarely exceeding one part per thousand.

Whenever Ken didn't need me, I'd race up the hill and check on our wells. They transitioned from frack water to naturally occurring brine, but for days there had been no show of oil, vexing me with sleepless worry. Until, one morning, I lifted the oil-water separator and saw it—a translucent, purple sheen like a sheet of cellophane spread across the water. Right away I tasted it, a salty brine with a silkiness that smeared my lips. It was oil. We had oil. That was the first part. The second was how much. That would be a matter of time that I unintentionally dragged out by running up every few hours, looking for hope in a barrel, praying it would pick up its pace.

All in all, between the work on the wells and the work on the trucks, we had a three-week run of nothing but shop work: installing a new oil cooler, wiring in new rheostats on the chemical pumps, adjusting the computer's K-factor to the actual results of an endless run of bucket tests, and a dozen other details that finally ended when we had more or less worked ourselves out of work.

I also made our first hire with money I didn't have, a skinny kid named Brian who could run equipment. After Brian, I started talking to a guy named Frank who was on disability with another frack company, a competitor, but was happy to come to work for us for cash "for as long as it don't mess up my disability."

I was looking outside of the Kanes and hiring on a cash basis because I was worried. With Wallace's inscrutable withdrawal, I didn't know what was coming next. I began preparing for the worst, for the day when he truly did disappear. Then, utterly confounding me, the opposite occurred. There was a rumor. The first of it was that Wallace had gotten us work, two jobs' worth.

The second was that "we better be fuckin' ready."

The first of the two jobs was going to be a small well for a guy who owned tow trucks. Neither that nor that we fracked the well right out of a parking lot made it memorable. What made it memorable was that it was a freebie. Wallace had gotten us a *freebie.*

No one mentioned that it was a freebie, not as we prepped the trucks, or even as we rolled out. It wasn't until after the job was set up, and just before pumping, that I learned. Right at the point of no escape.

"Guy's a fuckin' prince," Wallace explained through the open doors of the van, the first time we'd spoken in three weeks. "There's never been a time he wasn't right there to haul us outta a jam."

"We're not charging?" I mumbled, failing to mask my incredulity.

"This guy, he'll drop anything he's doin', right in the middle-a the night. Got me outta a lotta jams, he'll get you out, too."

"But we're not charging?"

Wallace's stare told me he was done, and that I was, too. He had delivered his edict. This guy, our customer, who owned a wrecker service, was an essential friend of the Kanes and their banged-up trucks. And the day had just come when the Kanes would make good on all those free and timely tows. As slow as I was to grasp it, blinking back at Wallace's opaque explanation, it finally dawned on me. Half the tow prince's bills were mine.

After the first stage, the customer stopped by to say hello and tell me of his profound respect for my partner Wallace.

"The best there is," he said. "His reputation precedes him. Dan, is it?"

"Right, Dan."

"The staggering depth of knowledge there."

"Yep."

Just agree, I thought as I nodded along stupidly. *Just keep agreeing.* Never mind that the job should have billed out at $13,000. Never mind that when I ran to Eli with my objections, all I got back was, "Don't worry about it, that's just Wallace."

When I finally made it home to Pittsburgh, Mary was in bed, awake. She was as unsettled as I was after I called her on my way home to tell her of a day that had gone both good and bad. The job had gone well—we were getting the hang of it—but not to be paid, that's what was keeping her up.

"Doesn't he know how bad it is for you?" Mary asked, charitably discounting her own stake in the day.

"I don't think he cares," I said, setting my electric alarm clock for 2:00 a.m. If I fell asleep, I'd get three hours before the next day's job.

"Maybe just focus on tomorrow's job," Mary added, trying to bring the temperature down.

"Yeah. Tomorrow."

Chapter 50

THIRD AND FOURTH CUSTOMER WELLS

Venango County, Pennsylvania

The very next day, we rolled out for our next job, the second of the two Wallace had just "sold." This one was for Ronnie Beck, a friend of the Kanes and a guy I knew back when he was a kid. Ronnie was the son of Lowell Beck, the neighboring operator who had enriched me with his surrounding gas drive two decades before, when I drilled my first Pennsylvania wells. Now Ronnie was grown and pumping the leases his dad had left behind when he died.

Twenty frack jobs was the word on Ronnie. If the first one flushed enough oil, especially with oil's recent run up to seventy dollars, it could be our way out, the first step down a path to some sort of reprieve.

That—and Ronnie paid his bills.

Immediately, though, there were troubles. Treating pressures were low once we got started. Determining that it wasn't our sensors and transducers, we moved on to the possibility that the stages were comingling, that they were coming around the packer and entering previously fracked zones. The rig was Ronnie's, and the packer sets were his, too; but after repeatedly setting and resetting the downhole packer, we all began to agree on the same thing, something none of us said aloud: The area was depleted. Ronnie had drilled into a tired formation. There was nothing left to it, not after a century of surrounding wells pumping off the natural gas drive.

When the job ended, it was on a hopeless note. Not much was said, other than all of us wondering if we'd be back. Quietly, we racked up the trucks. After they rolled out, I stayed behind to print the ream of paper it would take to memorialize the job.

Ronnie and his crew were nearby, running a string of two-inch tubing into the well. Once he finished, he walked over, and we caught up on the nineteen years it had been since we had last seen each other—me and him and his father, all those years ago.

"Sorry I couldn't give your dad all that gas," I apologized. "What a waste that was."

"Yeah, I know all about that."

"Your dad have a few words to say about that?" I laughed.

"Oh yeah, every night at dinner," Ronnie laughed right back. "That was just Joe," he trailed off, referring to his old neighbor Joe Ruot, the owner of the neighboring land I'd drilled on years back. Old by the time I met him, he became a mentor to me. He even forgave me for nearly blowing up his house when oil got into his basement and was creeping up on the gas-lit water heater. One day I brought Mary along with me. "Mr. Ruot" pulled me aside and told me I needed to marry that girl. "Don't let her get away, Dan. You hear me? She's a special one." On another day, his wife, "Mrs. Ruot," confided in me, "You know, Dan, Joe thinks of you as a son. I just thought you should know that."

"Him and dad," Ronnie continued, outside the data van. "He was somethin' else, and my poor dad sayin' we had to stay neighborly about it," Ronnie added, shaking his head.

"Your dad was a good man, Ronnie."

"You know the name of my company, IMOD? Why I named it IMOD?" he asked.

I shrugged.

"In. Memory. Of. Dad."

"Yeah, that's good," I smiled. "IMOD. That's really good. You know, I remember sitting with your father in that office right off your kitchen, that little placard above his desk, the one that said: 'Anyone can be a father, but not everyone's a daddy.' You remember that, Ronnie?"

Ronnie nodded. "Yeah, I remember it. I have it." He stepped out of the van, choked up, it seemed. "See ya on the next one," he added as he walked off, but then stopped and turned and stared straight back into me. "By the way, how's it goin' with Wallace?"

"Wallace? Yeah. It's going pretty good," I said unconvincingly.

"That so?" Ronnie replied, grinning at me in a way that made me understand he knew. "You finish your bill up, I'll be back with a check."

A week later, we were back for Ronnie's second job, our fourth customer well. This time, it was different, more workmanlike. There was no backslapping or joking. Everyone was serious, all of us sensing a discontented customer. The first well was still on brine but was already pumping down—meaning the pump was outpacing the fluid entering the annulus below, enough to conclude that the first well was no good.

Right away I was wondering how many of Ronnie's twenty wells we'd be doing. The easy answer was two—if absolutely everything didn't go well on this, the second one.

But things didn't.

Like most tragedies, there was no one single event to suggest what was coming. It was a series of events, all at such an aberrant level of dysfunction that they quickly built to a bad and final outcome.

It was the first stage when I noticed it. It wasn't the equipment or the job. It was Wallace, arguing with Ronnie, right outside my van window. It was hard to hear over the engine roar, at first, anyway, but I could see it in their faces. I could see Ronnie gesturing at Ford, hand-signaling for a lower rate. Ford saw it, too, and right away backed down the pump, until Wallace threw his arms in the air and started shouting at Ford right over the caterwauling engines.

"Bring that goddamn rate back up!"

That triggered Ronnie, and right away he and Wallace were back at each other, right there in front of me, their arms waving animatedly, fingers pointing, Wallace's jugular bulging at every word.

"Bring it up!"

"Back off! Back off!"

"You don't know what the fuck you're doin'!" Wallace roared.

I could see his and Ronnie's necks craning, their heads coming at each other like spears.

"That's it! Shut it down! Shut it down! We're done here! Shut it all down!" Ronnie screamed.

The two crews, ours and Ronnie's, began stiffening against whatever mayhem was coming next.

"Pack it up and get out of here. You're done! You hear me?" Ronnie yelled. *"You don't hear me? Pack it up and get offa my location!"*

Wallace stood there, in Ronnie's way, and I thought that was it, a fight, the service man brawling with the customer in an unheralded level of dysfunctional lunacy. Then, just as abruptly as it started, it ended. Ronnie waved Wallace off, then turned and stormed off his own location, his entire rig crew obediently following him, pushing right through us.

What the hell? I thought, trying to piece it together. *This madness. My God, this madness!*

"Cut sand!" came Ford's voice over the radio. "Cut sand, goddammit!"

The stage wasn't fully pumped, but the order was in. Cut sand. But sand kept puking out the back of the raised dump.

I jumped in on my walkie, as infected by the delirium as anyone else. "Keep pumping! Sand's still in the hole! Keep pumping! Gotta clear the hole."

Then Wallace detonated, right outside my window. *"Cut sand! Quit dumpin' sand, you dumb fuck! Lower that goddamn bed!"* he shouted at the kid on the dump controls.

But the kid was doing everything right, dropping all his weight onto a pipe extension stabbed over a dump-valve handle. Still, it wouldn't budge, not with the dump bed up and gushing sand.

Wallace levitated right across the pad, right for him. Doubling down, Ford was right with him, pushing off his pump-stand chair and waving and shouting, *"Lower the goddamned bed! How fuckin' hard is that?"*

Enraged, the kid on the dump shouted back, *"What? What? What!?,"* then threw the four-foot-long pipe across the well pad and jammed down on the dump controls. The body slammed down into the chassis, crushing the truck's springs and rebounding right off the ground, all seventy thousand pounds of it.

"Ten more barrels! Keep pumping!" I shouted into my walkie. "Nine, eight, seven..." I counted, everyone suddenly coming together, no one arguing or shouting as we pushed the downhole column of sand back into the formation, clearing the well so we could pull off. "Three, two, one, that's it. Sand's clear! Shut it down! Quit pumping!"

Instantly, the operators killed the pump and blender, and the location went almost quiet.

Until it erupted. Again.

"We're done! Get the fuck off this location now! Get these piece-a-shit trucks outta here, now!" Wallace screamed.

"No, no, no," I was mouthing, in staccato, over and over and out loud as I jumped out of the van, right in Wallace's way. He was coming straight at me, right through me if I didn't get the hell out of his way. But he blew past, a wind sucking along behind him. Maybe he was going for his truck—maybe—I didn't know, but I lost sight of him and turned back to everyone else. All of them were looking back at me with the same slack-jawed stupor that must have been hanging off my own face.

How? How? How?

It was all so fantastic, so far out of the realm of possibilities. Me just as stunned and shell-shocked as the rest of them, like witnesses to a crash, silently processing it, trying to make sense of it all, until none of it made sense—not a damn bit of it.

One by one, we pulled ourselves out of our collective shock and did what we always did. We worked. I coiled up data lines as the rest of the crew dragged themselves to the wellhead. No one was talking or bantering in their typical, chirpy back-and-forth. Instead, it was like a crime scene, where people silently regrouped and thought to themselves, *Thank God it wasn't me.*

Then there was Wallace. He was back, standing over us like an animal not to be approached. Imposing, but different now, contrite and repentant and muttering over and over, "This is bad, this is bad, this is bad…"

It seemed that I was watching remorse, or maybe regret, I didn't know, but I had never seen it in Wallace before. Then he was gone again and that was that, except for the absurdly improbable mess he had left behind.

How the hell? Only on our fourth well. How? I thought.

An hour later, our trucks rolled away, and the once-raucous frack location returned to a quiet meadow. Maybe I'd get thrown off the location all over again, but I remained behind, thinking I had to save this. If Wallace got us there with his relationship with Ronnie, I'd have to keep us there with mine. I'd appeal to Ronnie and ask of him what his father had once asked of me: "Can you help?" I'd ask him all by myself, because that's all that was left.

As I printed what little there was of the job, Ronnie returned. He pulled up alongside me in his truck, and I braced myself. But it was different now without Wallace. It was calm. I could see it in Ronnie as he walked over and stuck his head through the van's open doorway.

"How you holdin' up, Dan?"

"Holding up okay, Ronnie. How about you?"

"Me? Ha. Truthfully, I'm pretty pissed off."

Ronnie took a seat. "Little crazy, but it's *my* job," he started in. "Wallace wasn't wantin' to do it any way but his. He wouldn't even listen. I been doin' this shit all-a my whole life, too."

"I get it, Ronnie."

"I don't need any hand-holdin' from Wallace."

"No," I said carefully, hoping for just a chance.

"You're gonna have a hard time with him, Dan. I'll pay you for this, but you're gonna have a hard time." Ronnie stepped out of the van, turning to me as he slowly backpedaled away, carrying every bit of my hope along with him.

"I can't do it with him, Dan. I'm sorry you're in the middle of it, but I just can't do it."

With that, Ronnie walked off with his eighteen remaining wells, making it clear that all my problems were now so suddenly and easily decipherable.

People get damaged by life but don't stop. They move through it as reasonless wrecks, causing accidents as they go, one blunt-force trauma after another. Trying to find reason, and so far out of my league, I could only wonder if success was an absolutely intolerable construct to Wallace, if failure was some kind of moral imperative.

Chapter 51

FIFTH FRACK JOB

Venango County, Pennsylvania

Time had run out. Repaying old tow bills with frack jobs and getting thrown off wells had pushed me deeper into an insolvent abyss. I was completely out of money but still hadn't told my bank. Already I was into the thirty-day forgiveness period after missing my first principal due date. In a few days, the loan payment would be in technical default. But I'd already mailed an interest-only payment—my notice to the bank that a principal deferment was no longer a suggestion. Strangely, no one had reached out to me about it yet.

I was back at our shop with Ken, perpetually turning wrenches to make our trucks work better even though they weren't working, when the Kanes' crew pulled in with their lowboy trailer. They were packing up their rig and pulling out, headed for an eleven-well program that every one of them had forgotten to mention. Not a word about it.

I was incensed. Apoplectic. But in my suppressed anger, at least I knew. Every suspicion I had was just put to rest. Wallace had drawn an invisible line, nothing that I could see, but it was there. He had stopped selling us. He was going to let me fail. Beyond that, I didn't know what his plan was. Sole ownership? Fatigue? I didn't know. How could I know about such self-destructiveness other than it was driving my near-certain demise?

Back in better times, Wallace and I had talked about the operator with eleven wells, a rich guy out of Cleveland with a compound and a private airstrip on a Forest County hilltop. Wallace was sure he could get us on all eleven wells, too, right alongside his rig. I even used the eleven frack jobs in my pro forma with the bank, an example of my "in-the-bank" opportunities. Now, however, left alone and left out, and unconditionally needing the work, I found Eli. He was still findable, and I begged him to get the Company Man's number off Wallace.

To my great fortune, Eli had it, and I called the Company Man, a guy named Bruce, who was kind enough to stay on the phone and interested enough about meeting after I salted our conversation with promises to be cheaper than anyone else. When Bruce suggested I come up and see him, I did so in a headlong rush, meeting him at his boss's landing strip along a ridgeline above the Allegheny River. Right away we got along. Probably because Bruce was as curious about me as I was about him.

"He wants us to make it longer, like that's no big deal, Dan," Bruce said with a high-pitched laugh, sweeping his hand across the landing strip. "You know how hard it is to build a runway on top of a mountain? An' now he wants it longer!" he continued, referring to his boss.

"Why?" I laughed along, thrilled to be engaging with him, the best lead-up to work.

"He wants to buy a bigger plane that can make it all the way to Miami without refueling. His pilot's got to stop partway up, an' he says the girls don't like that."

"Girls? You mean his kids?"

"Hahaha!" Bruce went on, laughing like he might spit out a lung. "No. *Girls* girls. Prostitutes! He gets prostitutes from down in Miami an' has his pilot fly 'em up here. I'm tellin' ya, it's just crazy, Dan. But that's Mike, an' now he's thinkin' a bigger plane's gonna solve all-a his problems!"

I smiled stupidly, daring not to weigh in with an opinion. Eleven jobs. Eleven! But Jesus God, now hookers and planes?

"We counted thirteen different girls last year alone. They didn't all look like hookers, but they were hookers, sure's this is the woods."

"Thirteen!" I laughed along. "Boss likes the ladies, I guess."

"Must be some kinda good deal down in Miami. Nice girls, though. Real friendly. They'll even talk to you if you wanna talk to 'em. I'm tellin' ya, though, it's insane. Amazin' we get anythin' done at all. 'Specially with him wantin' the place immaculate for 'em. Got us chippin' out all the fallen logs and sticks in the woods so he can take 'em on walks an' not trip on nothin'. An' I'm tellin' you, Dan, not a one of 'em's fit for the woods at all. Not in those crazy shoes they all wear!" Bruce said, laughing but not all-the-way laughing as we wandered inside an enormous airplane hangar that didn't have any airplanes in it, just drilling rigs and compressors and assorted gear laid out perfectly on a spotless concrete floor.

He wanted me to meet his guys. A good sign, I thought. When I did, they were all just like Bruce, solid guys, utterly bemused by their boss and his girls and what I could see was their boss's second fetish: cleanliness.

"We kept wonderin' when Wallace was gonna ask 'bout gettin' his trucks on," Bruce's tool-pusher told me. "We knew about 'em cuz he talked about 'em, an' 'bout you, but then he kinda didn't anymore."

"An' we didn't want to bring it up, 'cause, you know, maybe like he never had any trucks in the first place," Bruce snickered.

"Yeah, sorry, that's my fault," I lied. "Sorry I didn't get up here sooner."

"Well, to tell you the truth, we were about to call Universal, 'cause we didn't know, but we'd be happy to give you an' Wallace a shot, Dan. You give us a good price, an' we'll just see how it works out on the first one."

It should have been an exhilarating moment. I should have been intoxicated with relief. I kept wondering when it would come, but it never did. None of them had heard of us getting kicked off of Ronnie's well. I'd been expecting they had, especially because oil-field gossip travels like wildfire. I had even worked up a few reasons why, ones about personalities and not performance. But they hadn't heard—I thought—not right then, anyway. And I was spared. Again.

That was it. I had just sold my first well. If we performed, the crew would sell the rest of them. Eleven wells, over $200,000 of work, enough to stall a workout on my $1.5 million loan. I became truly ecstatic as the realization of it gained momentum. This was the beginning, the way out of the hole. I shared the news with everyone, everything suddenly feeling different. Work changed, too. Getting the trucks just right became more of a pleasure than a burden. And more immediate, too. There'd be no room for breakdowns or glitches or cover-ups for things that weren't working. We had to be prepared for Bruce's first well and the unconditional need to do well on it.

Then, the irrationally absurd, the thoroughly unexpected, happened all over again.

Wallace cancelled Bruce's job, the day before we were to roll out and frack it.

Shocked, agog, at a loss too difficult to comprehend, I couldn't even assimilate it.

Wallace never gave Bruce his reasoning. But I knew. I heard. After the fact. Wallace wanted to frack another well for his buddy, the tow truck operator—the freebie guy. And for no reason other than of his own choosing, it had to be the same day. Given a choice between working for free and survival, Wallace had just picked oblivion.

"What the hell is this all about, Dan?" Bruce demanded, the first words out of his mouth when he called me.

"What's what about?"

"Let me tell you, you're not on my well first thing tomorrow mornin', you're not gonna be there *any* mornin'! You frack someone else's well instead-a mine, we're done! We been bustin' our asses off getting this well ready to frack! We got choices, you know, Dan!"

What I heard next was Bruce slamming the phone down on me.

I had been training on a patch for our computer, from a Pittsburgh guy in the frack software business. Sitting beside him at a console, I apologized, jumped up, and ran outside. Frantically, I began calling Wallace over and over again. Of course he didn't answer. Giving up, I jumped in my Silverado and sped north out of Pittsburgh toward him and our trucks and crew, calling everyone else, letting all of them know we had to be on Bruce's well in the morning.

With my world whipping by at eighty miles an hour, I learned that Wallace had changed our plan so he could take the trucks to frack for his super-swell tow truck operator friend instead. Given that we had done a freebie for him and were likely to do another, I didn't see how he could possibly object to me postponing his second well. He didn't seem to, either, when I called him and told him so. But Wallace would, when I saw him soon enough.

Next up, I called Bruce back and blathered through a rushed apology. "We'll be there just as planned, Bruce. Just a miscommunication. Sorry about this, but we'll be there and ready to pump at six. No problems. We got this. No problems at all," I exhorted, throwing cover over the slight, feigning that it was a simple matter of confusion.

That made things more or less right, but not without a warning.

"Maybe you should work on gettin' your shit together, Dan. That'd be a good place to start."

"I couldn't agree more."

With a detente in place and assurances from everyone I could find that they'd be there in the morning, I began settling down. Not enough to leave, though. I'd have to find Wallace and get his assurances, too. But I never did, not at his shop or up at our wells or over at his lease and barn. Going to his house was off-limits, but that didn't stop me from doing drive-bys into nightfall. Still no Wallace. When I finally gave up, I called Mary and told her I wasn't going to make it home that night.

"Where you going to stay?" she asked.

"In my truck."

I woke up behind our building the next morning. It was still dark, around two, when I heard trucks approaching. It was our crew. I had our crew. But still no Wallace.

Gathering up and getting the trucks started, my first direct employee, Brian, laughed when he saw me.

"You seriously sleep in your truck, man?"

I grinned back. "Yeah, Hotel Ford. Best night of sleep I've had in a year."

Then, as the fulcrum swung back, we rolled into the job, and everything turned to the dark side of worse.

It was 4:00 a.m. when we pulled the trucks up against a gate and waited for Bruce and his crew to let us in. Most places we just drove into, but here you didn't. Chaperones were required, and once Bruce and his crew arrived, we drove into the compound past a posted wire fence and a forty-foot perimeter of mown grass. The woods we entered were different, distinguishable even in the dark. An oddly manicured forest floor was thoroughly picked clean of fallen limbs and logs, nothing there at all to tangle up a pair of stilettos.

An hour later, under the hazy beginnings of daylight, the frack crew was hammering in their last connection. I had the van set up and the computer monitors glowing inside. Bruce and I had already gone over the job, and the crew and I had done a quick safety meeting, boiling down to which direction to run if everything went to hell. Coffee had been made, and I was tying an empty garbage bag to the van's sideview mirror when I heard someone coming. I turned, thinking it was Bruce, but it was Wallace, walking toward me.

Naively, I smiled, thinking there was still enough between us. "Hey, Wallace," I called out.

"Fuck you."

"Wha— What?" I stammered.

"Get the fuck outta my way."

As was his way, he was coming right at me.

"What the hell is— *Fuck you!*"

That stopped him, five feet away from knocking me down.

"I'm done with this. I'm done with you. You hear me? I'm fuckin' done!"

"What I do?"

"What I do? What I do?" Wallace mimicked in a high-pitched falsetto. "Fuck you, what you fuckin' did!"

"Come on, Wallace. We were going to lose this work—"

"Fuck it! Fuck you! All-a your fuckin' bullshit!"

"*My* bullshit?"

"Yeah. Your bullshit frack company bullshit."

"*Our* frack company bullshit."

"Yeah, fuck it an' fuck you!"

"You know what then, Wallace? *Fuck you, too!*"

Right there, right in front of each other. If there was a fight, I was going to lose, badly, but at least I'd have my say.

"Get outta my face, you little fuckin' asshole!"

"Hey, hey, hey!" someone came shouting. It was Bruce, rushing in between us. *"Cut the crap, will you two? I'm not gonna have this on my job, you two soundin' like a coupla damned babies! Cut it out!"*

Immediately, Wallace took off for the rig and I headed for the van. It might have been war between us, but we both still needed the money.

Keep moving. Keep moving. Momentum was better than inertia. Just keep moving. It won't stick if you're moving.

I pulled on my headset and rushed to call for water. If water was moving, it would be harder to shut us down and kick us off the site.

"Let's go. Everyone ready? Let's go. Let's go! Right now, we gotta go!"

That was it. With war, there was no going back. But how would I do this without Wallace? Everything I had been banking on with the Kanes—fiasco or not—was over, irreparably.

I had needed them for every bit of it, and now, incomprehensibly, it was over.

Chapter 52

JUST KEEP FRACKING

Venango County, Pennsylvania

Not this! This was beyond nightmare. This was madness, a reiteration of Conrad's *Heart of Darkness*, of Marlow's regard for Kurtz, his "I should be loyal to the nightmare of my choice" sentiment. This was our own journey up the river, right when we had work right in front of us. And now this!

My father. I wanted to reach out to my father. He'd understand. He'd tell the story of the partner he once had, a story I saw play out as a kid. My father's partner running unflaggingly into assured self-destruction, taking everyone along with him, enough so for my father to finally say he was done, that he would sell out. But there was no selling-out option for me. My stake was optionless—succeed or fail. There would be no other venture, because mine was too tied to debt. That left only one direction. "Go alone and get away," my father would tell me. Do what we had both dreamed of—find oil. His time had come and gone, he would say, a bittersweet reminder of him and his friend Norby drilling a well. But my time hadn't, not all the way yet. Shameful to me was that maybe—maybe—I had the slimmest of chances, while his were gone. That wouldn't matter to him, though, not to a father with a son. "Push harder," he would tell me, "and you might push through with this middle-aged-crazy idea of oil, of yours."

Surprising me, Ford came back over the radio.

"Got a charge. Water's on its way."

He was still on the location, still with me. And if he hadn't walked off, my thought was that Wallace hadn't, either.

I heard the pump coming up, grabbing water and pushing it downhole. *Jesus God! Jesus God! Jesus, they're all here!* I was thinking, my heart still racing with panic from my fight with Wallace.

The van's side door flew open, and I jumped because I thought it was Wallace coming back to finish it all. When I spun around, it was Bruce. Alone. Whatever part of the open doorway he didn't fill, his voice did.

"What the hell was that!? Was that you bein' a professional, Dan?" he shouted. "That just another one-a those 'miscommunications' between you two?" Bruce asked, making air quotes.

"I'm really sorry, Bruce."

"I don't know what's going on with you two, but not on my job! Not here! You understand me, Dan?

"I understand, Bruce. I understand," I demurred. "It was just a— It won't happen again. We're good now."

"It better not happen again, or you're gonna be gone! You two babies don't get this worked out, you're not coming back! I'm not gonna put everyone at risk because you two can't get your act together. You hear? Act your ages, would you? Am I being clear?"

"Hundred percent, Bruce. I'm really sorry. It won't happen again."

He dropped his voice. "For your sake, I hope not. You don't want to get thrown off another well, two in a row, Dan!"

Bruce slammed the door and left—leaving me with the answer to my question. He knew about us getting thrown off Ronnie's job, which meant the rest of the world would, too.

I sat still, watching him march off, bouncing between one panic and another, trying to regain my wits as gravel flushed out of the derrick's el in a grayish waterfall. I could see out the van's windows that the crew was still there, doing their jobs, like nothing had happened. Then I saw Wallace, standing calmly behind Ford, composed and unperturbed, like all of his menace, his rage, his threats were just ordinary.

I spent the next ten minutes trying to get myself back into the job, calling for water and rate, winding up for the fight with the rock below.

Then the van doors flew open and I spun around for whatever was next. It was Bruce, again, this time crawling into the van and ready to go.

"Let's frack this well, okay, Dan?"

"Yes, sir. You got it."

The formation broke, and we took off. Nothing more was said about Wallace and me and all that was between us. We just moved through the job, everything clicking as we worked our way deeper into the well with a cadence that was beginning to amaze me. Even my two hires, Frank and Brian, were coming along and fitting in. Frank was even running the blender, knowing right away what to do and having no struggles with his "disability."

After every stage, Bruce would jump out of the van and watch as our ground man opened the 15,000-psi in-line ball valve. The harder the released water hit the plastic-lined earthen backstop, the bigger Bruce's grin became. He'd comment on it each time he pulled himself back into the van for the next stage. And each time, I'd unceasingly apologize for the van's computer display, until it became as tiresome for me as it was for him.

"Long as you're getting' sand in that hole, it don't matter what that computer-a yours is doin'," Bruce laughed. "Or isn't doin'! Your pick! Hahaha!"

Then he'd shove his hand into a bag of Dolly Madison donuts he'd brought along and complain about his weight.

"God, these are good, though, Dan. Worth every pound they're puttin' on me." Bruce laughed. "You want one?"

"Sure, I'll take one," I said, pulling one out of the bag and instantly sprinkling myself with powdered sugar.

"That doggone Dolly really knows her way around a donut, don't she? I really like these little ones with the white—what is that?"

"The powdered-sugar coating?"

"Yeah, that. Gets everywhere, but my God, these're good donuts. Sometimes, I eat the little chocolate ones, but my wife's just been buying these lately. I don't know, maybe a deal or somethin'."

"Day-olds?" I laughed.

"I bet. Buyin' 'em off the bottom shelf for me," Bruce laughed.

You ever want to get to know somebody, sit with them in a frack van. Hours go by where you're sitting side by side, hearing their stories and telling yours. You get to hear everything, all the business stuff, the home stuff, and then the personal stuff. You hear all the stuff that you'd normally save for a brother or sister or a best friend, all while roaring through one stage after another at ungodly pressures and rates.

When our first job finally ended, I waited for Bruce to bring it up: would he have us back again? Would he even bring it up, or just disappear like Wallace did? Swallowing hard and restraining myself, I was almost certain he'd cut me loose and let me and my nuisance slip away. Why bother with all the drama?

"You gonna come back, Dan?" Bruce asked, right out of the blue.

"Yeah. Yeah, for sure, Bruce. We're coming back if you'll have us."

"Without all-a yours and Wallace's dysfunctional behavior, right?" he finally said, cutting right to it.

"You won't have any problems from us," I promised, holding Bruce's stare, letting him know I meant it.

"Good. I'll see you on the next one then, end of the week. I'll know better tomorrow what day, an' call you after."

That was Bruce. Bruce was good people. And good people want to see you succeed. They want to help. Over and over, I thanked and thanked and thanked him, without saying it out loud, keeping it to myself and my God. A stranger's kindness and his work would save me for just a little longer. Maybe into the beginning of winter, when work slowed or stopped altogether.

Chapter 53

CREWING UP

Mercer, Pennsylvania

I went to see Eli about his brother. All along, Eli had been my sounding board, me venting while Eli chafed, "That's just Wallace."

This time was different. I found him on a contract well he was drilling. We moved away from the noise and were followed by one of his drillers. Eli dismissed him, letting him know he was fine, but the message was there. They saw me as trouble, which meant I was in trouble.

Ken didn't know what to do about it, either. "He'll come around," he'd repeat, even though we both knew that was unlikely. Wallace had been best man in Ken's wedding. Now, since I'd shown up, they rarely spoke.

The last hanging thread was to appeal to someone who had the sense, or even self-interest, to help me stop a sinking ship. That was Cassie, Wallace's wife, the lovely, big-hearted woman with her grounded and sensible outlook on life. I found her in her cluttered office at the junkyard where she worked. I came bearing a peace offering of two ice creams from a Tastee Freez down the street. She smiled and took hers, and we both started in on our treats.

"It's getting out of control, Cassie. We're barely hanging on," I confessed. "It's been…it's been terrible, really hard. And Wallace's— I'm sorry, but it's all so crazy. We got kicked off a well, Cassie. We didn't even get to finish it."

"I heard all about Ronnie's well."

"Then how do I work it with Wallace? How do I, I don't know, get along with him? I just… If things were just more normal, you know?"

"Honestly, I don't know what to tell you, Dan." Cassie shrugged. "But if you're looking for normal, you're in the wrong place."

That was it. Cassie fell into silence and I followed her there. Mostly we just ate, talking about anything but her husband. There was no need to, I realized. She couldn't do anything about the situation, either. When I left Cassie, it was as friends, but I knew with finality that my partnership with her husband was all but over.

Feeling an end-of-the-world doom, adrift and alone, I drove a miserable two hours home to tell Mary all about it.

"It doesn't make any sense. It's finally starting to work," she said, looking down at me on the living room floor where Maria and Elena were crawling over me, rolling off my lap and gleefully gibbering as they climbed back up.

"Yeah. Everything but the partnership."

"Then what's the problem?"

"Me. Me, I guess."

"He's just trying to get you out. Don't let him. This is some kinda game he's playing."

"I don't know. Maybe. Just with Wallace, I don't know."

"It sounds like you're defending him."

"You're right. It does." I stood and scooped up Maria and Elena and loaded them into their big, blue side-by-side stroller. "Winter's coming. We got nothing once winter starts."

"Then what are we going to do?"

"I don't know. Eat each other once the food runs out, I guess," I said, taking a shot at funny. "I'm gonna take the girls for a walk. Then I'm gonna find a crew."

"You mean hire more people?"

"If I can."

"Don't you already have a crew? Isn't that what Wallace was doing for his cut?"

"Yeah. That's what I thought, too. I'm hearing they may have some work, like a lot of it, for their rig."

"Are they taking you with them?"

"I don't think so.... No. It might be just a rumor, but I think...I don't know."

"He's messing with you, Dan. Don't let him. You hear? Screw every one of them," Mary said, all 115 pounds of her, fiercer than me, every pound of her fuming and ready to swing.

I agreed because it was the better move and promised Mary we'd be back in an hour—then began my adventure with our girls, pushing them up and down the same streets we walked most every evening, consumed with the need to be ready for the day when Wallace and his crew stopped coming.

As soon as the girls drifted off to sleep, a recurring pattern in their big stroller, I called Frank, whom I found working out in his garage, not convalescing on the couch, as his primary employer assumed.

"What's up?" Frank answered, with nothing of the formality typical of an employee-boss relationship.

"I got a problem."

"You think?"

On Bruce's job, Frank's first one for us, it had taken him all of ten minutes to figure out our blender and run it himself. Afterward, as I counted out twenties into his upturned palm, he couldn't resist a jab: "You and Wallace, you two pretty tight, huh? You two should hang out."

"It's nothing."

"That's nothing? I'd like to see something," he laughed.

Now, as I pulled Maria and Elena's stroller to a stop, I said, "Frank, you think you could find me a crew?"

"What's wrong with the one you got?"

"I'm thinking they may be going. I think they got a rig on a program up in the national forest. Like fifty wells.

"He's not takin' you with him?"

"I don't think that's in the cards."

"Then you got any work even worth crewing up for?"

"We got some. Seven more for Bruce, and maybe, like a long shot, but maybe six for another guy that Wallace got us way back when... So, you think you got any other friends on disability, anyone, you know, looking to make some side money? Like some farm boys that can frack?"

"Farm boys that can frack? Probably, yeah, I got some of those. I got one guy for sure. Maybe more."

I stopped. "You do? Really? They got experience?"

"Yeah. From Superior. Maybe one guy from Universal. The one guy, Scooter, he's my right-hand man. You'd love him. Guy's like an ox. Total farm boy."

"You think you can get him?"

"Scooter? Yeah, Scooter's always available for cash."

Right away, I was pushing for a meeting, and by the next day, I was speeding north to buy Frank and his farm boy lunch. I arrived at the restaurant early, and I saw them coming from a distance. Scooter looked to be just like Frank said, built like a musk ox. But as they got closer, the whole farm-boy part began falling right off of him.

"Dan, this is Scooter. Scooter, this is Dan," Frank grinned as he and Scooter sat down at my table. I shook Scooter's hand, staring at him even though I tried not to.

"Good to meet you, Mr. Dan. I been hearin' only the best-a things."

"Yeah, you too, Scooter. So, what, Frank pull you right off the farm?" I asked, kind of kidding but not really.

"Oh yeah," Scooter laughed alongside Frank, with me staring in disbelief at his shaved head and the flames tattooed on his skull—this long before people tattooed their skulls and necks.

"I guess things've changed a little out on the farm."

"Yeah," Scooter grinned, running a hand over his bare pate. "The chickens don't seem to mind, long as I feed 'em." That really cracked him and Frank up. When they finally caught their breath, he went on.

"Dan, I can run any piece a frack equipment you got. I've run everythin' from fluid pumps to nitrogen pumps to blenders to transports to everythin' ever made."

"Can't run a blender worth a shit," Frank ribbed.

"Ha! Run any blender *you* can. Just don't want to. Have to pay attention, I did." That set the two of them off again. Like nothing had ever been funnier.

"You think if I needed a crew you could make it?" I butted in.

"Any time you want, Mr. Dan."

"But you working now?"

"Don't sweat it, Mr. Dan. I'll just call off sick, whenever you need me. Jus' like Frank said. Who's gonna know?" Scooter proclaimed, setting off another endless round of belly laughs.

This time I joined them. It was the funniest damned thing I'd ever heard, probably because, for once, it wasn't me.

Chapter 54

TOM HAVRANEK

Venango County, Pennsylvania

Tom Havranek had been on my mind, living there rent-free for a long time. In fact, he'd become an overwrought fixation. Havranek and his fifty-well program that the Kanes had their rig on both had me throwing fits.

As the consulting engineer on the program, the hired gun, it was Havranek's choice who would and wouldn't be working over the coming winter. Given the colossal amount of work a fifty-well program throws off, and the fact that there was no other work coming in the surrounding counties, Havranek—this de facto overlord, this kingmaker—suddenly had the power over life and death.

"Too gassy." "Too many stages." "You'd never keep up," I was warned. When I pulled a page out of Wallace's playbook—"Let's frack a well for him for free, see if that doesn't get us in"—I pleaded to Eli. What I got back was: "Forget about it. You'll get yourself killed."

Because Wallace had stopped talking to me, but had left me in limbo as to what or what not his intentions were, all I could do was pester everyone else in his orbit. I begged every one of them to appeal to Wallace, to use his influence—to please, please help get us in with Havranek.

"Forget it. Outta your league," went the drumbeat of refrain. "Tom loves Universal." "Universal's been workin' for him forever." "We can't compete with Universal."

Over and over again, I heard it, ad nauseum.

"Universal even gave 'im a coat with 'Universal' stitched right on the back. Same one he wears every day."

Making it all the more vexing was that the Kanes were set. They'd be working for Havranek right through the winter and into the spring, right alongside our biggest competitor, Universal. Worse was, it didn't bother any of them.

Outside of those problems, my first problem with Havranek was that I didn't know him. The second was that I desperately needed to meet him. The third was I needed Havranek's work to survive.

Then, strangely, only because everything was strange, Tom Havranek called. Us. Reliance. Not Universal.

It was Wallace he called, telling him he needed us "right now!" I was training again on the software program in Pittsburgh, on a patch to lay over Zahir's totalizer mess—the one that showed us running three or four times more water than was the actual—when I got the call. Immediately, I jumped to my feet, signaling to the program's creator to be quiet as I hung onto every word coming over my phone.

It was Ford, in one of our trucks. Something about "Universal cancelling…Tom Havranek pissed…needing a crew…right then and there…on their way…too hard to explain…and…and…no time to talk!"

"Hold it, hold it. You guys are on your way?"

"That's what I said," Ford sounded off, annoyed. "Universal called off, and Tom's pissed. No warning. Tom told Dad to frack it, so we're on our way. They're waitin' on us, an' we're in a big goddamn hurry!"

"No way. They just called off? Just like that?"

"Dad tol' me to tell you to forget the van. Too big a rush. Never make it up here in time. Tom don't care, just needs to get the well fracked."

"You sure? You sure? You— Ford? Ford?" He'd hung up, leaving me standing over a computer bank, unaware I was even standing.

"You okay, Dan?" It was the guy training me, Bruce Myers, an early innovator of frack software. Bemused, he was looking up at me and my confusion.

"Huh? Yeah, pretty okay. Just got a job."

"Nice. Good for you. We'll get you ready for it," Bruce said, turning back to the computer.

"They're running up to pump it now. My partners."

"Without you?"

"Yeah. I guess. They don't want to run the computer. No time."

Bruce stopped. "Really?"

"We're a little Stone Age I guess."

"Yeah. Well, we'll have to change that, right?"

I sat back down, politely trying to listen to Bruce but incapable of listening, not when I had a job for a guy with the keys to the kingdom. It didn't matter that I had just been voted off the island by my own partners. Or that, in a few hours, I'd be tipped off that Havranek's call for our frack trucks had come the day before, or that it wasn't so impromptu and unexpected, that all along my absence was planned.

Later that day, I was back in my Pittsburgh office, agitated and pacing and impatiently waiting for Ford's call. Earlier, I had left a message and asked him to call me after the job. When his call came, I jumped up from behind my desk.

"How'd it go?"

"Good. Nothin' broke. No computer to slow us down."

"Havranek happy?"

"Didn't say, so probably."

"Well, what he say?"

"I told you, nothin'. Maybe 'good job,' I don't know. I was off on the pump. He seemed all right."

"Anything about any more jobs?"

"You're gonna have to talk to Dad 'bout that."

We both knew that was a dead end, and the conversation stopped.

So, without guidance, I worked up a $12,000 invoice and emailed it to Havranek's partner at the well owner's address that Ford had given me. It took all of twelve hours before I got a response. But not a good one.

"You gotta fix that invoice," Ford demanded when he called me.

"I just billed what we would—"

"Tom called Dad. He ain't very happy, an' Dad says for you to fix it right now!"

"Fine, I'll fix it. But how?"

"He says you gotta cut it in half."

"In half?"

"Yeah. Cut it in half right now—"

"No one told me."

"He just did."

Left out of every conversation about the well was that we were fracking the few stages Universal didn't finish on their first attempt, when a surge in pressure forced them off. The deal had been for Universal to return and frack it for material charges only. Implicit, but untold to me, was that we were to do the same.

I gave in. Immediately. Not because I wanted to, but because the revised invoice was to go directly to Havranek. It was his email that Ford had just given me. And it was my way in.

I may have been broke, but it felt like the curtain to Oz had just been pulled open.

Chapter 55

FIFTY-WELL PROGRAM

Venango County, Pennsylvania

The next morning, I got an email from my loan officer, Emaline. Immediately, I opened it, praying it was the reprieve from the loan committee I had been waiting on.

> Happy Monday Morning! There are eight checks hitting the Reliance account this morning.
>
> You would be short about $3,500 if everything is covered.
>
> Do you have anything to deposit today?

It was not the news I was waiting for.

I was falling further and further behind in a constant game of catch-up. The NSFs kept rolling in, and the first principal payment on my $1.5 million loan—that should have been a $2.2 million loan—was overdue. Bills were spilling off my desk. Vendors were requiring prepayment. Meaning I couldn't build inventories. I was at the bitter end of being able to fund payroll. Economics had shifted, too. Cost overruns were requiring significantly more than I had projected. Discounting was far deeper than I'd expected. Getting thrown off wells was not good. Worse were the occasional and flippant freebies I had to endure, back when Wallace was still lining up jobs for us.

Yet saintly Emaline, one person away from the workout department, was still so thoughtful and considerate about it. Two months before, she had been covering my overdrafts and waiving my NSF fees. But no longer, not with the loan committee about to re-involve itself.

Oil production had come on and was helping, but the water cut was high, and oil's share of total fluid was less than hoped for. What started out as me staring enchantingly into the open lid of our ten-foot-high tank top, feeling the thrill and temperamental shake of oil and gas filling it, had stopped. The oil income that had helped us along was on decline as the wells pumped off and settled into a decades-long tail of very little. Truthfully, though, had all three wells been bangers, production still wouldn't have mattered much, given the depth of my hole.

Trying to get more, to finish the remaining two wells up on the lease, was looking more like fool's play, too. It didn't matter that I had fronted the cash to get them drilled. No way the Kanes were going to take them on, not with their sudden workload for Havranek. The bigger impediment, though, was that we had come to the beginning of a push-pull skirmish, creeping toward the first stages of a war. I had even stopped asking Eli to ask Wallace, because they weren't talking to each other, either. Besides, I no longer had the money to complete the two wells. Abandoning them became the one and only option.

My schedule of wells to frack for Bruce was running out, too, pushing me up against winter's wall, when the cold reality of abolition would write my story.

With nothing else, nothing after the few wells I already had, all that was left was the long shot I had at Havranek.

I *had* to get to Havranek.

In my emailed invoice to him, I made my pitch: Reliance was cheaper. We had all-new gear with old hands. We ran the same materials as the bigger guys, but we weren't distracted by the onset of enormous and hugely profitable shale work. We wouldn't be pulling out of the shallow basin chasing better, deeper deals. Finishing it, I added my cell number and asked, "Can we meet?"

Then I sent it.

And heard nothing.

Everyone, even poor Bruce, with whom I'd gone from strangers to fast friends in a few weeks' time, had to listen to me. I'd go on about

Havranek and Universal, green with envy as I suffered aloud under the unbearable, unending flog of being spurned, pouting like a homely high school kid without a homecoming date. All to which Bruce snickered, justifiably, because I was so pitiful.

"Tom's a good man, Dan. He's gonna call you. You just got to be more patient," he chided.

"He keeps giving away my wells, though. And to frigging Universal. I can't take it anymore."

"*Your* wells?" Bruce laughed. "That's a good one."

"Yeah, I thought you'd like that."

"He'll come around. Universal and Superior an' all-a those big boys are pullin' outta our little world. They're gonna be gone 'fore you know it."

"Yeah, if I can outlast them. I can probably make it one more week. Maybe two, if I stop eating."

I glanced at my phone, consciously palming it but putting it down when I saw that Bruce was watching. "Sorry. Bad habit."

"Give him a chance, Dan."

"Least we got some other work, besides yours. Some guy Wallace knows."

"See? You're gonna be okay. Wallace's right there for you," Bruce said, grinning.

"Yeah, he set it up a while ago. Six wells for a guy named Big Foot. You know Big Foot?"

"No, I don't know that one. Lemme guess, he got big feet?" Bruce laughed.

"Yeah, I was wondering that, too. I'll check and let you know. Six wells, though. Starting tomorrow, right alongside our wells in Reno. Right next door. Then after that, and your wells, I got nothing. Forever."

I checked my phone. Again.

"You want his number so bad, Dan, why don't I just give it to you?"

"Whose number?"

"Tom's."

"Havranek's? You got *Havranek's* number?"

"Sure, I got his number. I've known Tom forever."

"And you're just telling me?"

"Just too much fun watchin' you sweat. You shoulda just asked!" Bruce giggled as he wrote out the number on a piece of paper. "I only hesitated to keep you from screwin' it up."

"Like I could screw this up, Bruce!" I laughed alongside him, bemused, overjoyed, and not at all reluctant to join in on the self-lampooning.

"Hahaha," we went, as I took Havranek's number and tucked it into a chest pocket.

The entire rest of the job, I wore Tom's number thin, checking and rechecking it and swearing to Bruce I'd let Tom call first. "Good negotiating," I said with authority.

Afterward, at the end of the job, after writing out a $13,700 job ticket, and as soon as Bruce wasn't watching, I called Havranek.

It was all desperation. That's the way I justified it. The same way I justified eating my kids' Halloween candy, right after I swore off Halloween candy, by saying "no, never"—then losing my mind and eating it anyway.

Calling would move me past the sterility of emails. Meeting would move me past an impersonal phone call. "No" comes too easy over the phone. You have to meet, but a meeting required a phone call. So, just like eating every Snickers bar in a jack-o'-lantern pail, I called him.

And immediately hated myself for it.

It went straight to voicemail. All the workup, and he didn't even answer. And then, stupidly, I left a message, the death knell of the desperate. Voicemail and desperation, a commensurable mix. People don't return calls from desperate people. Desperation is best suited to surprise, and I just gave up surprise.

"God, was that stupid," was my loathsome mantra all through the rest of the day, through preparing for Big Foot's first job, through my three-hour drive home, right into a nighttime stroller walk through Pittsburgh with Mary and the girls. Most of our conversation was a relief, Mary telling me of the few things she was selling on eBay that I didn't even know were gone. That should have been enough for an escape, anything mundane should have been a breather, but my regret and repentant self-hatred for having called Havranek were just too inescapable. I should have been captivated, my chippering little girls out in front of me and my long-, longtime best friend, my wife, right beside me. But I wasn't there. I was still wretchedly checking and rechecking my phone until I willed it.

It was him. Havranek. An email.

"It's him," I said, stopping dead still and passing the stroller to Mary.

"Who?" she asked.

"Havranek."

Mary stopped, too. "What's it say?"

"I don't know. Please…something good."

I opened it. "FYI" was all there was in the body of the email, that and an attachment. Once it loaded, I stared, looking for the point—then understood. It was a Universal invoice from one of Havranek's frack jobs, deeply redacted, but still clear. It was an example. It was the job design, and blacked out was what Universal was billing.

This was Havranek opening the door between us, the one that Wallace had been blocking.

In a rush of enthusiastic indiscretion, a million miles away from Mary and the girls, I immediately called Havranek. Right away, though, I caught myself and hung up. Thinking for a moment, blunting my fervor, I came up with a better plan.

I emailed him instead.

"I'll have a price to you in an hour. If we're not cheaper, please tell me and we will be."

Chapter 56

BIG FOOT

Venango County, Pennsylvania

In the dark of the next morning, I was in a hurry. My first worry was the same as the one I had every day: Would the Kanes be there? My second was: Would my newly hired crew?

I wanted to get to my two hires before Wallace did. I was worried that he'd run them off with his fury and normalized bedlam. But I was stuck behind in the data van, trying to get up the same steep, deeply rutted road that led to our wells. In front of me, seemingly on top of me, was my blender, chained to a 'dozer, inching its way closer to the rock outcroppings marking the ridgeline on top.

It wasn't until the blender crested the hill that I saw him, a towering visage above me. It was Wallace, silhouetted by a flash of headlights behind him, his eyes burning like lit spears from his dusky face. He was staring straight down into me.

I felt it as much as I saw it, him holding his stare right through the pan of my headlights, which I should have dimmed, and which suddenly seemed provoking. It was the first time I'd seen him since our words. Watching him as I passed, he remained immovable, striking in me a despair and the wish to run.

"He don't bother me," Frank said when I found him mixed in among the trucks and crew on the location. "We get along good. He's always wantin' to talk to me 'bout Superior."

"Yeah, no big deal. He's just a big pussycat," added Brian, thin enough that Wallace could pinch him between his fingers.

"All right. Good enough. Just stay outta his way. Let him get used to you some more," I said to Brian more than Frank.

An hour later, the job was on. Ford called for water, and we began flushing the hole down to our first stage as Big Foot, a big guy with the birth name Dan, pulled open the van doors and stepped inside.

"You must be Dan," I said.

"I am. How you doin', Dan?"

We shook hands, reviewed the job design, and a few minutes later broke the first stage, just like our nearby wells. A minute after that, after settling into our targeted rate and adding sand, Dan was leaning into the monitors, seemingly confused.

"I don't know what I'm looking at," he said, pointing at one. "You've got three hundred barrels of water in. That's not even possible. That what that says? Right there," he said, rising off the bench and jabbing a finger at the monitor.

"No...no..." I started in, explaining the software glitch and stumbling over getting caught so quickly. "The totaler's off. I know what's in the hole, that's not a problem, but the reading..." I went on, ratcheting through my well-rehearsed excuses: "Getting it worked out...Myers software fix...tech genius...training...conversion chart right here, all worked out..." And finally, to close the matter: "Our frack price reflects all-a this."

That did it. Big Foot's concern ebbed off on the price concession, as I quietly muttered about artless Zahir and his jerry-rigged operating program.

"Okay. You know what you're doing, just run the job."

We got through the first stage and then the second without a problem. To gain Dan's trust even further, I jumped out of the van between stages to measure water left in the tanks. After a quick cubic-foot calculation and a conversion, I was able to show him a dead-nuts match between the physical and the computer. After another stage, he told me to make sure I was available for the other five wells on the lease.

That felt just right, but with the coming winter and the insurmountable gap of time it brought, it wasn't enough. Not without Havranek.

Worse, so much worse, abhorrently so, it all crashed.

The tiny bit of momentum it had taken me over a year to achieve suddenly throttled down and detonated.

Everything, without even a hint, went straight to hell.

An SUV, just a flash of white, flew past us on the lease road. Right behind its trailing vortex of dust was a white pickup, and right behind that, a third white vehicle, another SUV. Through the dust, I could see that they all bore the same green, white, and blue logo of Pennsylvania's Department of Environmental Protection—essentially, the environmental police.

"What's that all about?" Dan asked, sitting up in his seat for a better look out a van window. "Those DEP?"

"Looks like it."

"Well, I hope they're not here to see us."

"They're not stopping," I said, trying to inject some hope.

"Thank God."

"Yeah. Please keep going, please keep going, please keep…" I said, glued to the window, just like Dan.

"They look pretty serious out there, racing around, don't they?" he added uneasily. "Someone's going to be in some deep shit."

Though we were still pumping the stage, everyone who should have been watching the job was watching the DEP instead. When two more of them appeared, making it a full-on squadron of government vehicles circling us, half the crew stepped right out onto the pad to watch.

This couldn't be a coincidence.

Was it our wells a quarter of a mile away on the hilltop? Maybe a leak, a rupture in a gathering line? Maybe the separator spilling over? All of it unlikely. And anyway, the pumper would have picked it up. We'd have been the first to know. It couldn't be us. It had to be something or someone else.

When the stage ended, the entire crew gathered for a better view. Dan and I stepped out of the van and joined them, all of us transfixed by the weight of five white SUVs and pickups on a hillside where there shouldn't have been any. All our engines were dialed down, and I could hear one of the crew gushing about "countin' five sonuvabitch DEP so far."

"How you get five if I only got four?"

"You only got to four 'cause that's only high as you can count!"

"Yeah, ya dumbass."

"Department of Environmental Persecution," another one joked.

"Someone goin' to jail," said another of them.

"Already been there, an' ain't goin' back."

On and on they laughed, like a cackle of hyenas.

Then I saw Wallace, Rusty, and Ford talking quietly among themselves, out on the edge of our site. For just a moment I thought of joining them. But their look left me feeling shouldered out. Besides, me approaching Wallace…I didn't think so.

"Let's keep this going," Dan said, moving back for the van.

I agreed and called out to the others: "We better keep going before the well comes on"—stopping myself when I caught sight of our two water-truck drivers, quietly waving me over.

I knew the one guy. He and his family had a few wells on the hillside near us. The other driver was his employee, both of them dead serious as I approached in a hurry, an obligation, but also out of curiosity.

Both of them backed out of view, to the distant side of their tanker trucks as I stepped in.

"I just talked to one of those DEP fellows, an inspector, I think," the first driver, my neighbor, divulged to me conspiratorially. "I was comin' up the hill an' he was standin' there an' I stopped an' he told me brine water got into the township water supply. Into their cistern, the entire water supply for the whole pissin' township."

"Brine? You mean production water?" I naively asked.

"Yeah! Brine."

"How could brine…? In the water supply?" I asked, stumbling, thinking of little else but the possibility of my part in it.

"I don't know, but they're gonna put everyone on ration, the whole pissin' township."

"You think it's from our wells, the ones we just fracked?"

"Might be, but I know it ain't from mine. But yours, you ain't even got the water lines buried. You'd-a seen it if it was yours."

The driver held my stare, like he was holding something back.

"Well, where you think it's from?"

The man paused, like he might or might not say something, then stopped himself and turned away. Whatever he knew, he wasn't giving it up.

I hurried back to the frack job and van, feeling gut-punched and thinking *What now, what else?* Then I damned near ran right into Wallace—on a crash course with the gathered crew—all of them rubbernecking for a better look at a passing DEP truck.

"What the hell you all starin' at?" he shouted, charging into them like a dog into a flock of geese. *"Get to work right fuckin' now an' get this pissant well fracked!"*

His bark was like a whip snap. Everyone parted and bolted for their stations.

I climbed into the van with Dan and hurriedly, obediently, set up the computer for the next stage. I was busy, but my attention was hardly on the frack job, not as I stole glances out my window to see if the DEP was turning in toward us or still racing around.

"Just keep it clean, all right?" Dan said, surprising me from the bench seat.

"No, no. We keep it clean. We watch everything."

"Don't get me wrong. I'm no fanatic. But today's not the day. Nothing goes on the ground, right?"

"Nothing. Absolutely. We're careful. We carry diapers if there's ever any leaks or spills. I'll circle around between stages, too. Nothing will go on the ground. We don't do that."

Placated enough, Dan sat back and watched out the window as I slid on my headset and keyed my walkie.

"Ready in the van. Ready when you guys are. And listen," I said into my mic, "anyone sees anything, a leak or anything, let's shut it down and clean it up like always, all right? Call it in. Let's be really careful."

"Got it. I'm watching," I heard back from Frank on the blender.

Brian came back with a different tack. "Don't worry, Big Dan, we'll try an' keep you outta jail!" he cracked over the walkie.

The engines came up, and we were off and running and in no time had another stage in, then another, and another until we were done. The job had gone well, uneventful other than the circus revolving around us, where our ringmaster Wallace remained unapproachable, withdrawn, and huddled on the sidelines.

Little else was talked about but the DEP as we racked up the trucks. The crew jabbered gleefully about it—finally someone in trouble other than them—popping their heads up like a game of Whac-A-Mole, then excitedly reporting back on what they saw, postulating on why it was that the clutch of DEP, seemingly more than five vehicles now, had gathered right on top of Dan's lease.

Plodding along through all the distractions and all the theorizing, we eventually got the trucks racked up and rolling in a convoy through a field under a power line. Directly ahead of us was all the DEP activity, just past where we stopped to wait for our turn to drop down the thin and steep lease road into the valley.

All bottled up, I sat still in the line, trying not to return the stares I was sure were on me, as though doom's own eyes had sought me out. I had planned to check on our three nearby wells but thought better of it as I snuck glances at the DEP people, a hundred yards past me, where there were more than before. The racing around had stopped, and they were now gathered together, convulsing over something and buzzing about like a hive of antagonized bees. Unwittingly, we were all left on display for them, like suspects in a single-file lineup for the authorities, all of them wrapped up in their gang colors of blue, with big and prominent white DEP lettering stamped across their backs.

The horrendous wait was suddenly punctuated by a flash of red and a cloud of dust as Wallace shot past us in his pickup, cutting line and dropping down the hill in an obvious “fuck you” move meant for me, or the DEP, or whoever couldn’t get out of his way quickly enough.

And then I saw nothing more of the DEP. Like the improbable boom of a lightning strike. There and gone.

Chapter 57

BIG FOOT CANCELS: THE DEP FINDS ME

Venango County, Pennsylvania

The following morning, not even twenty-four hours after Big Foot's first job, we lost all five of his remaining wells. These were the ones he had promised me in the van just the day before.

"It's too hot on that hill right now," Dan told me when he called and woke me up. "I'm hearing all sorts of things. Something about someone might've been dumping brine up there. I don't know, I wasn't there. But it wasn't me and I doubt it was you. So I don't know anything, but we're not fracking any more of these. I change my mind, I'll let you know."

He never did let me know. Though later on, I heard he fracked the last five of them with one of our competitors.

This was after an investigation was announced, one that was bumped up from the DEP to the Pennsylvania attorney general's office.

The day before, once the dust had settled after Wallace raced by in his fuck-you move, I saw the water-truck driver from before. He and his second had been waiting for us to clear the road so they could haul off the unused water in the frack tanks. We caught each other's eye and, with the line absolutely still, I parked and walked over.

"They found a covered-up pit," the first one I kind of knew said as I approached.

"A 'pit'? What do you mean, a 'pit'?" I asked.

"A stone pit. They're gonna dig it up. They got a backhoe on the way."

"What pit?"

"Right about where your pit is. The one they found, I'm thinkin'. Right over there. 'Bout right there," he pointed, right where the DEP had huddled, and right at our shale pit. Then he shook a thumb at his friend.

"He just talked to one-a them DEP guys. Said it's filled in with fresh dirt, but there's tire tracks all 'round it."

"Like someone's been dumpin' brine," the second said, excitedly speaking up, "an' that's where it come from—"

"An' you know brine only comes from oil wells—'round here, anyways," the first interrupted.

"An' that pit's right above the township cisterns. Right about where he says, over there," the second said, pointing.

"Don't point, man!" the first exclaimed, knocking his buddy's hand down.

"Why? You think they see us?"

"Yeah. They might. They could be right in the woods, watchin."

"Well, anyways, ground's all fractured up here, according to 'em. Easy for water to channel through. An' that pit bein' right above their cisterns, an'...well, it's gonna be lights out 'round here."

"You gotta be kidding me!" I said, like I'd just been stabbed.

"The DEP boss says it's a federal offense, if it's intentional. It's like domestic or environmental terrorism or somethin', he called it, 'cause it's a water supply. An' jus' 'cause I got a water truck don' mean no one's gonna call me no goddamn terroris'," the second one finished.

"Me and my truck ain't been nowhere near that pit or them cisterns. Them tire tracks ain't mine. I don't do shit like that. I'll prove it. I'll take pictures of my tires an' then them tracks an' compare 'em, right?" the first one said to the second. "Let 'em try an' match our tires 'gainst them tracks—"

"Damn right, we should do that—"

"Then who the hell did it?" I interrupted.

"Well, that's the big question ain't it?" the first driver flatly stated. "An' I'm not sayin' a damn thing." He turned and walked off, his buddy following right behind him.

Chapter 58

HOME

Pittsburgh, Pennsylvania

The oil and gas industry is harsh. The environment down below and almost universally above is harsh. Its people—the ones who go and get it out of the ground—are accustomed to harsh. We have to be, operating in the mud and brittle cold of the Appalachians, the Front Range, the Bakken; in the heat of the West Texas Permian; in the hurricanes and blowouts and all-engulfing fires of the Gulf. And then there's the political unrest: clerics in the Middle East holding oil hostage; Hezbollah attacking Israel rigs in the eastern Mediterranean; Ayatollah Khomeini using oil to leverage unrest before dying and passing his malevolence onto the next generation; Iraqi Shi'ite cleric Muqtada al-Sadr's coup d'etat; armed militias pushing unrest in Yemen, launching missiles into Saudi oil installations; journalist Jamal Khashoggi's dismemberment; militias in gunboats patrolling the Niger oil delta; Venezuelan dictators and Russian oligarchs stealing oil and lives; Vladimir Putin co-opting European energy security.

Oil people also believe in freedom—unfettered, unrestricted, state and personal. We protect the environment, righteously, practically. We don't deny our carbon output but see carbon as the byproduct of something inherently essential: that carbon is the apex foundation of society. Without it, there would be few trees left on the planet. We do not settle well with a government that moves about disjointedly, out of sync with common sense, thrift, affordability. This conservatism among us embraces the spirit of effort, self-determination, self-reliance, self-sufficiency. It loathes regulation, the noose of government, the oversteps, and lately, the discrimination.

But a few of us, fewer and fewer, go too damn far...

It was the day after Big Foot's job when my phone rang around 9:00 a.m. I was still at my house that late in the morning but had only gotten four or five hours of sleep.

"Hey, dude." It was Adam at Lightspeed.

"Yeah. Hey, Adam," I said, the first words I'd spoken that morning.

"You coming into work today?"

"Yeah. Little bit. Late night."

"Well, you might want to get down here. Like, right now."

"Why? What's up?"

"Well, there's, like, some guy with a DEP jacket here that wants to talk to you."

I sat up in bed, trying to understand. "What do you mean, 'DEP'?"

"Like DEP. It's in huge white letters right on the dude's coat, man, D-E-P. Like a blue windbreaker thing."

"You mean Department of Environmental Protection? Like a government guy?"

"Yeah, man. He said that, too," Adam chuckled nervously.

"Jesus."

"Yeah, dude."

"He say what he wants?"

"Yeah. You."

Mary walked into our bedroom, holding two baby bottles and a towel, stood over me and listened.

"Well, can I talk to him?"

"I'll ask."

I could hear Adam's voice in the background, but nothing from anyone else.

"What's wrong?" Mary asked, sensing a pause in the conversation.

"I'm in trouble," I said, standing in my underwear, all I had time to say before Adam was back on the line.

"Hey, man, he doesn't want to talk to you, on the phone, I mean," he said, sounding like he was cupping the receiver. "This guy seems to think, like, you're going to run or something. It's really weird."

"I'm not going to run!"

"Dude, I know that. But he doesn't know that."

"Well, what's he doing?"

"Ahh…at the moment, he's looking at me."

"Let me just talk to him. This is ridiculous. Tell him I'm in my underwear."

"How about you tell him that?

I could hear some rustling over the phone and an indecipherable exchange. Then the man was on the phone, identifying himself as "an investigator for the Department of Environmental Protection."

"When do you think you'll be getting into work today, sir?"

"Well, honestly, I just got up. I got in really late last night. From work, not from out drinking or anything," I said, forcing an ill-timed laugh. "But, ahh, how can I help you?"

"The way for this to proceed is for the two of us to meet face to face."

"And you're really with the DEP? You're not—this isn't like a joke? Like this is supposed to be funny?"

"No, sir, this is not funny."

My God, he's going to arrest me was all I could think. *Domestic terrorism*, just like the driver said back on the job. The man was right. It wasn't funny.

"Can I at least ask what the problem is?" I asked meekly.

"That would require we meet—"

"Is it the frack job yesterday? In Reno? I know something was going on up on the hill, all the DEP trucks. Is that what—"

"Mr. Doyle, we need to meet. That's why I'm here waiting to see you."

"Well, I'll tell you what. If you want to come out this way—I'm still in my underwear, but I'm like a two-minute walk from a Starbucks."

"Meet you at a Starbucks?" the investigator asked, not doing much to mask his incredulity.

"If it's okay with you. It would give me a chance to get dressed. Be faster this way than me getting down there. Just like fifteen minutes is all. If you even like Starbucks—I don't really like Starbucks—but everyone knows where the Starbucks is...." I went on disjointedly. *Jesus*, I thought to myself, *quit talking about Starbucks!*

The investigator went silent, which only increased my troubled neurosis.

"Well, if you know Pittsburgh," I stumbled on, "it's in Shadyside, the Shadyside Starbucks. Adam there, the guy you're talking to, he can draw you a map, you know, if you're not from Pittsburgh...."

Finally: "You're going to be there, Mr. Doyle?"

"I'll be there," I started, then more fully understood. I went on firmly. "I said I'd be there, I'll be there."

"All right. If you say you'll be there, I'll meet you there."

"Hold it, I know you're wearing a DEP jacket, but...ahh...I'm like five-eight, I'll be wearing...ahh...I gotta see—"

"I'll find you. That won't be a problem."

After we hung up, I began pulling on clothes with little regard for a match. What was the difference? What do you even wear when you're wondering if you're going to be arrested, maybe incarcerated.

Then, it hit me. "That won't be a problem," the investigator had said. He already knew what I looked like.

Mary, who had disappeared, was back now with Maria in one arm and "Woof Puff Puff," a blue teddy bear with big translucent eyes, in the other.

"Who was that?"

"Don't freak out, but it was some guy with the DEP, Environmental Protection. An investigator—"

"About yesterday, you mean? About the domestic terrorism?"

"Yeah. He wants to talk."

"Jesus, Dan. An investigator? It's just not going to end, is it? It's just one thing after another.... And now *terrorism?*"

"Yeah, I know. Didn't think to cover that in my business plan."

"That's a criminal charge. Like, you go to jail for that, right?"

"I don't know."

"Can they arrest us for that?"

"I don't know."

"Can we get a lawyer?"

"I'm gonna try."

"Is that what I heard? That you're going to meet him at the Starbucks?"

"Yeah."

"You hate Starbucks."

"Yeah, we're not going for the coffee."

Chapter 59

MORE LAWYERS

Pittsburgh, Pennsylvania

I stepped outside of my house, the same one that would be up for sale in a few months, directly into another world of lawyers. More lawyers.

I dialed my Pittsburgh lawyer Scott and fortunately he answered. Skipping all pleasantries, I unleashed a tirade about the Kanes, the pit, domestic terrorism, and the DEP. On and on, and out of breath when I finished, I could hear Scott exhaling.

"Boy, Dan. Didn't see this one coming, did you?"

We both laughed a gallows kind of laugh that quickly faded off.

"No. This is a new one for me."

"You know this is serious—"

"Yeah. Terrorism. Like I'm guessing maybe *prison* serious."

"Well... You're just going to have to be very, very careful with this, you know that?"

"I know."

"You said he's an investigator?"

"Right."

"I don't know if a DEP Investigator can make criminal charges, but I think you need to get ready."

Shocked straight, I stopped in my tracks.

"Like, I'm going to get charged?" I asked, hearing it from a lawyer carrying disproportionately more weight than hearing it from my wife.

"Possibly. Not right now, I wouldn't say. But you should be ready for it."

"I don't even know what the hell this's all about. I didn't do—"

"Doesn't matter. Also, I don't do criminal law like this. You need a criminal defense lawyer."

"Jesus. Criminal defense lawyer—"

"Environmental, mostly. Can you hold this off, with your investigator?"

"I'd say no. Probably no way on that. I said I'd meet him, so, you know…I gotta."

"Man of your word, huh?"

"Ha! Yeah. You know any of those? Criminal defense lawyers?"

"Well, you're in luck. First time in a while, eh? I know a good one, if I can get her. Stacie does environmental law with McGuire."

"McGuireWoods? I've used them."

"Good. That'll move things along quicker. I'll call her right now and ask her as a favor—that she call you right away. She calls, you can take it, right?"

"Absolutely. As long as, you know, I'm alone." I started moving again toward the Starbucks.

"I'll call her now. Watch for her call. You don't want to miss Stacie's call."

"Okay, all right. I won't."

"And, hey, Dan. On a personal note…"

"Yeah?"

"You all right?"

"Yeah…I don't know. I don't think so. You think he's going to handcuff me, anything like that?"

"That seems a bit extreme. Listen, talk to Stacy. Take her call, Dan. Be careful. These guys will use you."

I was pretty certain I was ahead of the investigator but wanted to stay out of sight, anyway. *"I'll find you. That won't be a problem,"* he'd said, having gotten to me. I stopped around the corner from the Starbucks and waited for my *next* lawyer's phone call. Behind me was a boutique store window display filled with winsome, frolicky, come-hither tennis outfits. There I stood, watching without judgment.

My phone rang. It was a 412 area code, so I thought it had to be Stacie.

"Hi, this is Dan."

"Hi, Dan, this is Stacie Christman, with McGuireWoods.

"Yeah. Hi, Stacie. Thanks for calling. A lot going on."

"Well, it's nice to meet you. I understand you may have a matter."

"A 'matter.' Right. It seems like it."

"And you're about to meet with the DEP?"

"Right. An investigator. I'm waiting on him now."

"I wouldn't."

"No? You wouldn't?"

"No, I wouldn't. You have nothing to gain, Dan."

"Stacie, I didn't do anything, so I thought—"

"I understand that. But did anyone else in your company do anything? Can you offer the investigator assurances of that—that there's no way anyone—that the area is secure and locked and monitored, so there's no way anyone in your company could have been involved?"

I didn't answer because there was no answer.

"Do you see my point, Dan? And I understand you have wells in the area and they're on your bond. Do you see it…? You'll put yourself at a disadvantage."

"He's on his way, Stacie. I told him I'd meet him," I said from my perch in front of the store glass, watching for that blue windbreaker.

"Then meet him, but tell him on advice of counsel you're not able to talk at this time."

There he was! A fifty-year-old, barrel-chested man, in no hurry, wearing a DEP windbreaker and coming my way. He looked to be just as out of place as me in the tony little shopping area.

"He's coming, Stacie. That's got to be him."

"Would you like me to talk to him?"

"No. I'm okay. I'll just— Listen, I don't know what anyone else did. I don't know if they were on my payroll when they did it—*if* they did anything—I don't know, but I doubt it. We don't have a way to even move brine that far away, Stacie. But I gave the guy my word. I got to talk to him. I can talk to him and not say anything. I can just ask him what he knows."

"So, you've talked to investigators before? Officials with agendas, that sort of thing?"

"No. I know. I haven't. But listen, I said I'd meet with him, for Christ's sake. I invited him for a cup of coffee," I admitted, watching the man closing in. "I think he sees me."

"Then meet him for your cup of coffee, but you're doing it at your own risk. You'll make my job a lot harder—getting you out of the trouble you get yourself in."

"I'll just listen, Stacie. I'll tell him I'm doing it against advice of counsel."

"All right. Listen for another second, Dan. Don't offer up anything. All you know for certain is you didn't do it. That's what you tell him. Don't speculate and don't let him paint a picture for you. You don't know, and that's the all of it! You understand?"

"Understood," I said, having wandered to the front of another store window, where leather thongs were hanging. *Jesus*, I thought, *I better move away and maybe wave or something.*

"Be careful."

"I will."

"Call me the minute you're done."

"I will."

Stacie and I hung up, and a few seconds later I walked toward the man, holding my hand out.

"Hi, I'm Dan."

Chapter 60

QUIT!

Venango County, Pennsylvania

When Adam called out for me from Lightspeed's office, I didn't hear him at first. But then he was yelling again, holding out the phone toward me in the shop.

"Hey, man, I think it's that guy Tom."

"Who?" I called from the back of a grip truck that I was loading with light stands.

"Seriously, man, I think it's that Tom dude you've been obsessing over."

I should have jumped the forty-two inches off the back of the truck to the shop floor. I should have broken into an elated run. But I didn't because I really didn't much care anymore, not with the fear of arrest. Keeping my business afloat suddenly seemed a paltry, inconsiderable concern now that I was on this new precipice, where losing everything wasn't just worrisome speculation.

"So, Mr. Doyle, what can you tell me about yesterday's events?" the DEP investigator asked me as we sat down in the Starbucks. What followed went down in a staccato of questions followed by my attempts at answers that wouldn't incriminate me.

"I don't know anything about it."

"Who did you speak to?"

"No one."

"Can I get their names?"

"What names?"

"I can assure you, Mr. Doyle—"

"Of what? Of what? I can assure you, too. This will ruin me, even though I don't know what you're talking about."

By the end of it, after the inspector and I separated, I had no idea what would come next, other than it wasn't over. I had promised him I'd cooperate, which I fully intended to do, but I knew, too, that he'd keep coming back, that he wasn't going to stop.

When I got home, Mary was waiting in as much disbelief as me. We gathered up the girls for a stroll and began walking and talking and looking for a path out. No matter how many streets we walked and turns we took, we kept coming back to the same obvious place.

"You know what? Fuck those guys. Every one of them," Mary said, her fury surprising me. "This is a disaster!"

"I know.... I know."

By noon, I didn't know what to do next, so I defaulted to work. I went to Lightspeed to look for whiffs of money and help load a truck that was going out. Anything other than this.

I remained in the back of the grip truck, fearing it was a joke from Adam, or a "thanks but no thanks" from Tom. I had sent him a quote for his work but hadn't heard back. This was him calling to politely say no. I'd heard he was a good guy. Maybe that was why he was calling. That and kindness, nothing more. "Get fifty more under your belt, Dan, then gimme a call." And why would he talk to me and not Wallace, given all their years together and especially since I was the agitating newcomer beset with freshman problems? The DEP. The environmental terrorism. The Kanes. Once he heard, everything would be pointless, anyway.

But then, as my feet do, they began moving, a drumbeat to the cadence of my disillusionment, my fruitless and miscarried thoughts: *I'm done. I'm done. My God, the fantastic madness of it all...*

Dutifully, a beaten man, I took the phone from Adam and took Havranek's call, the guy with the lifeline who no longer mattered.

"Hello. This is Dan," I said with a toneless lack of enthusiasm, surprising even myself.

And then there he was, Havranek, on the phone, asking me if I had a few minutes, sounding normal, nothing like the heavyweight I had made of him.

"Well, Dan, your crew did a fine job the other day. Really saved my schedule. Universal pulled the rug out from under me on that one. No warning at all. Not much time for us small fries anymore," Tom said, pretending to chuckle.

"I know," I said. "They're moving on with shale."

"Yeah. Kind of hard to keep to a schedule with that. Especially with forty-one to go, and then there's some talk of a year-end program. That happens, we're gonna just keep going."

"Another program?" I asked, my sudden interest betraying my otherwise gloom. "On top of this program, the forty-one you have left?"

"Yeah. That's what my partner's saying. Another fifty if it gets sold. With oil prices going up, it just might, too."

"That's like ninety wells. Geez, Tom, that's a lotta wells," I said, feeling the stir of hope.

"Lot of work, that's for sure. Actually, that's why I'm calling. I wanted to gauge your interest. These wells we're doing, they're a lot bigger than the wells you been doing down your way in Venango County. Lotta pressure, these ones. But you finished that well the other day for me just fine, so I guess what I'm asking, you think you could keep up with this kinda work?"

"We can keep up, Tom," I rushed to say. "We could handle that, just like on the first one. Kept up just fine with an EnerVest well we just did."

"That's right. I heard that. Lotta pressure up there. That's good. So, what I need to tell my partner is, you think you can do a little better on your quote? And thanks for that, by the way. But given the number of wells, can you give a little thought to something better?"

Following was a long pause. Mine, not Havranek's. In that drawn-out moment, the DEP was slipping away from me, enough for me to realize that I had to stay alive. That I had to provide. That I had to go lower, because it was survival, and because I knew I could.

"I have. A lot, actually. I was thinking if there was some volume, maybe something like ten percent. And it sounds like there's a lot of volume, so I think I could do another ten percent."

Another long pause followed, long enough for me to wonder if Tom was still there.

"Thanks for that, Dan. We kind of need it, the size of the program. Why don't you let me talk to my partner? We've both been with Universal a long time, but times are changing. Anyways, if you could revise that quote and send it to me, I'll get back to you. I've gotta get my partner's blessing, too, if that's all right? You don't mind, let me do that."

"Yeah. Sure, Tom. I'll get it right out to you. No problem."

We hung up, and I thought forty-one plus fifty makes ninety-one. For ninety-one wells, I'd search harder for more money to buy more time. But the DEP...the DEP would change my newfound luck. The investigation, the ecoterrorism, the possible indictment would kick the legs right out from underneath Reliance Well Service and its short and unprosperous run.

That unexpected phone call from Tom, and then this...

This madness...

Chapter 61

MUTINY

Venango County, Pennsylvania

My phone rang. It was Ford.

"I been tryin' to reach you," was the first thing out of his mouth.

"Yeah, I'm up here at Bruce's," I said into my phone, standing on Bruce's next well site. "Water's on-site and he's got a pump set, so no problem for tomorrow."

"Hey," Ford continued.

"Little tight, so maybe we back the pump in first."

"*Hey*, I said. You keep talkin'—"

"Yeah, I thought—"

"*Listen*, all right? I got somethin' to say. Dad wanted me to tell you we can't make the job tomorrow. Our guys can't make it."

I stopped, trying to understand. "What do you mean?" I asked, thinking Ford was joking. Unlikely, though, given our humorless relationship.

"I just said it. The rig crew's stayin' on the rig. They're not gonna be on the trucks."

"They're gonna be there, but just on the rig?"

"Yeah."

"And you're not kidding, right?"

"No."

"There a reason why, Ford?"

"Yeah. Dad said so."

"Okay… He say why?"

"Yeah. He says it's too much for 'em to do both. Jumping back and forth's too messed up, he said to tell you."

"Okay, but that's like the whole premise of everything, you know? Same crew on the trucks and the rig. Like that's what we've been talking about and doing all along."

"That's what he says."

"And he knows we have this job for Bruce tomorrow?"

"Yep. He's going to be on it."

"Then how we gonna frack it?"

"I don't know. Find some more-a your crew guys, I guess. Or Bruce calls Universal. One or the other."

We hung up, and for a few minutes I sat with a head full of cement, stumbling through a hundred incoherent thoughts, all of them underlain by a simple unconstrained fear: *I knew this could come. I should have seen this coming. I should've been ready. I should've, would've. I didn't act. I didn't...*

I was hardly able to think, volleying back and forth between knowing I was optionless and hoping I was only mostly optionless. But if I could think, think my way through it, maybe, just maybe I could land on something. That small bit of effort gave me my first coherent thought. I'd take a seat on a nearby pipe boat and push away everything. I'd find the spine and follow it.

"*You can do anything you please, Daniel. You hear me? You listening? It just comes down to how much you can bear.*" My father had told me this back when I was a seven-year-old boy, as I watched him struggling under the weight of his own start-up. He told me of the ironworker showing up with a gun, how the man had laid it on his desk, looking for an exchange of money for job-site protection. "I'll make sure nuttin' goes wrong wit' yer job, Pat." The gun there to demonstrate the ironworker's fidelity to the plan, and me, all ears, wondering why.

I started thinking of Frank's "farm boy" friend, Scooter. The guy with the skull tats. How Frank had told me he knew more just like Scooter, more guys on disability, and some on vacation looking for side work.

I called him.

"Wow, looks like you're fucked, Dan," Frank said after I explained it all.

"Yeah, I know. Listen, Frank, you think you can get ahold of Scooter and see if he still wants to work?"

"Scooter'll work. Lazy ass's just home playin' video games."

"Okay, but can he work tomorrow, our job for Bruce?"

"Tomorrow, like *tomorrow* tomorrow?"

"Yeah. You think of anyone else, too? Any of your other friends that can drive and frack?"

"For tomorrow, too?"

"Yeah, Scooter plus two, maybe three. Ford might or might not be there."

"So that's three guys, maybe four for tomorrow? Probably getting up at two in the mornin'. No problem at all," Frank nearly laughed into the phone.

"Yeah. I know. Sorry."

"Alright. I ain't gonna promise anythin', but I'll call around. Gonna depend on what you're payin', too."

"I'll pay cash. Whatever they want. Long as they show up. And, Frank, I don't have much of anything, but I'll take care of you for this."

"That was my thought, too. Be a pretty good idea, somethin' like this!"

"Don't worry, I'll take care of you," I said, the words of a determinedly desperate man.

Chapter 62

MY COMPANY

Venango County, Pennsylvania

"That'll be me in the white Silverado in your parking lot, if you don't mind," I explained to the trooper on duty. "I won't get in anyone's way, but any chance I can use your bathroom, if, you know, I need it? Not now, I mean, but during the night?"

"We don't lend out the bathroom here, sir." The trooper said after a drawn-out appraisal of me.

"Oh, okay," I said. "No problem. I understand."

When I started away, the trooper called out after me. "Why're you sleeping in our lot, sir?"

I shrugged and admitted it. "Tell you the truth, it's the safest place I could think of."

It was a state police barracks, not too far from the shop. It's where I was spending the night in the parking lot under a bank of floodlights. My thought was that no one would bother me there, there'd be nothing startling, no confrontations, nothing mortal as I pushed ahead on my own. And no one bothered me, not even the troopers, leaving me alone even as I peed into a cup, filling and refilling it through the night and pouring it out my truck window.

I never really slept, or if I did, I wasn't sure, because my worries didn't stop. All night they continued, unbroken. The same nightmarish volley of will-they-show, won't-they-show; the midnight collection of keys from the truck ignitions so they didn't go missing; the scramble to round up enough cash for four guys unknown to me but who I knew well enough to know wouldn't endure default.

All day long, Frank and I had been going back and forth, both of us reaching out to everyone we knew. But in the end, it was Frank alone who found success. Earlier that night, on our last call, he told me we had a crew. Three friends of his from Superior Well were in, each one of them, he assured me, happy to shrug off an injury or call in a sick day for a straight cash deal.

"You think they'd stay on for Bruce's last job? Tom's, too, you know, if we get any of them?"

"Dan, you can talk anyone into anythin', you got enough Benjamins."

That was it. I had a crew, assuming Ford would show up, too. It was just a matter of the Benjamins.

At 3:00 a.m., I gave up on sleeping and gave in to the fear of oversleeping. I drove to the shop and circled the parking lot to make sure Wallace, or anyone else counting on a bad outcome, wasn't there. A half-hour later, I stepped out of my Silverado and walked from truck to truck, starting each of them with the keys I had earlier grabbed, letting air build and hoping to save some time when—if—everyone arrived.

After that, I sat on the blender's bumper and skittishly waited for headlights to appear. By 3:45 a.m., I had delusionally convinced myself that someone should have arrived by now, that it was statistically impossible not to have at least one early riser. In my deranged, sleep-deprived numbness, I started out across the lot for the highway, ready to flag down anyone even resembling my crew, whatever it was that they looked like.

Then, at 3:55, I saw headlights and ran out in the open. It was Brian. I started running right alongside him as he turned in and offered me his hand. Crazily, I shook it, right through his window. A few minutes later, it was Frank and Scooter arriving, Scooter bear-hugging us all. And then another man, Newman, a mountain of a man, pulling up in a tiny car that he had to wiggle out of, showing off his shoes with rubbers because boots weren't wide enough to cover his calves.

"Oh shit! Someone better piss-test Newman!" Scooter shouted as Newman popped free from his little clown car.

"Hahaha," everyone went, even me, the guy who should have been concerned.

"Get over here, Scooter, so's I can breathe on you!" Newman shouted, as he charged him.

"Ninety-proof piss, I guarantee you!" Scooter yelled as he ran.

So far that was five, including me.

Still not enough. Then Ken arrived, and right after him a guy named Jeff. But I was still one short. Ford.

Earlier that day, I'd called and pressed him on whether he was fracking with us or not. In the end, he texted to say he was in, only because he liked running the pump, and for no good reason beyond that. But now, a little after 4:00 a.m., I was beginning to doubt his arrival. Without him, it was going to be a problem, but I had a crew to show around and started directing them toward the pump and blender. Then, at 4:10 a.m., right about when I was saying "Let's go," Ford slow-rolled into the lot right alongside the pump, which should have been a flush of relief but came with mixed feelings instead.

"All right, everyone, follow me. Try and stay within CB range," I shouted over the idling trucks as I headed for the van, texting Bruce to say we'd be ready to pump at 6:00. Then adding that Wallace thought it was too much for the rig crew to take on the fracking, too, so I was bringing a crew of experienced frack hands from Universal and Superior. *Hope that's okay.*

As long as Bruce didn't text back and say no, or should I forget to look at my phone if he did, I thought we might just make it through the day.

With that, my gaggle of mismatched frackers started hopping in trucks and pulling out behind me into the night, treating our first job together like Old Home Week.

Chapter 63

GET TOM'S WORK

Venango County, Pennsylvania

"What happened, Dan?" Bruce asked as he pulled himself into the van. "Wallace pull a mutiny on you?"

It was the first I had seen of him, but the moment I'd been tormenting myself over all morning. And then there he was, grinning, and bringing nothing of a challenge. As much as I wanted to break down to my new friend, to come clean and admit to my precariousness—and the oncoming calamity—Bruce was a customer first, and that had to stay out front.

"Sorry about the short notice, Bruce. I should have told you earlier, but they're a really good crew. Most of them been fracking for like all-a their working lives," I said, watching him, wondering if he'd waver. "Just too much for one crew. All the back and forth, from the rig to the trucks, then back to the rig, you know?"

"Long as you say so, Dan. I ain't gonna say nothin', but I'll take your word for it."

I nodded along silently, but so very thankful, thank-you-God thankful for my friend's clemency. It was the best he could do, too, under the circumstances. His kindness, the mass of it, feeding my defining premise that people are good. Better even than what I could have guessed at that moment.

Two stages in, and these strangers who showed up for me in the middle of the night were becoming something of an intercession. They were so much beyond what I had hoped for, surprising me as we moved through the job with ease. First stage, second stage, third, all of it effortless for them, like jumping on the same bicycle they rode every day. All along, I'd been anticipating the worst between the frack and rig crews—bitter shoves escalating into a scrum, maybe even a riot, where everything on-site would be quickly converted into bludgeons. Instead, utterly unexpected, the two crews knew each other and were laughing and joking and talking smack, like they had everything but the beer.

If trouble was to come, it wouldn't be from them. It would come from elsewhere, but so far Wallace remained a no-show, and in fact never made it to the job. That meant peace instead of interruption. Everyone got their chance to shine, and at the end of the job, Bruce and I talked about the end of his work—*and mine*—with him asking if I had heard from Tom.

"We're talking a little," I said.

"That's it? A little?" Bruce prodded me.

"Yeah, well, maybe a little more than a little, but nothing, really."

"Well, give him some time, Dan. He's been with Universal a long time. It's hard to pull away, but he knows it an' you know it, an' all-a us know it's only a matter a time. It'll happen. You just gotta wait."

I nodded along, not letting on that I had no more wait left in me. That I was already into a technical default on my loan and had already decided on an unannounced trip to the bank, where I'd plead for more time, a stay on my execution. "What good am I to you if my company's dead?" was the opening I planned to use—if I got past security.

And then the DEP matter. On my mind nearly every minute, with all of my response amounting to nothing but worrying and waiting to see what would come of it.

But Bruce knew. I could see it.

"Maybe all Tom needs is to hear from someone that's worked with Reliance. Maybe that's all it'd take."

I snapped up, about to question what I'd heard, but Bruce was already out of the van and on his way to the rig, leaving whatever it was lie there.

Two hours later, after wrapping up the job, and within a half hour of our shop, where I planned to press rolls of dollars into everyone's hands, my phone rang.

Forever an optimist—blindly so, as entrepreneurs trend—I had entered Tom's number into my phone. Now it was him. Right on my phone. Calling. Tom Havranek.

My first flashing thought was that he was calling it all off, that I wasn't worth the risk. That he had heard…

I falteringly answered my phone, and half expecting a brush-off, I was instead surprised by his buoyancy, his upbeat tone, his sounding like a guy wanting to talk, something that sounded to me like deliverance.

"Listen, you around? I'm over in Oil City on a few things, and I didn't know if you were over at the Kanes?"

"I'm not. I mean, I can be. I'm on my way," I nearly shouted, my enthusiasm catching me by surprise.

"How far out are you?"

"Half hour."

"Good. I'm right in the neighborhood. See you then."

Then he hung up, leaving me gripping my phone like it was a lifeline, my last, thin tether to solvency.

"I gotta take off," I said into the van's CB. "I gotta get back to the shop. I'll see you all there." I hit the accelerator and jumped from 50 to 70 mph, leaving behind the lumbering convoy of trucks in my exhaust.

In short order, I was back at the shop, vacuuming the van like a teenager cleaning up for the prom. Doing everything I could to impress Tom, I even booted up the computer to run a frack simulation and bury all that talk about graphing versus charting. Last up was washing the van. As soon as I began hosing it off, a few of the Kanes' rig crew rolled in, pulling along a cloud of dust that stuck like Elmer's glue to everything wet.

I was about to quietly hose it off again until I saw a Toyota pickup approaching. When the crew ran toward it, I guessed it was Tom—certain of it when they greeted him in a chorus of friendly shouts. He knew their names and joked and prodded along, everyone getting just what they were looking for—laughs from the guy who was handing out all the work.

When my turn came, I was greeted by a guy about my size. A Division III college football quarterback with a degree in petroleum engineering. Just like me, he was dressed in Carhartts and a ball cap, like a guy who used his hands.

"You look like a farmer," I blurted out, instantly feeling foolish.

Tom laughed. "Well, what'd you think I'd look like?"

"I didn't know. I guess a businessman or something," I said, cursing my Irishness, the part of it where you said whatever landed in your head.

"A businessman, out here?" Tom said, waving at the surroundings and chuckling.

"Yeah, I guess not," I chuckled along, too, willing to laugh if it kept him in front of me.

"So, Dan, I guess I gotta ask, you think you can commit to my program? I know you'll say 'for sure,' but Universal thought so, too. Now I'm getting cancelled. Fact, I was just cancelled again for my next one, right before I called you."

"Again? Hard to keep up with that."

"Yeah. Well, I'm going to need to replace them or supplement them, depending on how—" Tom said, his stare on me. "I just got off the phone with Bruce. I wanted you to hear that from me first, but he was singing your praises."

"Bruce called you?"

"Yeah. An old friend. He says you haven't had any problems keeping up."

"We can keep up," I said, thinking back to Bruce in the van, better understanding his comment, his unwavering, unimaginable generosity. This oil-field friendship, the way it is with family. "We'd commit to it all, Tom," I said, instantly regretting my directness. Moving away from it, I stepped toward the van. "The first job, you didn't see the van, but I thought I could show you now. There's still a few graphing issues. I don't want to pretend. But we're working it out with a fix I can show you."

"That what Wallace was talking about?"

"Yeah," I admitted, wondering what all Wallace had said. "But we'll get it," I said, looking right at him. "We can graph."

"I don't doubt it. You can give me water, sand, and chemicals, though, right? I can see them going in?"

"Absolutely. Right. We're running Coriolis meters, just like Universal."

"Rate and volume, too? And sacks in?"

"I can. I was thinking I can run you a frack simulation I've been working on, so you can see."

Tom held up a hand. He'd heard enough. "Thanks, Dan. I bet it works just fine. Long as I can watch everything on a graph or chart, I really don't care. Just so its accurate, and I can get a printout at the end of the job, I'm good."

"You can absolutely get that."

"Okay, then. We got a deal."

"A deal?"

"Yeah. Maybe not for all of them. Let's see how it goes. But right now, I gotta move on."

Thunderstruck, but quiet, I stood dumbfounded, afraid that any utterance could upend it all. "Okay. Deal. Just see how we do," I finally stammered, euphoric, but cool and reaching for Tom's hand, as though a handshake would finalize and make whole his word.

"I'm going to take the rest of this week off and move some things around," he continued. "But I'd like to start back in next Tuesday, if you can make next Tuesday?"

"We can do Tuesday. We'll be there."

I shook his hand again—a bad habit of mine—a prolific handshaker.

"Oh, and, Dan. I talked it over with my partner, and that ten percent offer, if that gets too hard, let me know. We'd like to see you stick around."

So silly of me to shut down like I did. To show no emotion or joy. To feel only relief, a reprieve from some kind of death I'd been certain was ahead. But that's what I did. I stared blankly, right into my muddy boots.

Then everything changed again. Something in Tom, the way he was trying to ask me a question.

"Oh, Dan…hey…I wanted to ask you something," he started in, haltingly. "Wallace was telling me you rent equipment out for movies and commercials?"

"Huh? Movies?"

"Yeah, like lights for movies and commercials, in Pittsburgh."

“Right,” I answered with a thin laugh, embarrassed that it wasn’t Halliburton or Schlumberger on my resume instead of Lightspeed. “I started it, you know, and oil got bad. I was working as a geologist down in Texas, nothing much was going on, so there was an opportunity and I started it. Pays the frack bills, I guess.”

“My son’s in advertising down in Pittsburgh,” Tom said, interested and not at all ridiculing. “He went to school for it, and now he’s got a job in it. But to tell you the truth, I don’t know a damn thing about it.”

“Where’s he work?”

Tom told me and I perked up, knowing the agency and sensing there was a connection, something I might be able to do for his son. “We work with all the advertisers. We work with all those guys.”

“Well, maybe you’ll run across Tom Jr. one of these days. Looks just like me but still has his hair,” Tom said lifting his ballcap to show off a bad case of male-pattern baldness, making both of us laugh, like we might be friends.

Chapter 64

LOVE AND OTHER DRUGS

Pittsburgh, Pennsylvania

By the time the week was out, I found Tom Jr. in Pittsburgh. Before we'd even moved onto our first full well with his father, I was driving him to a movie set where Lightspeed was supplying equipment. Neither of us could believe our good luck, Tom touring his first set and me ingratiating myself to his father.

My plan was as simple as the two of us hot-shotting gel rolls to a set. After a few words with security and a backslap—I knew them all—we were waved through and stepped right onto a closed set.

It was *Love & Other Drugs*, a 20th Century Fox movie. Of course, Tom was thrilled, and I was thinking *mission accomplished*, especially as we walked past actors Jake Gyllenhaal and Judy Greer.

On our way to the camera, we were stopped by a few of the film crew that I knew, warning me to be careful, it was a closed set. That only made it a better show as I forged on with Tom Jr., hellbent on showing him a good time. Then, when actress Anne Hathaway walked past us, barefooted and in nothing but a bathrobe, I understood the warnings better.

Everyone was quiet, with averted eyes, making it a little too easy for me and Tom Jr. to walk right into a tiny and supposedly super-secure bedroom set. But there we were with the director, the director of photography, and a few lighting and camera techs, waiting on a set where even the producer was banned.

Aww, no, I thought, knowing what was coming, a forced exit at the hands of security. But Tom was grinning, and I was thinking just a little more about *mission accomplished*, about a happy son and a happy father—until the party crashed.

The key grip, a friend, leaned in, barely suppressing his quiet outrage. "What're you doing here with that guy?" he whispered, eyeing Tom Jr.

"I don't know, watching?"

"Seriously?"

"I know. But his dad's giving me some frack jobs."

"Come on, man. You gotta go."

"Bart, it's like ninety wells."

"You don't get the fuck outta here," he hissed, "I'm gonna throw you out myself!"

Chapter 65

THE BIG WOODS

Allegheny National Forest

I never made it home again, sleeping instead in the data van, in another state trooper barracks parking lot, this one a handful of miles from Tom's well.

When my Casio alarm rang at two, I was already up and working on my phone's calculator, factoring out the long-shot promise of two wells a week for Tom.

"*Maybe not all of them. Let's see how it goes. But right now, I gotta move on*," he'd said.

Tom's own words.

As long as we performed, as long as Wallace didn't self-combust, as long as the two crews didn't fight, or the bank's workout department didn't call with a cease and desist, maybe I'd get Tom to push Universal away. Forever. Maybe.

I called Frank. He answered over the engines idling in the background, letting me know everyone was at the shop and ready to pull out, and that I was holding them up. Relieved, I hung up and ate a sandwich Mary had packed for me the night before the day before.

It was time. I started the short drive to the well site, running headlong into a folded earth that rose higher and steeper as the "Big Woods" closed in around me, where blacktopped roads slipped into gravel roads, into shale roads, then into mud and the Kanes' towering rig. That was home base. I parked the van and pulled on my flame-retardant coveralls under a felt-black sky and its skirt of cloud cover and freckled patches of stars.

A little over an hour later, I heard them. A half minute later, I saw headlights grinding their way toward me. It was the pump and blender, and behind them our two sand dumps. Thank God we had two. Making Wallace right after all.

Before I could say what went where, Newman was already on the ground and guiding the pump truck in with a flashlight. The blender came next, then me in the data van, and finally the sand dumps, like this is what we did every day.

Immediately following were the hard strikes of sledgehammers breaking through the night as the setup began without pause.

Halfway into it, I saw the lights of a pickup approaching and knew it would be the Kanes' rig crew. They parked off location and walked in through my crew without disorder. Everyone was getting along, surprising me all over again and matching the last job in bro humor and good temperament. Similar, too, was that Wallace hadn't shown up on this one, either. So far.

At our 6:00 a.m. pump time, I rounded everyone up behind our sand dumps, the agreed-upon muster point. I had never run a safety meeting, a standard in the industry, but I'd seen them and knew we needed to do it here. Right then, just as I was beginning, Ford stepped in and I crumbled into an apprehensive unease. I had been ready to give the pump to Newman, though I knew it had to go to Ford.

Suddenly even more insecure, I started, "Hey, Ford. You all know Ford. He'll be on pump. Newman, if it's okay, you'll be ground man.

"No problem," came Newman, a relief after Ford said nothing.

I then covered the usual topics, most of them safety-related, like evacuation and muster points.

"Don't smoke at the wellhead," I went on with my most sage and ridiculously obvious advice. "Smoke out past the dumps and pocket your butts. Ahh...let's run chemicals across all of this. Make sure you got chemicals going downhole with first barrel."

"Yep," came Frank.

"Brian, you're covering sand, so you know the deal."

"Got it."

I turned to one of the new guys. I didn't even know his name, though I would soon enough, and asked, "Can you cover water? Up on the tank tops? Make sure we don't run dry? Gotta have at least two tanks full before we start a stage. Can you cover that?"

"In my sleep."

"All right," I smiled back.

"Okay. I'm not sure if Tom will want to shut in or release right away, so just beware on your headset. And on sand, we'll want to lower the dump every stage. Brian, if you can crawl up and have a look and gimme a best guess on sand level, I want to make sure the computer's lined out."

"You got it, Mr. Dan."

On I went, like a quarterback pretending to know what came next, with everyone strangely listening to me.

"All right. Anyone got anything?"

"Nope," came the first and only word from Ford. But he was there and knew how to run the pump, so that was good enough.

No one else spoke up, so I finished it. "All right, let's get this in the ground and get home before dark."

We broke up and everyone headed to their own piece of equipment. When I pulled myself into the van, there was Tom, surprising me, almost like I didn't know he was coming.

"We good?" he asked, wearing his Universal jacket and all business.

"All good, Tom," I said, offering nothing else.

"Okay, let's get on with it."

I pulled on my headset and mic. "Ready in the van. Anytime."

Over the din of engines throttling up, like racehorses prancing at a starting gate, Rusty whistled and spun his finger and cleared the well site with his crew. It was time to go.

Ford was next, calling over his walkie, "Gimme water."

The blender's C pumps engaged, and Ford shifted the pump into gear. Water started racing downhole, and the job was on. Fifteen stages on this one, easily twice what we'd been used to.

"Taking it pretty good," Tom said to me in the van, referring to sand hitting the formation face below.

"Yeah. Trending nice," I said.

"Good," he said, looking out the window. "Your crew's working out pretty well."

"Yeah. I got kinda lucky. We added it up, like thirty years of oil-field experience between 'em."

"That right? Few more years and they'll almost be caught up to me," Tom smiled.

An hour later, the sun came up. We were starting the fourth stage, then finishing it in no time, even when formation pressure came on and turned our valve releases into riotous jet blasts. Then the fifth stage and the sixth, and all the stress falling off as Tom told me how much Tom Jr. had enjoyed our field trip, the two of us laughing aloud over why anyone would ever allow me and his kid onto a closed movie set.

Then it all changed. Almost instantaneously.

When Wallace stepped on the location.

That's when it all came apart. It took ten minutes of the wrecking ball, the enraged, brooding chimera, the Armageddon, to make his arrival known. I shouldn't have been surprised, but I was, when Frank knocked and stuck his head in through the van's side doors.

"Sorry to interrupt, but, Dan, you got a minute?" he asked, engine noise flooding the van.

"Sure, what's up?"

"I mean, like alone, you know, the two of us alone."

Tom looked at me and I looked back at him, then shrugged like it was no big thing.

"It's probably nothing," I said as I stepped out. "Someone probably just ate someone else's Snickers bar," I quipped.

Outside, Frank turned to talk, but I kept going. No way I wanted to be within earshot of Tom. Marching a few truck lengths away, Frank finally caught up to me and was pissed.

"He's callin' me 'dildo breath.'"

"Huh?" I asked, confused.

"Motherfucker's callin' me, all-a us, dildo breath!"

"Dildo? You say 'dildo breath'?"

"Yeah. Dildo breath!"

"Who?"

"Who you think? Wallace!"

"What the hell is dildo breath?"

"Wallace should fuckin' know. He probably got it himself. An' 'sides that, the crazy fucker won't lift our pipe no more. Rusty says his dad says no more—we can lift our own goddamn pipe! I can deal with dildo breath, but the pipe—*who does that?*" Frank shouted, drawing a breath and spitting out disgust. "This ain't no good, Dan. An' Wallace's tellin' us he's gonna fuckin' bury you—get you run off, is how he said it. His words. Not mine."

All of it, and stupid me, struggling at first for words.

"Wallace's full of shit," I cried out, losing control. Everything abruptly unraveling and so damned close. "He's got no fucking say!"

"Yeah, well, my guys ain't gonna stick aroun' for this!"

I caught sight of Frank's crew, gathered around the back of the blender, watching me and Frank and waiting to see what I'd do.

Then I saw him: Wallace up on the rig deck with Rusty.

The son of a bitch. The son of a bitch and his standoff!

"Gimme a second. Tell the guys to hang on. Let me fix this," I told Frank as I feigned composure.

Trudging back to the van like it was ten miles away, I stumbled forward with no game plan other than the compulsive need to survive.

I pulled myself into the van, shut the door, and sat there in its quiet shell.

"Everything okay?" Tom finally asked.

I had nothing. Nothing materialized. I was sitting with the guy who had my life in his hands, who had known the other guy for the better part of his life, each of them pulling the other out of a hundred different jams over the years.

Think. I needed to think, but he was waiting, wondering, until reflexively, I caught my head lifting and wearily mouthing words.

"You don't know me from Adam, Tom. I know that. But— I know this is crazy. I know it's not your problem. But it's…it's… I got a problem. Wallace, I mean Wallace Kane. I'm really sorry, but I got this problem where Wallace's…where Wallace's threatening my crew."

"Threatening them?"

"I mean, not physically, but he's…ahh…calling them names for starters, and it's not setting real well."

"What's he calling them?" Tom asked, sitting up.

"Well, he's…ahh…calling them all…ahh…dildo breath, for starters."

There it sat. Right there between us, with Tom screwing up his face just as I had.

"You said 'dildo breath'?" he asked, incredulously.

"Yeah. That, and he's gonna run us off the location. Get us fired."

"Yeah, but *dildo breath*?" Tom exclaimed.

"Right. Dildo breath. I'm really sorry about all-a this. But I thought if something happens, I should say something, because I'm gonna have to go and deal with this. I want to let you know…in case all the sudden I'm in a fight, or my crew walks off."

Judgment was what would come next. There I sat, waiting on it, on bankruptcy or breakthrough, on some amorphous trouble with the government I didn't understand, wishing I could pull it all back in, every damn bit of it, and hide from my own ego, my arrogance, my audacity, from all the unrestrained self-bravado that made me jump and—preposterously—start a frack company. And from everything else my father told me I could be, if only I tried.

"You can do anything you damn well please, Daniel. You hear me? You listening? It only comes down to how much you can bear!"

Judgment was coming. In slow motion. Tom was looking at me and talking, but my fear was damning any chance of comprehension. I was left deciphering his words from the muddled sounds I struggled to understand.

"Known Wallace Kane for thirty year...sounds just like...bully... miscreant...don't need this," Tom was saying, shaking his head. "I got all these wells to get done, and now this."

The two of us sat on a seesaw that I was sensing could go either way.

"This is my fight, Tom. I gotta go deal with it. I just wanted you to know, in case things start gettin' out of hand," I said and started for the van door.

"Hold on. Hold on. I don't need this, okay? I got a well to frack. Maybe you should sit down."

That's when I perceived something like empathy coming from Tom.

"You're doing a fine job, Dan. I don't have a single complaint. But this is my job, and I'll handle this." With that, he stepped out of the van and started across the location.

I sat still, safe for just that minute, watching what I thought was a man walking on water toward the rig with Wallace up on it. I couldn't help my own stupidity and jumped out of the van, because no way was I going to sit inside it hiding. There was still too much I had to prove yet, and that started with Wallace.

"I hope he puts that son of a bitch in his place," Frank said as I was passing by him and our crew.

Waiting on an explosion, all of them were staring as Tom sprang up onto the rig floor, right at Wallace. Gradually, they became disappointed. There was no fight, just two guys up there talking over the rig noise. I stopped short of the rig and watched.

What I saw was Wallace listening more than talking. Until he started in on something that looked like reason to me. Like he was validating himself. Like I was about to lose. Me, altogether exposed and about to be thrown off the location. I started edging forward like this was it, until Tom raised his hands, not in surrender but in something that looked firm. As in "stop."

After that it was only Tom talking, the paymaster and resident adult. In a no-nonsense way, he was making his point. It wasn't him asking for feedback or an opinion. It was him putting a stop to the bullshit.

Two minutes later, Tom was double-timing back to the van, spinning his finger in the air as Rusty would do, letting everyone know it was time to get back to work. Right away, everyone including myself began moving. The rig and frack crews got back in position. Everyone was getting ready to go again. Everyone except Wallace—who began flailing his arms as he erupted into an argument with Rusty. Each of them was shouting, but nothing I could hear over the surging engine noise.

Unruffled and levelheaded, Tom pulled himself back into the van as though nothing had happened. Ninety-one wells ahead of him, and he simply said, "Let's go."

I pulled on my headset and shouted into my mic, "Let's frack this. Let's go. Let's get some water moving, right now!" I was rushing it, afraid if I didn't, it would all stop. Just as I'd done on Bruce's first well.

Keep moving. Keep the water moving. Hard to shut down a job with water moving.

Then I saw Wallace in all of his disarranged strength, his bullish strides carrying him off my location and up the adjoining lease road. He had lost, but you wouldn't know it, not from his rage, not from his pervading madness, not from the fear and uneasy awe he struck.

"Dan," Tom said, as we settled into the stage, looking right at me. "What are you doing Thursday?"

"Nothing."

"Ink me in, all right? Every Tuesday and Thursday, if that works for you."

"That works, Tom."

"And I wouldn't worry about Wallace. He can stick around, but he's gonna stay at least one location away on all the frack jobs going forward. Tell your guys Rusty's gonna lift your iron, too."

Then we sat still, equipment spinning all around us, water pushing through pipe, engines screaming, and Tom finally shaking his head, trying to make sense of it, just as I had been for months.

"I don't know what Wallace's thinking," he said. "Life may have got the better of him. I don't know.... It's a real riddle.... I don't know he should be threatening your guys, either, not with the size of some of them."

And then the job played out just like it should, with me ducking inside my headset, privately overwhelmed with a relief I had never known before, saved and so gratified by this unfathomable kindness. Nothing more about troubles and me wearing them on my sleeve, so easy to see.

"You holding up all right?" Tom asked, breaking the silence I was afraid to fill for fear of embarrassing myself, afraid I'd lose all poise in a place where there was no such thing as poise.

"Been a bit of a long road, Tom."

"That's all right. I've been on a few of those."

"Yeah."

I wanted to reach out to the friendly face, tell him everything, unload it all. But not then. The time would come, as would friendship. We had ninety wells ahead of us to talk about everything. We'd have our chance, because the truth always finds its way in a frack van.

A few stages later, I caught sight of Wallace, six hundred feet away, on a location firmly footed on a hilltop crest, banished and haunting the job with a stare that dared me to come and push him off.

That's when I saw something different in him, looking at him at that moment, standing alone over a job and a fate that was no longer his to control. I'd leave it at bewilderment, as something I'd never understand. "A riddle," as Tom had said.

• • •

Later, Wallace and Eli would buy me out of the Arcade wells and would exit Reliance. The DEP would turn the hilltop matter over to the Pennsylvania attorney general's office, which would show an interest in the Kanes but none in me. Work would turn on without them as Reliance's reputation built. A few investors would even come in alongside me. All family, the first was my brother Pete, who called me one day from his car.

"Hey, Dan, you still looking for investors?"

"No. I gave up."

"Nah. You didn't."

"Yeah. I'd rather stick a pencil in my eye."

"Well, let me in. I got it worked out. I can come in with four hundred."

"Uh-huh. Four hundred what?"

"Four hundred thousand dollars. How much of Reliance would I get for it? And Arcade?"

"Haha. April fool, right?"

"No. We want to come in."

"Uh-huh."

"No, we're serious."

"He's serious, Dan," came a woman's voice. Pete's wife, Libby.

"What do you mean, 'serious'?" I asked.

"Serious-as-a-heart-attack serious," Libby pronounced in her Mississippi twang. "Will four hundred thousand do it for you, Danny boy?" Libby laughed, along with Pete.

Little in life is as stone-cold sobering as a sister-in-law's edict. As great as it felt, I sensed they felt even better about it than I did.

Later on, two more siblings would join us, Annie and Dave. They came in with another $300,000, because the $400,000 still wasn't enough.

When the time came to buy them out, their return was seven times their investment.

Their help, and growing revenues, made it so I could replace Zahir's computers and pay off my loan with Emaline's bank. It helped me build more crews, facilities, and a stand-alone business. In time, although not much of it would be easy, I'd have crews across five different frack camps in the Appalachians, Ohio, southern Illinois, and out into Wyoming's remote and deep Powder River Basin. I'd have remarkably competent people working alongside me, doing what I had once done myself.

But right then, before all of that, I forgave Wallace for every damned bit of it, for every last piece of it.

I had survived him and everything and everyone else. But in the beginning, it was Wallace. He was the one who saw it could work. The one who said yes. Who had the background and experience that helped me get my loan.

Whatever else he was, he was an oil man through and through, tough and unrestrained, a heavy who had suffered incalculable losses yet remained standing, a brawler, an immovable force who became a brother to me in work.

Work and more work.

My God, the effort!

Wallace's regard, his hatred for me, didn't matter any longer. All that mattered was that I didn't hate him.

After the job, on the long drive home, I'd call Mary and tell her that we might just be okay with this dream of my doing. The dream that she had backed only because it was my dream, then holding me up when I didn't have the knees for it, covering me at home and putting our tiny daughters on the phone, coaxing them to make any sort of sound at all. "Tell Daddy you and Mommy love him," she'd whisper into the phone long before Maria or Elena could say a word.

After that, I'd call my sounding boards, my brothers and sisters, and after that my mother, to tell her I was okay after all and not to worry.

And later, I'd tell my father everything. I'd sit with him and explain it all away, loading him with everything I had been carrying, telling him what had happened and what I did and how I did it, just the way he told me to. I'd tell him how he would have been proud of the way I stood up and got punched and got knocked down, but got back up, just like he did, just like I saw when I was a boy.

I'd tell him that he had always been right, and how lucky I was to be his son. Then I'd tell him how I missed him, as I talked and talked to him at his bedside, where he would never know and never again understand, as he lay alone in a rented and barren room, a prisoner of Alzheimer's.

ACKNOWLEDGMENTS

I didn't travel this road alone—my oil and gas family were constant companions.